# Assessment Methods for Student Affairs

John H. Schuh and Associates

JOSSEY-BASS
A Wiley Imprint
www.josseybass.com

Published by Jossey-Bass.
A Wiley Imprint
989 Market Street, San Francisco, CA 94103-1741—www.josseybass.com

Jossey-Bass books and products are available through most bookstores. To contact Jossey-Bass
directly call our Customer Care Department within the U.S. at 800-956-7739, outside the U.S.
at 317-572-3986, or fax 317-572-4002.

Jossey-Bass also publishes its books in a variety of electronic formats. Some content that appears
in print may not be available in electronic books.

**Library of Congress Cataloging-in-Publication Data**

Schuh, John H.
   Assessment methods for student affairs / John H. Schuh and associates.
      p. cm.—(The Jossey-Bass higher and adult education series)
   Includes bibliographical references and index.
   ISBN 978-0-7879-8791-6 (cloth)
  1. Student affairs services—United States—Evaluation. 2. Educational
evaluation—Methodology. I. Title.
   LB2342.9.S38 2009
   378.1'97—dc22
                               2008027254

Printed in the United States of America
FIRST EDITION

*HB Printing*        10 9 8 7 6 5 4 3 2 1

The Jossey-Bass

Higher and Adult Education Series

# Contents

Tables, Figures, and Exhibits     vii

Foreword     ix

Preface     xi

About the Author     xxi

About the Contributors     xxiii

1.    Assessment as an Essential Dimension
of Contemporary Student Affairs Practice     1

2.    Using Existing Databases     23
*Kevin Saunders and Darin R. Wohlgemuth*

3.    Planning for and Implementing Data Collection     51
*R. M. Cooper*

4.    Selecting, Sampling, and Soliciting Subjects     77
*Ann M. Gansemer-Topf and Darin R. Wohlgemuth*

5.    Instrumentation     107
*Kevin Saunders and R. M. Cooper*

6.    Data Analysis     141
*R. M. Cooper and Mack C. Shelley, II*

7.   Writing Reports and Conducting Briefings                    171

8.   Ethics                                                       191

9.   Using a Mixed Methodological Approach
     to Assessment: A Case Study                                 211

10.  Looking to the Future of Assessment: Some Ideas
     and Musings                                                 231

Appendixes

1.   Example of a Focus Group Protocol                           249

2.   Using Microsoft Excel to Develop a Random Sample
     and a Stratified Random Sample                             255

3.   Listing of Commonly Used Instruments, Purpose,
     and Information Collected                                   257

4.   Computer Syntax Code for Table 6.1                          261

5.   Further Explanation of Table 6.2                            263

6.   Sample Methods Paragraph                                    265

7.   Informed Consent Checklist: Basic and Additional
     Elements                                                    267

8.   Codes of Ethics of Relevant Professional
     Organizations to Conducting Assessment Studies
     in Student Affairs                                          269

Index                                                            271

# Tables, Figures, and Exhibits

**Tables**

2.1.  IPEDS Information Categories                                    36

3.1.  Process and Outcomes                                           55

3.2.  Examples of Specific and General Questions                     59

3.3.  When and When Not to Use Focus Group Interview                 69

3.4.  Role of the Observer                                           71

5.1.  Resources for Selecting Published Instruments                 115

6.1.  Crosstabulation of Student Learning Community
      Participation with Whether Student Is Retained
      from First Fall to Second Fall Semester                       154

6.2.  Chi-square Measures of Association Between
      Learning Community Participation and
      Undergraduate Student Retention                               155

**Figures**

3.1.  Suggestions and Considerations for the Successful
      Interview                                                      67

**Exhibits**

4.1.  Checklist for Developing a Sample                             102

# FOREWORD

When my colleague and friend John Schuh asked me to write a Foreword for this book, I had two reactions. The first was "We wrote a book on assessment just a couple of years ago; isn't it too soon to write another?" Then (at John's insistence) I did the math, and sure enough, our last book was about eight years ago, so another is definitely very timely and needed. My second reaction was "Is there that much new in the field of assessment in the last eight years to write another?" And once again, John was right. After reading the manuscript, I concluded that more than enough has been learned over the past eight years by both scholars and practitioners to justify an update.

John and his colleagues attempted to meet an almost impossible challenge. On the one hand, there must be enough of the "basics" of assessment in student affairs to inform those practitioners who may not know much about the topic. On the other hand, those practitioners with more knowledge and experience with assessment will want a book that "takes them to the next level" in developing and conducting assessments that inform policy and practice.

I believe this book successfully meets this challenge. For those with little or no familiarity with assessment, John and his colleagues have restated, extended, and updated basics of assessment, beginning with the most important question of all: "Why are we doing this assessment?" Other basics include the many different types of assessment, getting started, data collection, selecting/sampling/soliciting subjects, data analysis, and perhaps most important, communicating assessment results in ways that influence policy and practice.

But this book is not simply a badly needed review and update of assessment practices. It also includes many topics that deserve far greater attention than they have received in the past. For example, too often practitioners assume that assessments require collecting new data, while in fact there may be already existing local or nationally accessible data that could answer the assessment question under consideration. Moreover, practitioners sometimes assume that the methodology question is "either/or" while in fact a mixed methodology study may yield the most useful and useable results. Instrumentation is always a moving target, with new and more psychometrically sound instruments available. And the ethics of assessment are often overlooked, with sometimes negative consequences, particularly for students. All of these and many other topics previously neglected in the literature are highlighted, discussed and explained in this book.

As the authors of this book correctly point out, the assessment "movement" has come a long way since the early 1990s, when the whole notion of the importance of assessment was questioned, the tools to conduct assessments were less sophisticated and accessible, and many student affairs practitioners were naïve about or intimidated by the prospect of "doing" assessment. Thanks to John Schuh and his colleagues, this book is an excellent "next step" in the continuing effort to make assessment a necessary and routine part of informing, influencing, and framing student affairs policy and practice.

Lee Upcraft

# PREFACE

In 1976 while I was working as assistant director of housing at Arizona State University, the department received a notice from the Western Interstate Commission for Higher Education (WICHE) announcing that a workshop on the ecosystems approach to environmental assessment was going to be held in Phoenix. Representatives from WICHE member institutions were invited to attend this workshop at no cost. It was to be led by Dr. Ursula Delworth, a WICHE staff person. Since the topic was interesting, I organized a team from ASU to attend. The only obligation we had to fulfill was to try to field test the model the next academic year. We agreed to do that and attended the workshop.

That experience was my introduction to assessment in student affairs. The footnote to the experience was that we did field test the model during the next two academic years, and then I moved on to Indiana University, where we applied the model each of the next nine academic years. I also used it several times in my days as associate vice president at Wichita State.

In the early 1990s I had an idea that a *New Directions for Student Services* sourcebook might be written on assessment in student affairs. I approached Peggy Barr, one of the editors at the time, about the project. She referred me to Gale Erlandson, the editor for books on higher education at Jossey-Bass, who had been in communication with Lee Upcraft about doing a book on assessment in student affairs. Gale then brought us together and asked that we consider collaborating on a book on assessment in student affairs. We agreed to undertake the project, and that led to our first book on assessment, *Assessment in Student Affairs* (Upcraft & Schuh, 1996). A few years later she asked us to prepare a companion volume, *Assessment Practice in Student Affairs* (Schuh & Upcraft, 2001). In the intervening years Lee and I wrote several articles and conducted a number of workshops on assessment practice at professional conferences, as well for specific campuses.

Over time I began to focus less on trying to convince the participants at our workshops that conducting assessment projects is a necessary element in student affairs practice and more on how to conduct assessment projects. Specific issues addressed were how to deal with the nuts and bolts of conducting assessments, including exploring such issues as how to get started, how to select an instrument, how to collect and analyze data, and how to present information in a meaningful form to the various stakeholders of the assessment project.

Based on that experience I concluded that a book on assessment methods was needed. That is, practitioners were seeking ideas about how to conduct assessment projects. They had moved beyond the "convincing" stage in their thinking about assessment and needed practical advice about how to conduct assessments. With that in mind I proposed a third book in what has become an assessment series. David Brightman, Gale's successor at Jossey-Bass, quickly agreed, and this project was launched.

## Purpose of This Book

The book discusses the methodological aspects of conducting assessment projects. It is designed for the student affairs practitioner who is ready to conduct assessment projects but is not quite sure how to manage the technical aspects of the project. With that purpose in mind, the book should help student affairs staff who are not sure how to address sampling issues in assessment projects, how to collect and analyze data, how to report results, and so on. Our writing team has provided much more detail about the "how to" aspects of assessment projects than Lee and I did in our previous volumes. We see this book as complementary to the previous books that we prepared on assessment, as well as providing an update on the methodology of assessment.

## Audience for This Book

The book is written primarily for student affairs practitioners who are preparing to undertake assessment projects. In preparing the book I have made several assumptions:

1. That the readers of the book are ready to conduct an assessment project. That is, they do not need to be convinced that conducting assessment projects is a worthwhile use of their time and resources.

2. That the readers are interested in ideas, suggestions, and recommendations for how to conduct assessment projects. In short, they are looking for useful advice about the process of conducting assessment projects.

3. That readers have institutional assets in place or such assets can be secured to conduct assessment projects. By that I mean that they can secure help as is necessary to complete a project. An example might be that although the person conducting the assessment may not be an expert on statistical techniques, the person knows where to go on campus to get this sort of help.

The secondary audience for this book is graduate students in student affairs preparation programs who want to learn more about assessment techniques. This volume can be helpful to graduate students once they understand the basic elements of the research process, which they should learn in a foundational course. It is not a primer in statistics, nor does it claim to be a foundational publication in qualitative methodologies. Instead, it focuses on solving practical problems related to assessment in student affairs.

The book is not written for statisticians, qualitative methodologists, theoreticians, psychometrists, or others whose careers are centered on the development or refinement of various research paradigms. Rather, it is prepared primarily by practitioners for practitioners, based on our combined decades of experience with assessment projects.

## Some Caveats

We offer some caveats about what this book is and is not.

First, this book does not discuss theory. We understand that theories are foundational in the work in assessment and evaluation, but our purpose for the book was to focus on practical issues and practical problems. Topics such as sampling theory, theories under girding statistical techniques, instrument development, and various theoretical foundations that support qualitative inquiry are not addressed. We recognize that an extensive and important body of literature provides the theories that support work described in this volume but we saw no reason to repeat that information. Part Two of *Building a Scholarship of Assessment* (Banta & Associates, 2002) provides an excellent discussion of theoretical foundations of assessment, and I recommend that resource to readers interested in the topic.

Second, we do not use the terms *assessment* and *evaluation* interchangeably (see Upcraft & Schuh, 1996). For the purpose of this book, we define *assessment* as we did in our previous volumes: "any effort to gather, analyze, and interpret evidence which describes institutional, departmental, divisional, or agency effectiveness" (Upcraft & Schuh, 1996, p. 18). We define evaluation as "any effort to use assessment evidence to improve institutional, departmental, divisional or agency effectiveness" (Upcraft & Schuh, 1996, p. 19).

Third, this is not a text about research methods, even though we use the term *research methods* from time to time in this book. Lee Upcraft and I differentiated *assessment* and *research* years ago (Upcraft & Schuh, 2002). I reiterate that we understand the difference between research and assessment, but we wanted to develop a volume that focuses on assessment in student affairs, which has a practical framework, and not deviate from our focus.

Fourth, we do not have a preference in terms of our methodological approach to assessment. Our view is that the problem being assessed should drive the decision about the methodological approach to employ. Therefore, the kind of data that are necessary to provide answers to the questions framing our inquiry should determine the methods employed. This book is not intended to advance a particular methodology; if readers are looking for advocacy in favor of qualitative or quantitative methods, they will be disappointed. Both methodological approaches have great value in our view, and the decision to choose one over the other in an assessment project hinges on the dynamics of the project and its goals. In fact, we advocate the use of mixed methodologies, as is explained in detail in Chapter Nine.

Fifth, I have used the "royal we" extensively. When I use the term *we*, I am referring to the collective thinking of Lee Upcraft and me. Lee and I worked closely for the better part of a decade on the development of literature focusing on assessment, and in the end, it became impossible for us to identify which ideas were his and which were mine. Although he is not an author of this book, his ideas can be found on virtually every page. Lee's thinking on assessment is brilliant, and I want to acknowledge his contributions to the assessment movement in general and to my thinking and learning in particular.

Finally, the book is not about assessing student learning that is part of students' classroom or formal curricular experiences. Although student affairs practitioners may teach classes or contribute to the formal curriculum in many ways, this book focuses on student learning that occurs under the purview of student

affairs practitioners, who, typically, are not members of an institution's teaching faculty. We think this learning is central to a
student's education, as has been demonstrated at many colleges
and universities (see, for example, Kuh, Schuh, & Whitt, 1991;
Kuh, Kinzie, Schuh, & Whitt, 2005). Wonderful resources are
available to assess student learning in the context of the formal
curriculum, among them Suskie (2004), Huba and Freed (2000),
and Angelo and Cross (1993).

## Overview of the Contents

We have organized the contents of this book differently than had
we prepared a research report or taught a class on appropriate
steps in writing a dissertation. The book has been organized
more closely to resemble the assessment process rather than
an assessment report. For example, in an assessment report you
would describe the selection of participants, choice of instrument, and then data analysis methods. However, when you begin
the assessment process, it is important to think about the bigger picture—what methodological approach would most likely
answer your assessment goals, what data are currently available,
what instruments should be used, and who are the participants.

Fundamental to our approach is the nature of the assessment
that we are contemplating, and it can be explained best with
an illustration. If, on the one hand, we were responsible for
a study abroad program that involved ten students spending a
month in another country, we would not consider conducting a
quantitative assessment of their experiences. Rather, we would
consider some combination of qualitative methods, including,
but not necessarily limited to, conducting a series of focus groups
with the participants before, during, and after their experience,
perhaps asking them to keep journals of their experiences and
possibly using other techniques, such as photographic inquiry. On
the other hand, if we wanted to collect baseline data related to the
perceptions of a student body consisting of 20,000 undergraduates

regarding a proposed new food service program, we probably would want to conduct a survey.

We begin the book with getting started in assessment in student affairs. We present various reasons for conducting assessment projects, introduce some ideas about how to begin assessment in student affairs, and identify different types of assessment projects. We conclude Chapter One with a few success stories from campuses that have been very successful in conducting assessment projects.

Sometimes data are available and ready to be mined for assessment projects. Kevin Saunders and Darin R. Wohlgemuth provide details about using databases in assessment projects in Chapter Two. Their perspective is that many offices on campus are potential sources of data and resources for assessment projects and should not be overlooked as wonderful institutional assets. They also identify national databases that can be accessed through the World Wide Web.

In Chapter Three, R. M. Cooper presents strategies about how best to develop and implement data collection from students and other student affairs constituencies. The author presents advantages and disadvantages of various data collection techniques.

Ann M. Gansemer-Topf and Darin R. Wohlgemuth examine topics related to sampling and attracting subjects to assessment projects in Chapter Four. Typically, assessment projects are about people, and securing their participation can be challenging but is absolutely essential in the success of an assessment project. The authors also discuss problems with survey fatigue and use of incentives to increase participation.

Kevin Saunders and R. M. Cooper examine the challenges of identifying appropriate instruments for assessment projects in Chapter Five. They discuss using commercially prepared instruments or developing local instruments for quantitative studies, and they also take a look at developing protocols for interviewing participants, reviewing documents, and conducting observations in qualitative assessment.

R. M. Cooper and Mack C. Shelley, II address data analysis in Chapter Six. They provide examples for various data analysis procedures and present a number of choices (that is, statistical procedures) for quantitative data analysis. Our thinking is that in reviewing these choices, if a person is not deeply versed in statistics, after selecting the statistics of interest, assistance can be identified to work through the technical aspects of the analysis. The authors also discuss data analysis in qualitative studies.

The next step after analyzing the data is to share the information with interested in stakeholders. In Chapter Seven we present ideas about preparing reports and conducting briefings, with a special emphasis on identifying recommendations for practice and change. Those engaged in an assessment project should take the initiative in setting the agenda for change, based on the findings of the study.

The ethical dimensions of assessment are central in any project. This includes protecting the participants from risk and adhering to federal and institutional requirements. In Chapter Eight we provide detailed information about the ethical dimensions of assessment.

The use of mixed methodologies can result in particularly rich assessment studies. This means that the methodologies are complementary and can be used to inform each other. In Chapter Nine we offer a case study that uses mixed methodological approaches.

Finally, we present some ideas about the future of assessment in Chapter Ten. Institutions will be called upon to engage in assessment projects at an increasing rate in the future, and student affairs practitioners will need to meet this challenge. We think that they are well positioned to provide institutional leadership in meeting the demands for accountability in the future.

## About the Contributors

The writing team that was assembled for this volume consists of faculty and administrators at Iowa State University. The team's members have been engaged extensively in assessment projects over the past decade, and much of their current work focuses on using data to inform decision making and professional practice. They advise practitioners on assessment projects on a routine basis and conduct studies of their own. I am very grateful to each of them for contributing their ideas to this publication.

## A Final Word

At the beginning of this introduction I noted my first exposure to assessment in 1976 through attendance at a workshop led by Ursula Delworth. Her thinking about how to conduct assessment projects has influenced me over the past thirty years. I will always be grateful to her for her assistance and encouragement. My colleagues at Arizona State University, Indiana University, Wichita State University, and Iowa State University have been extraordinary with their help, guidance, expertise, and support as I have taken on assessment projects with them to improve the experiences of college students. Gale Erlandson and David Brightman have been so helpful in encouraging me to put my ideas regarding assessment on paper, and without their help, none of these books would have been published. But most of all I want to acknowledge and thank my colleague and friend, Lee Upcraft, from whom I have learned so much about assessment and student affairs practice over the years.

John H. Schuh
Ames, Iowa

# References

Angelo, T. A., & Cross, K. P. (1993). *Classroom assessment techniques*. San Francisco: Jossey-Bass.

Banta, T. W. & Associates. (2002). *Building a scholarship of assessment*. San Francisco: Jossey-Bass.

Huba, M. E., & Freed, J. E. (2000). *Learner-centered assessment on college campuses*. Boston: Allyn & Bacon.

Kuh, G. D., Schuh, J. H., & Whitt, E. J. (1991). *Involving colleges*. San Francisco: Jossey-Bass.

Kuh, G. D., Kinzie, J., Schuh, J. H., & Whitt, E. J. (2005). *Student success in college*. San Francisco: Jossey-Bass.

Schuh, J. H., & Upcraft, M. L. (2001). *Assessment practice in student affairs*. San Francisco: Jossey-Bass.

Suskie, L. (2004). *Assessing student learning: A common sense guide*. Bolton, MA: Anker.

Upcraft, M. L., & Schuh, J.H. (1996). *Assessment in student affairs*. San Francisco: Jossey-Bass.

Upcraft, M. L., & Schuh, J. H. (2002). Assessment vs. research: Why we should care about the difference. *About Campus, 7* (1), 16–20.

# ABOUT THE AUTHOR

John H. Schuh is distinguished professor of educational leadership and policy studies at Iowa State University. Previously he held administrative and faculty assignments at Wichita State University, Indiana University (Bloomington) and Arizona State University.

Schuh is the author, coauthor, or editor of over 235 publications, including 24 books and monographs and over 60 book chapters and 110 articles. His most recent books are *One Size Does Not Fit All: Traditional and Innovative Models of Student Affairs Practice* (with Kathleen Manning and Jillian Kinzie), *Student Success in College* (with George D. Kuh, Jillian Kinzie and Elizabeth Whitt), and *Promoting Reasonable Expectations* (with Thomas E. Miller and Barbara E. Bender). He is coauthor of *Assessment Practice in Student Affairs* and *Assessment in Student Affairs* (both with M. Lee Upcraft). Currently he is editor-in-chief of the *New Directions for Student Services* sourcebook series.

John Schuh has received the Contribution to Knowledge Award and the Presidential Service Award from the American College Personnel Association, and the Contribution to Research or Literature Award and the Robert H. Shaffer Award for Academic Excellence as a Graduate Faculty Member from the National Association of Student Personnel Administrators. Schuh received a Fulbright award to study higher education in Germany in 1994.

# ABOUT THE CONTRIBUTORS

R. M. Cooper is a social scientist for the Research Institute for Studies in Education (RISE) and an instructor of research and evaluation courses for the Department of Educational Leadership and Policy Studies at Iowa State University.

Ann M. Gansemer-Topf is the associate director of research for the Office of Admissions at Iowa State University. Prior to her current assignment, she was the associate director of institutional research at Grinnell College.

Kevin P. Saunders is the coordinator of continuous academic program improvement in the Office of the Executive Vice President and Provost at Iowa State University. He also serves as chair for the Learning Communities Assessment Subcommittee at Iowa State University.

Mack C. Shelley is University Professor of Educational Leadership and Policy Studies, Statistics, and Political Science at Iowa State University. From 2003 to 2007, he served as director of the Research Institute for Studies in Education at Iowa State University.

Darin R. Wohlgemuth is the director of budget research and analysis in the Office of the Executive Vice President and Provost and the director of research for Enrollment Services at Iowa State University.

# 1

# ASSESSMENT AS AN ESSENTIAL DIMENSION OF CONTEMPORARY STUDENT AFFAIRS PRACTICE

When Lee Upcraft and I wrote our first book about assessment (Upcraft & Schuh, 1996), we asserted that conducting assessment projects was an essential element of student affairs practice. At the time, assessment in student affairs was a relatively recent phenomenon, although the concept of doing assessments had been around for several decades (see, for example, Aulepp & Delworth, 1976). We asserted that studies would have to be undertaken by student affairs practitioners because we thought that the stakeholders of their units would demand data that would confirm the important contributions of student affairs programs and services to student learning and growth.

Much of our thinking had a financial lens to it. We thought, for example, that institutions might choose to outsource programs and services that historically had been assigned to student affairs if they were not cost effective. We also thought that student affairs units had to be able to demonstrate that they contributed to student learning and development. If they could not, questions as to their efficacy would be raised, and they might be outsourced or eliminated.

We really did not have a crystal ball when we made these assertions, but if we were to look back over the past decade, it is clear that assessment has emerged as an activity of increasing significance in the work of student affairs practitioners, as well as faculty members. Moreover, studies conducted of institutions of higher education that have been successful in achieving their educational goals for students (Kuh, Kinzie, Schuh & Whitt,

2005) have shown that assessment has become an important element in student affairs practice.

In this chapter, we identify and discuss reasons that contribute to why accountability in student affairs has become an essential dimension of contemporary student affairs practice. We also describe how assessment is linked to other organizational functions in student affairs. We then provide suggestions about how to get started in conducting assessment projects and identify a number of different kinds of assessment projects that student affairs leaders might consider. We conclude with a few examples of institutions that are undertaking ongoing assessment projects in student affairs.

## The Current Press for Accountability

As is the case in many elements of our society (medicine, K–12 schools, state government), the emphasis on accountability in higher education has accelerated in the past decade or two (Leveille, 2006). The Commission of the Secretary of Education (U.S. Department of Education, 2006) made it clear that assessment of student learning outcomes needs to be central in the process of accountability. The Commission added, "Accreditation agencies should make performance outcomes, including completion rates and student learning, the core of their assessment as a priority over inputs or processes" (p. 25). Berger and Lyon describe the situation this way: "The past fifteen years have seen accountability become a more important mandate in higher education" (2005, p. 26). In addition, governing boards and legislatures are increasing influential in the priorities and operations of institutions (National Association of Student Personnel Administrators and American College Personnel Association, 2004). Colleges and universities increasingly are being asked to demonstrate how they make a difference in the lives of students, how they contribute to the economic development of their communities and states, and how they contribute to the national welfare.

Although some institutions may have the luxury of ignoring this increasing pressure perhaps due to an extraordinary endowment or a unique niche in American higher education, the fact is that in contemporary higher education, the vast majority of institutions cannot afford to ignore the multidimensional contemporary press for accountability. In turn, various units of institutions of higher education, including student affairs, are being asked to demonstrate various forms of accountability. Several of these forms of accountability are discussed below.

## Contributions to Student Learning

Certainly since the release of two reports, *Involvement in Learning* (Study Group on the Conditions of Excellence in Higher Education, 1984) and *An American Imperative: Higher Expectations for Higher Education* (Wingspread Group on Higher Education, 1993), interest has focused in higher education on enriching the undergraduate experience. The Study Group's report recommended ways that institutions could provide experiences for undergraduates that would increase student involvement and raise expectations for student achievement. It also provided recommendations for assessment and feedback. Taking this work a step further, the Wingspread Group asserted, "society must hold higher education to much higher expectations or risk national decline" (p. 1). Other reports built on this report including *The Student Learning Imperative* (American College Personnel Association, 1996) and *Learning Reconsidered* (National Association of Student Personnel Administrators and American College Personnel Association, 2004). All of these documents urged higher standards for higher education, better communication, and the production of evidence on the part of higher education that students were being held to rigorous standards. In short, higher education was being asked to demonstrate that students were learning what institutions said they were learning. Since student affairs units have asserted for decades that students learn from the experiences provided in out-of-class expediencies (see Baird, 2003), they, too, have to produce evidence to sustain their claims.

## Retention

Closely related to learning is the extent to which various units on college campuses contribute to institutional retention efforts. Retention has several dimensions to it. Most important, retention data are linked to the extent to which students are able to achieve their educational goals. For example, over 95% of entering students planned to earn a bachelor's degree or higher in 2006 (Almanac Edition, 2007, p. A18), but the six-year graduation rate of students who entered college in 1999–2000 was 55.9% (Almanac Edition, 2007, p. A14). Also important are the financial implications of students' dropping out. Students incur debt and institutions suffer financial losses when students drop out. No one benefits from students' not being retained.

Tinto (2005) described the situation his way: "Today it is more important than ever for institutions to respond to the challenge of increasing student success. Forced to cope with tight, if not shrinking, budgets, institutions face mounting pressure to improve their rates of student retention and graduation" (p. ix). Consequently, student affairs practitioners might choose to explore the following questions. Does the first year experience program contribute to retention? If students live in residence halls are they more likely to be retained from the first year to the second and ultimately graduate? If the college has an extensive learning communities program, does participation in this program improve a student's chances for being retained and ultimately graduating?

## Political Pressure

Not only is this pressure coming from study groups, think tanks, and the like, but the political environment, for various reasons, has also placed higher education under the microscope. At times this scrutiny is related to the cost of attendance (Boehner & McKeon, 2003); sometimes it reflects concerns about public accountability (Business-Higher Education Forum, n.d.) and the relationship between public institutions and the states in which they are located (American Council on Education, n.d.). Regardless of the presenting problem, greater controls over higher education, particularly in the public sector, have been applied (American Council on Education, n.d.). Institutions are being called upon to provide evidence of the success of their various operations, or they can expect more involvement of politicians and various governmental agencies and greater scrutiny of their operations.

## Accreditation

For nearly a hundred years (Millard, 1994) regional associations have engaged in the accreditation of colleges and universities. Specialized accreditation of programs has developed during similar period of time. Until recently, this form of providing public assurance has been the accepted standard, but in recent years, calls for federal involvement in the accreditation of institutions have become more vigorous (Dickeson, 2006). The essence of the criticism is that higher education has not undergone appropriate scrutiny; more rigorous measures of evaluation are necessary, since institutional accreditation has been voluntary and is conducted by peers as opposed to governmental or other external bodies. At the time of this writing it is unknown how or whether this situation will be resolved.

What is known, however, is that the regional accreditation agencies have increasingly stressed that institutions provide solid, empirical data that illustrate what students are learning. The Middle States Commission, for example, provides a Web site that includes publications for assessing student learning and institutional effectiveness (Middle States Commission, 2005a), and exemplar programs including student affairs (Middle States Commission, 2005b). The Southern Association of Colleges and Schools Commission on Colleges (2004) in its resource manual on principles of accreditation identifies relevant questions for student support programs, services, and activities that include providing evidence for the effectiveness and adequacy of support programs and services, and evidence that student support services and programs meet the needs of students of all types and promote student learning and development. Requirements such as these are unambiguous; assessment data are needed or the questions cannot be answered satisfactorily.

## Cost

The cost of attendance at institutions of higher education is an issue that has been explored widely in the literature on contemporary concerns in higher education (see, for example, Yeager, Nelson, Potter, Weidman & Zullo, 2001). The cost of attendance has been rising faster than the Consumer Price Index (see The College Board, 2007). For example, the cost of attendance at a four year public institution increased by 7.1% from the 2004–2005 academic year to the 2005–2006 academic year whereas the consumer price index increased by 3.4% from December 2004 to December 2005 (Bureau of Labor Statistics, 2006). Those students who rely on federal financial aid, especially Pell Grants, are finding that relief in this from the increasing cost of attendance has not kept pace (King, 2003). Moreover, students and their parents do not have a good sense of the cost of attendance, and they often overestimate the cost of going to college (Horn, Chen, & Chapman, 2003).

Student affairs units are not immune from price increases and in some cases contribute to the increasing cost of attendance. At public universities it is not uncommon for the cost of room and board to be greater than the cost of tuition and fees (Schuh & Shelley, 2001). In this environment, those who are responsible for units that charge special fees, or are supported substantially or perhaps entirely by student fees or fees for service, will have their operations and costs placed under the fiscal microscope. At this point a case has to be made for the level of the fees charged, and the extent to which students and other stakeholders are receiving value for their expenditure. Very, very few institutions can ignore the cost of attendance and its effect on students.

## Benchmarking

One other form of accountability has to do with how institutions compare with each other, against industry standards, or against institutionally adopted standards. "[B]enchmarking and other strategies for assessing and improving quality have, and will continue to have, great value...The underlying concepts and goals are anything but new or revolutionary; they have a long tradition or application in our work in higher education" (Doerfel and Ruben, 2002, p. 23). Not only do institutions conduct studies of how they compare on various dimensions with other institutions, private consultants also are available to conduct those studies for institutional clients (see, for example, Educational Benchmarking, Inc.). In addition, the Council for the Advancement of Standards in Higher Education provides functional standards that can be used for benchmarking purposes (http://www.cas.edu/).

Benchmarking may not answer all the questions that might arise related to providing evidence that various units are competitive when compared with similar units at other institutions of higher education or other sectors of our society, but they provide guidance as to whether industry standards are being met and whether the approach taken at the institution of interest is similar to that being taken at comparable institutions. At a minimum, the data resulting from benchmarking assessments can demonstrate that a unit or program is on track within a predetermined framework, that is, the standards used for the benchmarking exercise.

## Linking Assessment to Organizational Functions in Student Affairs

Assessment activities are central elements in program planning and program development in student affairs. Brief descriptions of the role of assessment in these functions in student affairs are provided hereafter.

## Strategic Planning

As with most organizational functions in higher education, assessment stands in relation to and has an influence on other organizational functions. In fact, assessment plays a central role in organizational renewal. Typically, organizations participate in strategic planning exercises that include a review of their mission statements and goals, and then adopt action steps that are designed to achieve their goals (Schuh, 2003). The action steps can include such activities as developing upgraded facilities for recreational sports, implementing leadership development programs in student activities, or raising external funds designed to provide scholarships that are more robust for students from modest economic backgrounds in financial aid. All of these planning activities require effort and resources; in the end they are designed to help student affairs units achieve their goals, thus moving these units in concert with the division's mission.

Assessment plays an important role in helping these units determine the extent to which their initiatives have achieved their desired intent. In the case of the illustrations above, questions such as the following need to be answered: Do the upgraded facilities result in increased satisfaction by the users of the recreation complex? Do the leadership development programs result in more effective leaders for student organizations? Do the scholarship initiatives contribute to the retention of the students who receive the enhanced scholarships? Each of these initiatives should be assessed to determine whether they had the desired effect. If the desired effect is achieved, the programs can be continued, but if the initiatives do not achieve their desired results, they should be modified or perhaps eliminated.

## Organizational Effectiveness

Closely related to its role in strategic planning is how assessment can assist in measuring the effectiveness of various elements of departments in student affairs. For example, is the current theoretical framework for program development yielding the desired student learning in the residence halls? Is the student health service providing high-quality services for reasonable costs? Are tutoring programs having their desired effect? Is the matriculation rate of admitted students comparable to that in peer institutions?

Questions related to organizational effectiveness can be answered through a comprehensive assessment program. Without a systematic approach to gathering information and using that information to determine the effectiveness of student affairs units, initiatives, programs, and procedures, unit leaders will have difficulty determining whether organizational goals are being met, thus making their organizations vulnerable to reorganization, outsourcing, or even elimination.

## Getting Started in Assessment

Assessment looks to be a complex, time- and resource-intensive process that at first blush might appear to be overwhelming. There is no question that student affairs practitioners are busy people. The crisis of the day can take precedence over long-term thinking, so to be able to step back and take the long view of what needs to be accomplished in the division of student affairs might appear to be a luxury. We find, however, that taking the long view is essential. Central to this long view is assessment, and central to developing an assessment program is knowing how to get started.

Although it might seem trite to claim that a long journey begins with the first step, the fact of the matter is that in taking a journey, a series of steps have to be accomplished for the journey to be completed successfully. This was what Karl Weick had in mind when he introduced the concept of "small wins" (1984). Weick's idea was that to bring about social change one needed to think in terms of effecting small changes before one could bring about a large change. "The massive scale on which social problems are conceived often precludes innovative action because the limits of bounded rationality are exceeded and arousal is raised to dysfunctionally high levels" (1984, p. 40). Pascarella and Terenzini (1991) came to the same conclusion in writing about how to bring about change on a college campus. Their thinking is instructive on this point.

> Thus, instead of singular, large, specially designed, and cam-puswide programs to achieve a particular institutional goal, efforts might more profitably focus on ways to embed the pursuit of that goal in all appropriate institutional activities...In short, rather than seeking single large levers to pull in order to promote change on a large scale, it may well be more effective to pull more small levers more often. [1991, p. 655]

The approach advocated by Pascarella and Terenzini also can be applied to starting assessment programs. On the one hand, if one conceptualizes getting started on assessment programs as a massive effort, involving virtually all the activities of a division of student affairs, ranging from keeping track of who uses facilities to measuring the student learning outcomes of all the experiences and activities in a single year, it is likely that the process will not get off the ground. On the other hand, using the advice of Weick and Pascarella and Terenzini, a division should start modestly and attempt to conduct a few assessment projects rather than undertake a study of massive proportions. The chances of success are much greater if the division starts with a manageable project with modest but important goals rather than with a highly complex project. In fact, success will build upon success. Our advice is for student affairs practitioners to think about various assessments in this way:

> Small wins are not a matter of decoration but a matter of structure, an integral part of work. They fit perfectly into larger strategies because they are understandable, doable, and generally nonthreatening. [Rhatigan & Schuh, 2003, p. 19]

Assessment needs to start with reasonable projects that are not necessarily complex and that can be completed in a reasonable time. The surest way to dampen enthusiasm for conducting assessments is to conceptualize projects that are time consuming, technically complex, and beyond the expertise of the staff who are available to conduct them. But if assessments require a manageable amount of time, are simple in design, and demand nothing more than the skills already possessed by the staff that will conduct them, a recipe for success is in place. Let us suggest a few kinds of assessments that can be conducted within the already established calendar of events in student affairs.

## Measuring Participation

Measuring participation is an assessment technique that should be done on annual basis and probably is being done already at your institution. This approach is designed to keep track of who uses the various services and who participates in the programs offered by the units in the division, as well as those students who do not. Certainly, student housing can produce basic numbers about who lives in the residence halls and their identifiable characteristics, financial aid staff can develop a profile of who receives how much and what kinds of aid in an academic year, career services can develop a profile of the companies that interview on campus and the students who have received help from the staff in preparing their credentials or have attended workshops, the counseling center should have a profile of the various clients who come to the office for assistance, and so on. Publishing these data and distributing them widely is a wonderful start. It begins to get the word to various stakeholders on and off campus about who is served by the various units of student affairs. The units themselves can develop the strategies for collecting and analyzing the data, but it makes good sense to have material available on a Web site to begin to tell the story of the contributions of the division of student affairs to student life.

## Needs Assessment

The population of a typical four-year institution will turn over by around 50 percent every two years or so and obviously much more frequently than that at a two-year college. Conducting a needs assessment approximately every other year will fit the concept of trying to stay abreast of the needs of the student body. It is important to remember, however, that needs are not the same as wants, so needs can be framed by the institution's mission and academic program. For example, just because some people want to develop graduate programs at a baccalaureate college does not mean that it is a good idea to develop them. But it is good idea to understand how students' needs change over time, and a very good strategy is to conduct a needs assessment when over 50 percent of the student body has turned over.

For example, once upon a time a strategy was developed to build a large of number of computer labs at a university so that students would have access to computing facilities. That approach became obsolete when it was discovered that over 90 percent of the students attending the institution brought their own laptops; what they really needed was wireless access, not the computing hardware. The consequence was that the institution's strategy for providing computing access had to be altered. That is an example of how students' needs will change over time.

## Satisfaction Assessment

After an institution develops strategies to meet student needs, the next step is to measure the extent to which students and others are satisfied. This can be accomplished through an assessment conducted the year after a needs assessment is conducted. So if a needs assessment is conducted in year two, a satisfaction assessment can be conducted in year three. This is the perfect follow-up to institutional change and an appropriate way of checking on whether changes have their desired effect.

Suppose that the institution, after doing an exhaustive study, makes a change in its approach to food service. In this example, the institution has gone from being a traditional food service to one in which students can eat at any food service on campus through the use of a declining-balance system to improve customer convenience; the desired result is improved satisfaction with the food service. Since this is a major change for the institution, it is important to determine whether the change had the desired effect and that students and other stakeholders' expectations for the new food service were satisfied.

## Outcomes

An argument can be made that the reason that campuses offer many programs and activities is that these can be framed by the institution's objectives for student learning and that they contribute to student learning and growth (National Association of Student Personnel Administrators and American College Personnel Association, 2004). But for various units to claim that they contribute to the student experience (for example, living in the residence halls contributes to the institution's retention rate), data are required. The various experiences and learning opportunities that typically are available on most campuses are numerous, so it is impractical to assess the educational potency of each one of them, every year. So, our advice is that on a periodic basis, a few programs be selected for assessment. This could be intramural football one year, a speaker series the next, the volunteer services bureau the next, and so on.

Any time a major commitment is made to a new program, such as implementing a leadership development program, it is a good idea to have an assessment component, because those providing the funding will want to know whether their investment was fruitful. Outcomes assessments are challenging to conduct, but they are essential in making the case for value that is contributed to student learning by specific programs and other student experiences.

## Cost Effectiveness

Can a private, off-campus vendor provide services more cheaply than what is being provided on-campus? This is a typical question that student affairs administrators face in the course of their work. Off-campus challenges come from apartments, bookstores, child-care centers, computer vendors, and so on. Probably on an annual basis an environmental scan should be conducted to determine how costs compare for various services that are provided off-campus with those that are provided on-campus. The time that is required to conduct such a scan is minimal, but the data are very useful in answering questions such as the following: Are our costs competitive? Are our services comparable to what is available off-campus? It should also be noted that the definition of *off-campus* has evolved over the years. Although it might be important to recognize that the bookstore down the street from the campus may provide competition for selling books and supplies, so will online book providers that can have a student's order delivered the next day.

Determining cost effectiveness with local vendors is an approach that is a cousin to the process of conducting benchmarking surveys with other institutions of higher education. Various approaches are available to conducting benchmarking, and these can be done on a periodic basis, say every three or four years.

Some data will be relatively easy to identify (for example, room and board rates) but other data are more difficult to discern (such as how training programs for resident assistants compare across institutions).

## Other Assessments

Other assessments can be conducted on a periodic, but certainly not annual, basis; for example, conducting a campus culture assessment or an environmental assessment. These forms of assessment are very complex, can be expensive, and may even require the use of external consultants. We do not have a specific formula for when to conduct these forms of assessment other than to suggest that every few years, meaning every five years or so, might be the right interval to conduct them. They can provide very useful information, but the utility of the information has to be balanced with the effort that it takes to conduct this type of study.

## Framing Questions

We have written this volume to help student affairs staff members integrate assessment into their administrative practice. But a number of aspects of the assessment process must be reviewed and considered before making methodological decisions. Specifically the following questions must be answered before moving into other aspects of assessment:

1. What is the issue at hand? That is, is the proposed assessment part of a routine, ongoing process, the result of a special request (by the governing board or senior officers, for example), the consequence of a specific event (such as a tragedy) or data that suggest that further analysis is needed (such as a graduation rate that has declined for two consecutive years)?

2. What is the purpose of the assessment? Defining the issue at hand will generate a second question. If, for example, a declining graduation rate triggers an assessment, the purpose of the assessment might be to delineate the variation of graduation rates of specific groups of students (such as commuter students or residential students), or it might be to determine whether the graduation rates of all students have declined. In this case, the assessment takes on a diagnostic dimension, since it will help clarify the nature of the decline in graduation rates.

3. Who should be studied? Will the assessment involve all students, a subset of them, or others associated with the institution, such as graduates? In the example described in number 2, if we learn that the decline in graduation rates has been especially pronounced for commuter students, the next step would be to initiate a study of them and their experiences and eliminate residential students from further study. Selecting participants is the focus of Chapter Four.

4. What is the best assessment method? At this point, we begin to consider various designs that are available to us. If the population is particularly large, we might want to start with a study designed to generate baseline data. This process might be conducted with a database available on campus. Chapter Two describes how existing databases can be used for assessment purposes. Alternatively, we might think about developing a qualitative study that would include conducting focus groups with commuting students to understand how they describe their experiences on campus. If time and other resources permit, we advocate the development of mixed methods assessment, an example of which is the focus of Chapter Nine.

5. How should we collect our data? Do we want to use a telephone survey or a Web-based survey; do we conduct focus groups or use another approach to collecting our

data? The methodology we have selected will help us determine our data collection process. Chapter Three provides an in-depth discussion of data collection.

6. What instrument should we use? This question has to do with developing our own questionnaire, or purchasing a commercial instrument if we plan a Web-based survey. If we choose to conduct focus groups, what will our interview protocol look like? Should we develop several protocols based on the groups we plan to interview? Instrumentation is discussed in Chapter Five.

7. How should we analyze the data? The different assessment designs identified above will demand different approaches to data analysis. Chapter Six provides more information on data analysis.

8. How should we report the results? Results can be reported through executive summaries, short reports, targeted reports, oral briefings, Web sites, or a combination of these. The report needs to be more than a rendition of findings, however. Reports should also include action steps for reasons that are enumerated in Chapter Seven.

These questions provide a map for thinking about the assessment process, as well as offering a framework for how to structure the design of an assessment. Implicit in the process is the protection of and respect for the participants. More details about the requirements for working with participants are provided in Chapter Eight.

## Some Illustrations of Assessment in Student Affairs

Examples in student affairs assessment are available on institutional Web sites. Those that are particularly well known include student affairs assessment at Penn State University, the

University of Massachusetts at Amherst, Syracuse University, and many others that are available on the World Wide Web. What is so encouraging about these Web sites is that they reflect that the culture of evidence that we referenced in the introduction to this chapter has developed at many institutions of higher education.

North Dakota State University has developed a wonderful student involvement transcript that is designed to help students assess the skills they have developed by participating in a variety of out-of-class programs (NDSU Student Life, 2006). Oregon State University similarly has identified learning goals for students and provides information about how various student affairs units can contribute to student learning (Oregon State University, 2008) Syracuse University has published a detailed plan related to assessment projects that cut across the units of the division. Guiding questions have been identified for assessment projects (Syracuse University Division of Student Affairs, 2006). Assessment reports are then made available to the campus community and other stakeholders through postings on Web sites (Syracuse University Office of Residence Life, 2005). Penn State University has published 149 studies as of May, 2007 related to student life under the umbrella of the *Penn State Pulse* program. "Penn State Pulse was initiated in Spring of 1995 by Student Affairs to gather feedback on student issues, expectations, usage, and satisfaction" (Research and Assessment, 2007, n.p.).

After reading this discussion as to how to get started and examining a couple of illustrations, we hope it becomes clear that one does not have to do every assessment every year. We recommend that institutions start with keeping track of those who use the various services and move into more complex assessments, which do not have be conducted every year. We think this approach will result in a more manageable strategy to conducting assessments successfully.

## Conclusion

In this chapter we presented the case for why assessment in student affairs is an essential dimension of contemporary practice in student affairs. Stakeholders, many of whom are external to our institutions of higher education, expect and demand accountability on the part of our colleges and universities. We then introduced ideas about how to get started in assessment and discussed various types of assessment projects. Finally, we presented a few examples from institutions that do an especially good job of conducting assessments. These exemplars are important because they illustrate not only how to do assessment but also that assessment can be done well in the context of the myriad responsibilities that fall to student affairs officers.

In the next chapters we look at the elements of the methods of assessment. Our authors will review mining existing databases, collecting data, soliciting participants, making decisions about instruments, and analyzing data. Then we bring this process together with a discussion about presenting results to various stakeholders. The book concludes with a discussion of the ethical dimensions that frame assessment, a presentation of a hypothetical mixed methods assessment project, and our vision for the future of assessment projects.

## References

Almanac Edition. (2007, August 31). *The Chronicle of Higher Education*, p. A14, p. A18.

American College Personnel Association. (1996). The student learning imperative: Implications for student affairs. *Journal of College Student Development, 37,* 118–122.

American Council on Education. (n.d.). *Shifting accountability: Autonomy, accountability, and privatization in public higher education.* Washington, DC: ACE—The Futures Project.

Aulepp, L., & Delworth, U. (1976). *Training manual for an ecosystem model.* Boulder, CO: Western Interstate Commission for Higher Education.

Baird, L. L. (2003). New lessons from research on student outcomes. In S. R. Komives, D. B. Woodard, Jr., and Associates, *Student services: A handbook for the profession* (4th ed., pp. 595–617). San Francisco: Jossey-Bass.

Berger, J. B., & Lyon, S. C. (2005). Past to present: A historical look at retention. In A. Seidman (Ed.), *College student retention: Formula for success* (pp. 1–29). Westport, CT: Praeger.

Boehner, J. A., & McKeon, H. P. (2003, September 4). *The college cost crisis.* Retrieved April 21, 2006 from http://edworkforce.house.gov/issues /108th/education/highereducation/highereducation.htm

Bureau of Labor Statistics. (2006, January 18). *Consumer price index 2005.* Washington, DC: United States Department of Labor.

Business-Higher Education Forum. (n.d.). *Public accountability for student learning in higher education: Issues and options.* Washington, DC: American Council on Education.

College Board. (2007). *Trends in college pricing.* Washington, D.C.: Author.

Dickeson, R. C. (2006). *The need for accreditation reform.* Retrieved April 20, 2006, from http://www.ed.gov/about/bdscomm/list/ hiedfuture/reports.html

Doerfel, M. L., & Ruben, B. D. (2002). Developing more adaptive, innovative and interactive organizations. In B. E. Bender & J. H. Schuh (Eds.), *Using benchmarking to inform practice in higher education* (pp. 5–27). New Directions for Higher Education, no. 118. San Francisco: Jossey-Bass.

Horn, Chen, X., & Chapman, C. (2003). *Getting ready to pay for college: What students and their parents know about the cost of college tuition and what they are doing to find out.* NCES 2003–030. Washington, DC: National Center for Education Statistics.

King, J. E. (2003). *2003 status report on the Pell grant program.* Washington, DC; American Council on Education

Kuh, G., D., Kinzie, J. Schuh, J. H., Whitt, E. J., & Associates. (2005). *Student success in college: Creating conditions that matter.* San Francisco: Jossey-Bass.

Leveille, D. E. (2006). *Accountability in higher education: A public agenda for trust and cultural change.* Berkeley, CA: University of California, Center for Studies in Higher Education.

Middle States Commission on Higher Education. (2005a). *Assessing student learning and institutional effectiveness.* Philadelphia, PA: Author. Retrieved May 18, 2006 from http://www.msche.org/publications_ view.asp?idPublicationType=5&txtPublicationType=Guidelines+ for+Institutional+Improvement

Middle States Commission on Higher Education. (2005b). *Best practices in outcomes assessment.* Philadelphia, PA: Author. Retrieved

May 18, 2006 from http://www.msche.org/publications_view.asp?
idPublicationType=5&txtPublicationType=Guidelines+for+
Institutional+Improvement

Millard, R. M. (1994). Accreditation. In. J. S. Stark & A. Thomas (Eds.),
*Assessment & program evaluation* (pp. 151–164). Needham Heights,
CT: Simon & Schuster.

National Association of Student Personnel Administrators and American College Personnel Association. (2004). *Learning reconsidered:
A campus-wide focus on the student experience.* Retrieved April 20,
2006, from www.naspa.org/membership/leader_ex_pdf/lr_long.pdf

Pascarella, E. T., & Terenzini, P. T. (1991). *How college affects students.* San
Francisco: Jossey-Bass.

Rhatigan, J. J., and Schuh, J. H. (2003, March-April). Small wins. *About
Campus, 8* (1), 17–22.

Schuh, J. H. (2003). Strategic planning and finance. In S. R. Komives, D.
B. Woodard, Jr., and Associates, *Student services: A handbook for the
profession* (4th ed., pp. 358–378). San Francisco: Jossey-Bass.

Schuh, J. H., & Shelley, M.C., II. (2001). External factors affecting room
and board rates: How much influence does the housing director
have? *The Journal of College and University Student Housing, 30* (1),
41–47.

Southern Association of Colleges and Schools, Commission on Colleges.
(2004). *Handbook of reaffirmation of accreditation.* Decatur,
GA: Author. Retrieved May 3, 2006, from http://www/sacscoc.org
/handbooks.asp

Study Group on the Conditions of Excellence in Higher Education. (1984).
*Involvement in learning: Realizing the potential of American higher edu-
cation.* Washington, DC: National Institute of Education.

Tinto, V. (2005). Foreword. In A. Seidman (Ed.), *College student retention:
Formula for success* (pp. ix–x). Westport, CT: Praeger.

Upcraft, M. L., & Schuh, J. H. (1996). *Assessment in student affairs: A guide for
practitioners.* San Francisco: Jossey-Bass.

U.S. Department of Education. (2006). *A test of leadership: Charting the future
of U.S. higher education.* Washington, DC: Author.

Weick, K. E. (1984). Small wins: Redefining the state of social problems.
*American Psychologist, 39* (1), 40–49.

Wingspread Group on Higher Education. (1993). *An American imperative: Higher expectations for higher education.* Racine, WI: Johnson
Foundation.

Yeager, J. L., Nelson, G. M., Potter, E. R., Weidman, J. C., & Zullo, T. G.
(Eds.). (2001). *ASHE reader on finance in higher education.* (2nd ed.).
Boston, MA: Pearson.

## Web Sites

NDSU Student Life. (2006). *Student involvement transcript*. Fargo, ND: Author. Retrieved July 13, 2006 from http://studentlife.ndsu.nodak .edu/index.php?action=page_manager_view_single&page_id=7

Educational Benchmarking, Inc. (2008). Complete assessment solutions. Springfield, MO: Author. Available at http://www.webebi.com /default.aspx

Oregon State University. (2008). *Learning in the division of student affairs*. Corvallis, OR: Author. Retrieved January 29, 2008 from http://oregonstate.edu/studentaffairs/assessment/index.html

Research and Assessment. (2007). *Penn State Pulse*. University Park, PA: Division of Student Affairs, Penn State University. Retrieved September 18, 2007 from http://www.sa.psu.edu/sara/pulse.shtml

Syracuse University Division of Student Affairs (2006). *Assessment work plan*. Syracuse, NY: Author. Retrieved July 13, 2006 from http://assessment.syr.edu/assessment/planFrames.htm

Syracuse University Office of Residence Life, (2005). *The orange slice*. Syracuse, NY: Author. Retrieved April 20, 2006, from http://assessment.syr.edu/assessment/reports/orl/ORLindex.htm

# 2

# USING EXISTING DATABASES

## Kevin Saunders and Darin R. Wohlgemuth

This chapter examines how student affairs practitioners can use existing data sources to provide useful assessment information. At the outset of a new assessment project, a good place to start is to consider what information is already available that fits the purpose of the project. In addition to the variety of existing data sources outside of the institution, many campuses are developing integrated databases or data warehouses that can provide answers to questions through successful data mining efforts. This chapter does not provide an exhaustive listing of the entire collection of existing data sources. Instead, we use a case study to illustrate a scenario in which multiple existing data sources can be helpful. We first consider how institutions can use data sources that are external to the institution to address several assessment questions. Next we consider ways that student affairs practitioners might take advantage of information collected within an institution. The discussion of internal data use considers issues in accessing data, general recommendations for enhancing the use of collected data, and effective practices for improvement in combining data. Because of the breadth of data collection activities on various campuses and the variety of information needs across institutions, this chapter is meant to provide a framework for enhancing assessment efforts through the use of existing data sources.

This chapter discusses how to maximize use of existing data in ways that demonstrate the value of student affairs efforts across students' experiences. Sometimes it is easy to overlook the fact that existing data can be used to address assessment questions.

Once planners identify the focus and assessment questions, it is important to ask the following additional questions (Fitzpatrick, Sanders, & Worthen, 2004):

- What public information sources and databases may provide useful information that is relevant to the questions?
- Is the manner of data collection, definition of constructs, and sampling methods appropriate for the current assessment?
- Within the institution, are existing reports, documents, or data collected for other purposes available that might provide answers to some of the questions?
- Are internal sources of information collected and organized in a valid and reliable manner?
- Does existing information adequately answer the identified assessment questions?
- What assessment questions are only partially answered by existing data?
- Which institutional offices maintain information that may be relevant to the assessment?

In short, planners will want to consider how existing data sources can assist with answering the identified assessment questions.

One clear reason for efforts to further the use of existing data sources is the limited number of resources available to student affairs staff for assessment or research effort. Consider that a 1999 study identified only 37 student affairs research offices nationwide (Malaney, 1999). Because of the national trend of budget cuts, the current number of student affairs research or assessment offices probably has not grown substantially. One implication of limited student affairs researchers is the need to collaborate with others across campus, including faculty members affiliated with student affairs, institutional research offices, and registrar offices. Sandeen and Barr (2006) suggest that in order to improve student affairs assessment there is a need to decrease separation from academic program assessment and reduce isolation from campus institutional assessment efforts. One way of coordinating assessment efforts is to collaborate with others across campus to review and analyze existing data sources. The following case study presents a campuswide issue regarding recruitment and retention and offers a context for exploring how collaboration can promote effective assessment efforts through the use of existing data.

## Case Study

Eastern University (EU) is a public, land-grant institution. In addition to using enrollment management information to support the fiscal operations of the institution, EU is also sensitive to its need to attract and retain a diverse student body that will enhance the learning environment. Eastern University recently has struggled to meet its enrollment goals for a diverse student population. Specifically, institutional and state leaders have noted that there is a growing gap between the percentage of African American students enrolled at the institution compared to the percentage of African Americans in colleges nationwide. In addition to a decline in African American students attending EU, the institution notes that African American students are less likely to persist to graduation. The director of admissions has been asked to form a task force to examine the factors influencing the recruitment and retention of African American students at the institution.

In thinking about the potential data sources that could be helpful for the work of the task force, it is helpful to break down the admissions process and the persistence process into different stages. In other words, if we consider the different pieces that relate to the overall assessment question, then we may be able to better identify the existing sources of information that are already available. Chang (2006) parses the admissions process into the following stages: prospects, inquirers, applicants, admitted, confirmed, and enrolled. Each term represents a different stage in the matriculation process. Similarly, the question regarding student retention involves several different decisions that can influence an end measure of student graduation.

The task force formed the following guiding questions to assist their assessment efforts:

- What do we know about the demographic characteristics of our applicant pool?
- What regional and national trends have an impact on the applicant pool?
- What do we know about the characteristics of students who apply to EU?
- Are there trends that inform us about the types of students who matriculate (enroll) at the institution?
- What benchmarking information is available regarding enrollment data of peer institutions?
- How do student experiences at EU affect their retention decisions?

The task force considered the first framing question posed at the beginning of the chapter: What public information sources and databases may provide useful information that is relevant to the questions?

## External Data

The admissions director and committee would be likely to consider several different information sources in order to examine the trends that shape the prospect pool. For example, a publication entitled *Knocking at the College Door* is provided through the Western Interstate Commission for Higher Education (http://www.wiche.edu/policy/knocking/1988–2018/),

ACT, and the College Board. This publication offers detailed projections of high school graduates by state, income, and race/ethnicity that can help identify demographic changes that influence future college populations. Here the committee considering the issue of recruiting a diverse student population could review detailed information about the projected number of high school graduates within neighboring or high-yield states to determine the number of diverse students represented in past applicant pools and the number of high school graduates in the primary recruiting areas.

Other sources of trend data include information from the U.S. and State Departments of Education. For example, the National Center for Education Statistics (NCES) (http://nces.ed.gov) provides an annual digest that offers information regarding national and state trends. The task force at EU might be interested in information regarding the estimated total and school-aged population by state (Snyder, Dillow, & Hoffman, 2007). It is worthwhile to note here that NCES uses several different survey programs to collect information at various levels, including elementary/secondary and postsecondary. Although the data are accessible to researchers, a number of existing publications also provide national level analyses of trends and issues facing education institutions. Using the search function in the NCES Web site allows individuals to search for relevant publications. Often these reports use information from several survey programs. For example, Peter and Horn (2005) use several of the NCES postsecondary datasets to provide a detailed account of gender differences in undergraduate education. An additional benefit of these reports is that they often offer a longitudinal perspective. Peter and Horn provide trends in high school academic preparation, postsecondary persistence and degree completion, and early labor market degree outcomes. Although this kind of information does not give an institution specific view, individuals looking to understand issues and develop effective information resources may find a useful framework and methodology in addition to an

understanding of national trends. In the case study presented for this chapter, the committee considering matriculation and retention decisions of African American students will find a large number of relevant NCES reports that may be useful.

Colleges and universities increasingly are using student information databases to better understand the characteristics of students who apply, are admitted, and enroll at institutions (Murray, 1991). The next step in the admissions cycle narrows the focus from the general population of students attending high school to high school students who take college entrance examinations. At this stage, institutions are able to access a variety of information sources that move beyond trend data to provide a listing of students who represent current prospects.

Both ACT and the College Board have search tools that may be used to identify counts of students in specific areas and with specific characteristics. Many aggregate reports are available on their Web pages. Individuals who register for the exam provide detailed profile information on categories such as educational plans, extracurricular plans, demographic background, factors influencing college choice, characteristics of high school, and high school extracurricular activities. Institutions can design specific queries of student test takers who match characteristics in the profile information. This is especially important if the school has admission criteria that restrict a set of students from being offered admission. For example, EU requires that students have a core set of high school courses and that they rank in the top half of their high school class. It would be helpful to identify those students who are eligible for admission. This allows the institution to target its marketing and attention to specific segments of the prospect pool.

Applying this data source to our case study, we note that groups interested in recruitment issues can look at different reports of ACT test data based on such variables as gender, type of high school, ethnicity, high school rank, high school grade point average (GPA), course-taking patterns, intended college

major, and degree-level goal. Specifically, one could examine the number of African American test takers who are in the top half of their graduating class and have taken the ACT exam to define the population of students.

These databases assist institutions in targeting their recruitment efforts by combining "information on lifestyle decisions, purchasing patterns, and even the types of colleges to which prospective students apply" (Hossler, Kuh, & Olsen, 2001a, p. 218). Typical information available through these database systems include geographic variables (state of residence, high school district, distance from campus), academic performance (for example, GPA, high school rank, standardized test scores), gender, anticipated major, race or ethnicity, family income, religious preference, and desired college characteristics (for example, state, type, size). Either the ACT search tool (called Enrollment Information Service, EIS) or the College Board tool (Enrollment Planning Service, EPS) could be used to develop this type of customized report. In many cases, the admissions office will have one of these tools for recruitment planning.

To this point, we have discussed some of the available data sources and tools that a campus may use to examine concerns regarding recruitment of African American students. The director of admissions and the committee will make use of demographic trends to see broad changes that affect the applicant pool. They also can make use of compiled databases that offer insights into the characteristics of students who apply, are admitted, and enroll at the institution. Although there are several other steps that students follow in the admissions process before they enroll at an institution (for example, application, admission, confirmation), the following discussion moves on to consider existing data that relate to students who enroll at the institution. Recall that in the case of EU, not only is the institution concerned about attracting African American students but it also recognizes the needs and the institutional challenges in retaining students.

Suppose that the admissions director also is interested in seeing how neighboring institutions are faring in the area of recruitment and retention of African American students. The Integrated Postsecondary Education Data System (IPEDS) is a federal database provided by the National Center for Education Statistics (http://nces.ed.gov/ipeds/). IPEDS offers a Peer Analysis System online that allows, among other things, institutions to gather comprehensive data for benchmarking against other institutions (Schuh, 2002). First-time users of the IPEDS system can follow a helpful tutorial that offers an overview of the features available within the system and details about how to log in. Use of the Peer Analysis System requires individuals to locate a six-digit institution number from the College Opportunities On-Line (COOL) link. Once individuals log into the Peer Analysis System, they are able to create a peer comparison group, select variables for data collection, and generate comparison reports. Another useful tool in developing peer comparison groups is available through the Carnegie Foundation for the Advancement of Teaching. A classification Web site (http://www.carnegiefoundation.org/classifications/sub.asp?key =784) provides tools for using the Carnegie Classifications to develop custom listings of institutions. Institutions can use classifications, classification categories (for example, undergraduate instructional program, graduate instructional program, enrollment profile, undergraduate profile, size and setting, and community engagement), or both to create a custom listing of institutions for comparison purposes.

The information collected through IPEDS is robust because it contains an enormous amount of data about higher education institutions. The information collected includes areas such as institutional characteristics, degree completions, human resources, fall enrollment, finance, and graduation. Bailey (2006) noted over a thousand variables listed in the data dictionary from the IPEDS Peer Analysis System. In addition to the large number of institutions and data fields, the data span multiple years, thus allowing institutions to examine patterns and trends over time. One important feature for users to understand before using the IPEDS data is that the data can be used to generate summary information at the institutional level but cannot be used for measures at the student unit record level. For example, although the admissions director may be interested in finding out how many African American students are enrolled at other institutions within the state (institution level), the IPEDS system will not allow an examination of the amount of financial aid provided to African American students (student level).

The Peer Analysis System now includes a listing of frequently derived/used variables that allows users to quickly generate benchmarking data with relative ease. For example, the director of admissions and committee in our case study would be able to select a number of these frequently used variables such as "percentage admitted—total," "admissions yield—total," "percentage of total enrollment that are black, non-Hispanic," "graduation rate—bachelor's degree within six years, black, non-Hispanic," or changes in the pattern of price or financial aid. Once the key variables of interest are selected, the system allows the user to generate a benchmarking report of these variables for the selected comparison group. Consider the following scenarios and how online information can be used to provide information quickly and relatively accurately.

## How Do Our Room and Board Costs Compare?

It's a Tuesday afternoon in the middle of the fall semester and the vice president for student affairs at Eastern University has been reflecting on what a good semester it has been to date. Enrollment in the university has been strong, the number of students living in the residence halls has been on target so that the budget for the year will be met or even exceeded if retention from the fall to the spring occurs as anticipated, and the number of student problems has been minimal and addressed very well by the staff. In short, the term is going well and the vice president is pleased.

Then the telephone rings. The president is on the line and she is a bit worried. Several new members of the governing board have a strong business background, and early indications were that they would be more activist than the board members they were replacing. The next board meeting is in three weeks and the president was just presented with a series of questions related to how the expenditures of the college compared with ten peer institutions (the "Peer Ten"). The president has parceled out questions related to expenditures to the vice presidents who provide oversight for the areas in which the questions fall. In the case of this call, she needs to know how room and board costs at EU compare with those at the "Peer Ten." She also needs to know how expenditures for student affairs at EU compare with those at the "Peer Ten."

A decade ago or so the answer to the first question would have required the vice president to call in the housing director and ask for the information related to room and board charges to see whether he knew what the room and board charges were for the "Peer Ten." If he did not, he would or his staff members would have to place calls to the housing offices of the "Peer Ten" and get the information. This is not a hard question to answer, and pre-sumably within a day or two the information could be collected. In the current environment, making telephone calls would not be necessary, since the data are available on the Web sites of the various institutions and could be collected quickly. So the answer to the first question is easy to ascertain, and the information can be made available to the president in a matter of hours. In fact, the president could have had a member of her staff get the data from institutional Web sites and be done with the process.

## How Do Our Expenditures for Student Affairs Compare?

The second question is a bit more difficult to answer. The president wants to know whether the institution is spending more, less, or about the same on student affairs as the "Peer Ten." Years ago this would have been a question that would have been very difficult to answer. Among the problems would have been defining what to include in the definition of "student affairs" because units at some institutions that are part of student affairs, such as an office of career services, might be part of academic units. So, defining what is included could be difficult.

Fortunately for the vice president, with the development of the executive peer tool of IPEDS, the answer to this question is easily attained. Since the vice president is quite familiar with IPEDS, all it takes is to access the Web site (http://nces.ed.gov/ipedspas/ExPT/index.asp), type in the institution's name, add the names of the "Peer Ten," and go to the page where variables are available to investigators. One of the sets of variables available is core expenses per FTE in six specific categories: instruction, research, public service, academic support, institutional support, and student services. With a simple click the average (mean) data per FTE student are available for the "Peer Ten," and with another click the data are available for each of the institutions. So in a matter of minutes the vice president can provide the information to the president and fulfill the second request.

To be sure, IPEDS is not perfect (see Schuh, 2002), but it does provide a central database that is easy to locate and navigate. Although there can always be problems associated with a database of this type, including how those who supply the data interpret the questions they are responding to, and the extent to which they accurately key in the information, there is no question that this database is much more efficient than if one had to collect the data via other techniques. So this database can be used to answer a variety of questions from room and board rates to retention rates to financial aid questions and so on.

## How Do Our Crime Statistics Compare?

When the vice president provided this expenditure information to the president, the president was grateful and then said that she had one more question that had been sent to her just a few minutes ago. This one had to do with crime statistics.

A board member wondered how the crime statistics for the campus compared with the "Peer Ten." The president thought that since the vice president had been so successful and prompt in providing answers to the first questions that maybe the vice president could come up with the answer to this question. The vice president indicated that an answer was something that could be developed through another data set and the information would be available soon. The president asked whether information could be provided not only for the previous reporting year but also perhaps for the two years preceding as well. The vice president said that this was possible, but that it would take a bit of time to gather the information.

As a consequence of the Student Right to Know and Campus Security Act of 1990 (Barr, 2003) institutions of higher education have been required to make crime statistics available to the public on an annual basis. These data are reported to the federal government in addition to being published through various campus media, and the federal government also makes the information available to the public.

Crime statistics are available on an institution-by-institution basis through the College Opportunities Online (COOL) Data System, also part of the IPEDS Web site. The specific Web site for entrance into the COOL Web site is http://nces.ed.gov/ipeds/cool/. To get the answer for the crimes statistics, the vice president clicked on the Web site and noted that it took an additional couple of clicks and the crime statistics were available for the most recent reporting year and the two previous years, including criminal offenses, hate offenses, and arrests. These data were copied and placed in an EXCEL spreadsheet for each of the "Peer Ten" in addition to the baseline data for EU. The data then were made available to the president, who, in turn, provided the material as part of a report for the governing board. The president was particularly grateful to the vice president for providing the data on such a timely basis.

## Observations About IPEDS

Schuh (2002) outlined the strengths and weaknesses of the IPEDS system. Strengths include the wide range of participating institutions, the ability to customize peer groups, the consistency of data-gathering instruments, the accessibility of information and speed of comparisons, and the availability of longitudinal information. Weaknesses include the broad categories of variables that prevent narrowly defined comparisons, the need for other software tools for sophisticated analysis, and the possible confusion between survey year and fiscal year when reporting data. Schuh concluded: "knowledgeable use of IPEDS...can assist investigators in more fully understanding their institutions and how they compare with peers" (p. 37).

Earlier we noted that there are over a thousand variables available in the IPEDS data dictionary. Rather than provide a comprehensive listing of the data elements that student affairs practitioners might find valuable, we instead offer Table 2.1, which describes the broad categories of information collected.

We've offered some of the additional examples of ways to use existing external data in an effort to encourage readers to consider the breadth of available information sources. As we return to the case study of recruitment and retention at EU, the task force can use another of the initial framing questions to consider additional information sources: Within the institution, are existing reports, documents, or data collected for other purposes available that might provide answers to some of the questions?

## Internal Data

Although most of the examples thus far address the use of information for recruitment of new students, there are ample tools and services that use student data for ongoing assessment in areas such as student retention, satisfaction, engagement, and academic performance. Previous research indicates that certain

## Table 2.1  IPEDS Information Categories

| Information Collected | Data Description |
| --- | --- |
| Institutional characteristics | Include educational offerings, control/affiliation, award levels, admission requirements, student charges (including tuition and fees, room and board, and other expenses). |
| Degree completions | Completions data include demographic information on race/ethnicity, gender of recipient, and field of study. Data collected by level or type of degree and non-degree programs. |
| Twelve-month enrollment | Headcount, instructional activity (contact or credit hours), and full-time equivalent (FTE) enrollment. Data include demographic information on race/ethnicity and gender. |
| Human resources | Headcount information on employees by assigned position. Information on staff, including number of faculty, non-faculty, part-time employees, tenure of full-time faculty, and number of new hires. |
| Fall enrollment | Number of full and part-time students enrolled in the fall. Demographics include race/ethnicity, gender, residence, and age. |
| Finance | Revenues by source, expenses by function, physical plant assets and indebtedness, and endowment investments. |
| Financial aid | Data regarding number of students receiving federal grants, state and local government grants, and loans. Data on average amount received by type of aid. |
| Graduation rates | Number of students entering the institution in a particular year, number of students completing program within a period equal to one and a half times the normal period of time, and number of students who transferred to other institutions. |

Source: Table adapted from http://nces.ed.gov/IPEDS/about/info_collected.asp.

college experiences, such as peer relationships, extracurricular involvement, and interactions with faculty, enhance educational attainment (Pascarella & Terenzini, 1991, 2005). Beyond gathering benchmarking information, it is important to gather information about students' experiences at an institution. Tinto (2000) stated that students' "interactions across the academic and social geography of a campus shape the educational opportunity structure..." (p. 94). An important question facing student affairs professionals is how to best gather and use this type of information to assist student learning.

One place to start is to identify any national surveys that the institution has participated in over the past couple of years to see whether there may be useful information to answer specific questions. Chapter Five offers an overview of many existing national instruments that gather specific information about students' experiences at an institution. Interested readers are encouraged to consult that chapter for additional details about available instruments and ways to maximize institutional use of existing data when participating in these studies. Imagine that EU participates in one of two national surveys: the National Survey of Student Engagement (NSSE) or the Cooperative Institutional Research Program (CIRP). Here are some ways that the data could be further mined beyond the overall institutional report.

Sandeen and Barr (2006) note that the National Survey of Student Engagement is one of the most encouraging developments in recent years that provides colleges, students, and the public with information regarding students' participation in a number of educational practices demonstrated to be associated with learning. Instead of focusing on academic reputation or resources, this instrument provides institutions with information to improve educational programs. The NSSE annual reports, which are available on the NSSE website (http://nsse.iub.edu/index.cfm), offer several examples of different ways that institutions are using the data.

In the case of EU, the campus may be interested in reviewing several of the NSSE benchmarks of effective educational practice. Based on forty-two key questions that capture "some of the more powerful contributors to learning and personal development," the five benchmarks include level of academic challenge, student interactions with faculty, active and collaborative learning, supportive campus environment, and enriching educational experiences. EU may be interested in finding out whether underrepresented students report different experiences in these five benchmarks compared to other students. University of Massachusetts, Lowell recently compared the NSSE benchmark scores between students who returned to the institution and those who left the institution. The comparison indicated that students who leave scored lower on each of the five benchmarks (NSSE, 2006). Institutions who participate in the NSSE should review the work resulting from the Documenting Effective Educational Practice (DEEP) project that examined the practices of institutions that had higher-than-predicted scores on the NSSE benchmarks and predicted graduation rates. *Student Success in College* (Kuh, Kinzie, Schuh, & Whitt, 2005) describes the DEEP project and offers insight into ways to enhance student learning, student engagement, and educational effectiveness.

Another commonly administered national instrument is the Cooperative Institutional Research Program (CIRP, http://www.gseis.ucla.edu/heri/cirp.html). One instrument, the Freshman Survey, is administered annually at around 700 institutions during new student orientation or registration. This instrument offers information about students' characteristics before their institutional experiences, including areas such as parental income and education, ethnicity, financial aid, secondary school achievement and activities, educational plans, attitudes, and self-concept. Information from the CIRP can be used to provide the campus community with an annual profile of students at the institution. If EU participated in this survey, the student affairs staff might find value in examining the characteristics, attitudes, self-concept, and goals of African American students attending the institution.

It may be helpful to note that both survey programs mentioned here (NSSE, CIRP) have designed instruments that may be used for longitudinal data analysis (see Chapter Five). Although institutions that participate in these survey programs can use the datasets for subsequent analysis, there may be some value in exploring the potential benefits of how these could support the collection of longitudinal data that might assist assessment efforts in new ways.

Perhaps EU does not participate in national surveys and has not systematically collected information from students using institutional surveys. Institutions use several different administrative systems to support operations and management that offer a wealth of available data. The next sections of this chapter consider issues in accessing these data, the typical data collected by most campuses, and how these data can be combined with other data.

## Accessing Data

Although we previously discussed the possible use of survey-based information for retention assessment, some research suggests that widely available institutional data also hold promise in this area. For example, Caison (2006) tested an alternative to the resource intensive methodology of student surveys. The study presented a model that included commonly collected data (for example, high school GPA, entrance exam scores, in-state residency, and total semester hours) combined with other frequently collected information (for example, parental education, certainty of major, and intention to work). This model provided a better prediction of retention than using an institutional integration survey scale as a single measure. Nichols (1995) estimated that between 30 and 35 percent of the assessment data needed by an institution is already available on campus and can be identified by an inventory of existing assessment activities. A publication of this inventory allows individuals to see examples of assessment activities and information that are in place at the institution.

However, institutions often encounter difficulties when trying to access existing information in meaningful ways that support decision making. This challenge can be the result of trying to extract information from administrative systems that are designed to manage student, financial, human resource, and payroll processes (Norman, 2003). As Norman explains, "the primary function of an institution's administrative system is to support the critical day-to-day transactions...designing a solid reporting solution that runs beside your administrative system will save you time, money, and frustration" (pp. 59–60).

Consider the initial struggles EU experienced in trying to collect information regarding the recruitment and retention of African American students. Separate pockets within EU may be collecting and analyzing different information regarding African American students' experiences at the institution. Perhaps there is attention to the types of activities students participate in, disaggregated by ethnicity through student affairs. There might also be an effort to examine student participation in academic learning communities by ethnicity. A committee exploring campus climate issues may have hosted several focus groups with a diverse set of students to learn more about their campus experiences. In addition, the Office of Institutional Research has information about academic majors, academic performance, and withdrawal trends by ethnicity. Although these groups each take an important look at critical issues from different perspectives, a lack of coordination, communication, and integration may make it difficult to gain a clear understanding of the overall assessment question. If institutions strive to support consensual decision-making processes that involve several different constituents, there is a need to provide a common body of information (Friedman & Hoffman, 2001). As Hossler and Gorr (2006) explain, institutions invested historically in stand-alone systems for financial aid, registration and records, or student financials. By the 1990s campuses turned

a database system, staff will need additional skills such as developing queries or using spreadsheets to analyze and present data. In other words, rather than simply concentrating on the business functions that technology supports, student affairs staff should integrate assessment functions into their understanding of technology tools.

As institutions move to increase sharing of information through integration of separate subsystems, new challenges arise. For example, the ability to easily extract student data from institutional systems presents risk-management concerns related to the Family Educational Rights and Privacy Act (FERPA) and the Health Insurance Portability Accountability Act (HIPPA) regulations (Moneta, 2005). Not only do staff need proficiency in using database management and use, but there is also a need for ongoing education and training efforts to ensure proper use of the information. Readers should consult Chapter Eight for insight into the ethical issues relevant to data collection and use of existing data records.

We would like to touch on one final area of consideration as professionals contemplate the use of relational databases for assessment information, which is a fundamental understanding of how data are collected and how a relational database functions. One important understanding is the difference between what might be called snapshot or point-in-time data and ongoing student records. In our case, envision that the committee is interested in learning about the retention of African American students who are in the College of Liberal Arts and Sciences (LAS). Depending on how we define *membership* would have a lot to do with how we would try to look at existing data. In short, students who are pursuing LAS majors represent a moving target. Some students enter with a declared major, some students decide later, and other students change majors. This same issue warrants consideration when using existing data and requires careful attention to the parameters. Are we interested in individuals who had LAS majors during a specific period or individuals who ever had LAS majors? The process of aligning data can be difficult. Friedman and Hoffman (2001) explain that one of the largest tasks in database development is finding a way to revise the structure of data stored in disparate university systems to "fit" a common relational database environment. They also caution that the fit will never be perfect, cannot anticipate all future contingencies, and will experience mistakes.

## Typical Data

After considering some of the issues outlined above, institutions will begin to determine and define the variables of interest that will be used in a relational database. One of the best places to begin when considering the types of data available at an institution would be to spend time visiting with the "keepers" of information at the institution. This might include institutional research, an assessment office, the registrar's office, or the provost's office. One might consider reviewing some areas of data commonly collected at institutions as a way to think about the potential benefits of coordinating assessment efforts at an institution. For example, a review of the Common Data Set (CDS) initiative would offer insight into the types of information collected at several institutions. CDS is a joint effort among the College Board, Peterson's, and U.S. News and World Report. The goal is to improve the quality and accuracy of shared information through the development of consistent and clear data definitions. A review of the website (http://www.commondataset.org/default.asp) provides access to the current data set definitions, which include the broad topical areas of enrollment and persistence, admissions, academic offerings and policies, student life, expenses, financial aid, instructional faculty and class size, and degrees conferred.

Many of these categories overlap with the most commonly used performance or "dashboard" indicators noted by Volkwein (2007). These dashboards commonly include measures of "admissions, enrollments, faculty and student profiles, and finances...but few have gotten beyond retention and graduation rates, degrees awarded, class size, student/faculty ratios, honor and study abroad participation, student/faculty/alumni satisfaction, research funding/expenditures/patents, employment/ graduate school attendance by graduates, library rankings, and reputational ratings" (p. 154). Institutions noted by Volkwein that use these indicators to track and monitor progress include Pennsylvania State University, Ohio State University, Miami University, Tufts University, and Illinois State University.

The increased use of online course management systems also offers potential as an additional source of data. For example, Purdue University is looking at ways of using its course management system to develop an early warning intervention system designed to improve student retention (Wanger, King, & Guentert, 2006). Course management systems are essentially Web-based systems that allow instructors to create and manage online courses. In a pilot study that examined the feasibility of using course management information (for example, number of sessions accessed, time accessing sessions, response to e-mail or discussion postings, information reviewed), the authors developed a prediction model for course grades that included a combination of background characteristics and course interaction behaviors including session times, composite SAT, information viewed (URLs accessed), academic status, and cumulative GPA. As institutions collect more information regarding student learning behaviors demonstrated through course management systems, there may be additional ways of using that information to enhance student learning and success.

In no way is this section meant to be representative of the universe of existing information that can contribute to assessment. There are several other examples nationwide that offer new insights about ways to maximize the use of commonly collected information. Hossler, Kuh, and Olsen (2001b) advocated for using a combination of theory from higher education research and data from institutional research to guide institutional policies and strategies. They provided the example of institutional research that demonstrated students in high-risk courses were more likely to seek tutoring available in their residence halls than when the tutoring service was provided in other locations. The analysis of student tutoring participation by location had important programmatic implications for the institution. The point here is that there are multiple ways to use existing information to support assessment efforts.

## Building a Database

Some institutions may be in the process of developing relational databases to enhance the use of data across the institution. Interested readers can consult several resources that offer ideas about how to effectively develop relational databases (for example, Friedman & Hoffman, 2001; Gorr & Hossler, 2006; Hossler & Gorr, 2006; Moneta, 2005). These resources also detail the challenges involved in this process. Friedman and Hoffman (2001) acknowledge that the process requires a paradigm shift in how institutions approach information from isolated, independent, and static views of data to an understanding that information is a shared resource, that databases serve multiple purposes and are relational, and that databases change in response to new needs. Moneta (2005) cautions that the complexity of developing common data definitions and standardizing business practices requires a level of ongoing effort that is underpredicted and underresourced by institutions. For a complete discussion of strengths and weaknesses of commercial versus build-your-own enterprise systems see Gorr and Hossler (2006).

## Conclusion

In conclusion, we offer one example to highlight the need to consider ways of using existing data that are collected at the institution. The director of an honors program at the institution was asked to present information to the board of trustees. A recent initiative within the program was an effort to enhance students' participation in research with faculty members at the institution, and the director wanted to quickly gather some information about the need for this effort. The director of the program contacted the provost office, seeking assistance in the development and administration of an assessment tool to capture information about student research at the institution. Before developing a new instrument, however, the provost office developed a report of existing data from the National Survey of Student Engagement. This report not only provided a longitudinal view of students' participation in faculty research but also allowed the director to compare student engagement at the institution between students who had participated in faculty research and those who had not.

Our final point is to emphasize the potential of using existing information to support assessment efforts. By coordinating with other individuals across the institution to maximize institution-specific data, analyze the information, and widely share the results, student affairs professionals can help effect positive change, demonstrate impact, and improve our understanding of student and institutional performance.

## References

Bailey, B. L. (2006). Let the data talk: Developing models to explain IPEDS graduation rates. In J. Luan and C. M. Zhao (Eds.), *Data mining in action: Case studies of enrollment management* (pp. 101–115) New Directions for Institutional Research, no. 131. San Francisco: Jossey-Bass.

Barr, M. J. (2003). Legal foundations of student affairs practice. In S. R. Komives, D. B. Woodard, Jr., & Associates, *Student services: A handbook for the profession* (4th ed., pp. 128–149). San Francisco: Jossey-Bass.

Caison, A. L. (2006). Analysis of institutionally specific retention research: A comparison between survey and institutional database methods. *Research in Higher Education, 48* (4), 435–451.

Chang, L. (2006). Applying data mining to predict college admissions yield: A case study. In J. Luan and C. M. Zhao (Eds.), *Data mining in action:*

*Case studies of enrollment management* (pp. 53–68). New Directions for Institutional Research, no. 131. San Francisco: Jossey-Bass.

Fitzpatrick, J. L., Sanders, J. R., & Worthen, B. R. (2004). *Program evaluation: Alternative approaches and practical guidelines* (3rd ed.). Boston: Pearson.

Friedman, D., & Hoffman, P. H. (2001). The politics of information: Building a relational database to support decision-making at a public university. *Change, 33* (3), 50–57.

Gorr, W., & Hossler, D. (2006). Why all the fuss about information systems? Or information systems as golden anchors in higher education. In D. Hossler and S. Pape (Eds.), *Building a student information system: Strategies for success and implications for campus policy* (pp. 7–20). New Directions for Higher Education, no. 136. San Francisco: Jossey-Bass.

Hossler, D., & Gorr, W. (2006). Enterprise systems. In D. Priest and E. St. John (Eds.), *Privatization and public universities* (pp. 203–227). Indianapolis, IN: Indiana University Press.

Hossler, D., Kuh, G. D., & Olsen, D. (2001a). Finding fruit on the vines: Using higher education research and institutional research to guide institutional policies and strategies. *Research in Higher Education, 42* (2), 211–221.

Hossler, D., Kuh, G. D., & Olsen, D. (2001b). Finding fruit on the vines: Using higher education research and institutional research to guide institutional policies and strategies (Part II). *Research in Higher Education, 42* (2), 223–235.

Kleinglass, N. (2005). Who is driving the changing landscape in student affairs? In K. Kruger (Ed.), *Technology in student affairs: Supporting student learning and services* (pp. 25–38). New Directions in Student Services, no. 112. San Francisco: Jossey-Bass.

Kuh, G. D., Kinzie, J., Schuh, J. H., & Whitt, E. J. (2005). *Student success in college: Creating conditions that matter.* San Francisco: Jossey-Bass.

Malaney, G. (1999). The structure and function of student affairs research offices: A national study. In G. Malaney (Ed.), *Student affairs research, evaluation, and assessment: structure and practice in an era of change.* New Directions for Student Services, no. 85. San Francisco: Jossey-Bass.

Moneta, L. (2005). Technology and student affairs: Redux. In K. Kruger (Ed.), *Technology in student affairs: Supporting student learning and services.* New Directions in Student Services, no. 112. San Francisco: Jossey-Bass.

Murray, D. (1991). Monitoring shifts in campus image and recruitment efforts in small colleges. In D. Hossler (Ed.), *Evaluating student recruitment and retention programs.* New Directions for Institutional Research, no. 70. San Francisco: Jossey-Bass.

National Survey of Student Engagement. (2006). *Engaged learning: Fostering success for all students, Annual Report.* Center for Postsecondary Research: Indiana University Bloomington.

Nichols, J. O. (1995). Assessment Planning. In J. O. Nichols (Ed.), *A practitioner's handbook for institutional effectiveness and student outcomes assessment implementation.* New York: Agathon.

Norman, W. (2003) Data, data everywhere—Not a report in sight. *Educause Quarterly, 4,* 59–62.

Pascarella, E. T., & Terenzini, P. T. (1991). *How college affects students: Findings and insights from twenty years of research.* San Francisco: Jossey-Bass.

Pascarella, E. T., & Terenzini, P. T. (2005). *How college affects students: A third decade of research.* San Francisco: Jossey-Bass.

Peter, K., & Horn, L. (2005). *Gender differences in participation and completion of undergraduate education and how they have changed over time (NCES 2005–169). U.S. Department of Education, National Center for Education Statistics. Washington, DC: U.S. Government Printing Office.*

Sandeen, A., & Barr, M. (2006). *Critical Issues for Student Affairs: Challenges and Opportunities.* San Francisco: Jossey-Bass.

Schuh, J. H. (2002). The integrated postsecondary education data system. In B. E. Bender & J. H. Schuh (Eds.), *Using benchmarking to inform practice in higher education* (pp. 29–38). New Directions for Higher Education, no. 118. San Francisco: Jossey-Bass.

Snyder, T. D., Dillow, S. A., and Hoffman, C. M. (2007). *Digest.* National Center for Education Statistics, Institute of Education Washington, DC: U.S. Government Printing Office.

Tinto, V. (2000). Linking learning and leaving: Exploring the role of the college classroom in student departure. In J. M. Braxton (Ed.), *Reworking the student departure puzzle* (pp. 81–94). Nashville, TN: Vanderbilt University Press.

Upcraft, M. L. (2003). Assessment and evaluation. In S. R. Komives, D. B. Woodard, Jr., & Associates, *Student services: A foundation for the profession* (4th ed., pp. 555–572). San Francisco: Jossey-Bass.

Upcraft, M. L., & Schuh, J. H. (1996). *Assessment in student affairs: A guide for practitioners.* San Francisco: Jossey-Bass.

Volkwein, J. F. (2007). Assessing institutional effectiveness and connecting the pieces of a fragmented university. In J. C. Burke (Ed.), *Fixing the Fragmented University.* Bolton, MA: Anker.

Wanger, S. P., King, J. A., & Guentert, L. G (2006, June). *Student retention: Using the course management system for an early warning and intervention system.* Paper presented at the International Assessment and Retention Conference, National Administration of Student Personnel Administrators, Phoenix, AZ.

## Databases

Association for Institutional Research. http://www.airweb.org/?page=309

Carnegie Foundation. http://www.carnegiefoundation.org/classifications/sub
.asp?key=784

College Opportunities Online (COOL). http://nces.ed.gov/ipeds/cool/

Integrated Post Secondary Data System (IPEDS). http://nces.ed.gov/ipedspas/
ExPT/index.asp

The Education Trust. College Opportunities Online. http://www.collegeresults
.org/mainMenu.aspx

# 3

# PLANNING FOR AND IMPLEMENTING DATA COLLECTION

## R. M. Cooper

All decisions regarding research, evaluation, or assessment projects are strongly linked with the purpose for conducting the project, the research questions asked, and the objectives addressed. Therefore, the first step in any assessment project is to determine the purpose for the project, which then leads to developing the questions and identifying the objectives of the project. From the objectives one can determine who the participants will be, as well as what methods of data collection are best suited for the project. Without a clearly defined purpose, data collection can be an exercise that consumes a great deal of time, yielding mounds of data that have no direct connection to the assessment inquiry. A clearly defined purpose helps identify the data collection methods most appropriate for the inquiry. For example, if the purpose of the inquiry is to review the admission standards at a university with the intent of revising these standards, one method would be to examine incoming student academic records. For this reason, document review would be an appropriate data collection method. If the inquiry was to review how students experience the admission process at the university, appropriate data collection methods might include a Web-based survey (if the institution wanted a census or a large sample) or focus groups (if the goal was to gather information that was not bounded by the limits of survey questions).

The goal of this chapter is to provide information that will help those responsible for assessment inquiries in developing and implementing data collection plans. Consideration should be given to (1) data collection methods that align with the purpose and objectives of the assessment, (2) how different methods of data collection are implemented and carried out, and (3) advantages and challenges of using various data collection methods.

Before moving forward in the discussion of data collection methods, it is important to mention that on most campuses all data collection efforts that involve campus community members (for example, students, staff, and faculty) should be reviewed by and approved through the institution's human subjects review board. Please check with your institution's institutional review board (IRB) for the policies and guidelines relevant to conducting human subjects research at your institution. Ethical considerations of working with human subjects are discussed in Chapter Eight.

The data collection methods discussed in this chapter are not meant to be an all inclusive list of methods but those most likely to be used in student affairs assessments; these include surveys and questionnaires, interviews (individual and group), observations, and document reviews.

## Surveys and Questionnaires

Surveys and questionnaires can be used to explore relationships and obtain sensitive information; they may also be combined with other data-gathering approaches (Colton & Covert, 2007). Typically, they are used with a sample to make inferences about characteristics, attitudes, or behaviors of a population. For the most part, surveys can be a very cost effective and efficient method for collecting data which makes them the primary method for collecting assessment data on college campuses. Colton and Covert (2007), however, point out that "surveys are mistakenly perceived to be more time and cost effective than other approaches to information gathering" (p. 11). This may be the case when the choice is to develop a local instrument because of the time and costs that go into creating questions and ensuring that the instrument is reliable and valid. One approach to offset costs incurred with developing a local instrument is to use a published instrument (see Chapter Five).

## Why Use a Survey Design Method?

Nardi (2003) explains that surveys are best designed for (1) measuring variables with numerous values or response categories, (2) investigating attitudes and opinions that are not usually observable, (3) describing characteristics of a large population, and (4) studying behaviors that may be more stigmatizing or difficult for people to tell someone else face-to-face (pp. 58–59).

Surveys can be administered through pencil and paper versions, Web-based technology, or by telephone polling, although the latter is not particularly common, Penn State's assessment unit being a notable exception. Often a Web-based survey design can be implemented with a large sample or with an entire population (for example, census survey) efficiently and cost-effectively. Furthermore, the use of probability sampling (see Chapter Four) works well with a survey design; hence it is an appealing method of data collection when results need to be generalized to a larger population. Reliability and validity of a survey instrument (see discussion in Chapter Five) adds to the quality of the results thus making it an appealing method for data collection when the results are to be compared with preestablished benchmarks. An obstacle to using a survey design for data collection is the possibility of low response rates that affect the ability to generalize the results. As the number of surveys increases, so does the potential for the decrease in overall response rates.

One advantage to using a survey method is the confidentiality (i.e., participant identifiers are kept and could be linked with the data, but data are stored securely) or anonymity (i.e., no potential connections between the participant and the data collected) afforded to participants. As a result, participants are often more likely to be open (that is, candid, sincere) in their responses.

When considering a survey design for data collection, there are a number of questions to consider and address. For instance:

- What do you want to measure by using a survey data collection method?
- Are the population and method identified for selecting a sample? Will it be a random or convenience sample?
- What is the size of the sample? Or is it a census survey?
- Will this survey be used at more than one point in time and over the course of time (for example, longitudinal)?
- What type of instrument will be used? A published instrument or an instrument developed locally?
- How will the survey be pilot tested?
- What is the time line for collecting data?
- How will the survey be implemented (for example, Web-based or paper and pencil)?
- Will participants be compensated?

Several of these questions are examined in the following subsections.

## What Do You Want to Measure by Using a Survey Data Collection Method?

Once the assessment focus of inquiry has been identified, and objectives determined, the next step is to ascertain what information (that is, what you want to measure) will be useful in carrying out the goals of the assessment inquiry. Colton and Covert (2007) suggest considering whether what you want to understand is the processes or the outcomes. Table 3.1

### Table 3.1  Process and Outcomes

| | Process<br>Efficiency (doing things<br>right) —productivity | Outcome<br>Effectiveness (doing the<br>right things) —quality |
|---|---|---|
| What to Measure | Inputs | Outcomes |
| | Resources needed<br>Resources used | Goals and objectives attained |
| | Outputs | Impacts |
| | Services rendered | Long-term, socially beneficial results |
| Questions | Did it occur? | What was achieved? |
| | How often? | Did it accomplish what it was suppose to do? |
| | How much?<br>When?<br>Where? | Does it make a difference? |

Source: Colton and Covert (2007), p. 102.

summarizes the different focus between process-oriented information and outcome-oriented information.

Suppose a senior student affairs administrator wants to know whether she should increase the budget for a learning community on her campus. Before the administrator increases the budget, she might want to know whether the current funding the learning community receives is being used efficiently. Thus, a survey or questionnaire with process-type questions would be beneficial. If the administrator already has information that demonstrates the efficient use of funds for the learning community, she might then want to know how effective the learning community is in achieving its goals. In this case, the survey will be more focused on measuring the outcomes of the program. It is possible to address both process and outcome questions on the same survey as long as there is a clear understanding of what is being measured by each specific item.

If the goal is to measure attitudes and opinions, Nardi (2003) suggests doing this through open-ended questions to get the most information. However, close-ended questions are useful when attempting to standardize responses, but this can often frustrate participants who want to further explain their answers or do not find a response category that matches with their opinion. One method of compromise is to use closed-ended questions for their efficiency and standardization but also include opportunities in the survey for participants to further explain their answers or select an "other" option that then provides space for clarification.

Filtering questions are also useful in determining whether participants know something about the questions they are being asked. For example, if the purpose of the assessment was to inquire about the effectiveness of a learning community in meeting specific outcomes, it would be very important to ask survey participants a filtering question on their level of involvement with the learning community.

Intensity measures are a key piece to asking participants about their behaviors or attitudes, particularly with closed-ended questions for which a "yes" or "no" is too limiting a response. Typically, intensity measures follow some ordinal scale of measurement (see Chapter Six) that can be ranked. For example, a commonly used intensity measure is a Likert-type scale in which 1 means strongly agree, 2 means agree, 3 is neutral, 4 means disagree, and 5 is strongly disagree. (See Chapter Five for more information on developing a survey instrument.)

## Are the Population and Method Identified for Selecting a Sample?

Part of determining and examining the purpose of your assessment project includes identifying from whom you will collect information; in other words, this process identifies the individuals who have the information that you seek. This may include more than one type of participant. For example, if you are assessing the effectiveness of a learning community you might have multiple participant groups—students in the learning community, faculty supervisors, and learning community peer leaders might all be participants in your assessment. You might also have different data collection methods (for example, surveys, focus groups) for each group.

The groups you choose to invite to participate in your assessment, in many cases, will have an impact on the methods you use to collect data. If your goal is to collect information from students living in rural areas regarding extracurricular activities on campus, you will want to consider how accessible a Web-based survey will be for these students, whose access to the Internet might be limited by geography. In this case, a paper and pencil survey mailed to the students' home address with a postage paid return envelope might yield better return rates than a Web-based survey. Through this example, it is easy to see how the participant groups might have an effect on the data collection methods used.

## What Is the Size of the Sample? Census Survey or Sample?

Another consideration in using a survey method is how many participants to survey. Do you want to survey an entire population (for example, all incoming, first-year students at Midwestern Community College), thus conducting a census survey, or do you want to sample a portion of this population? Web-based surveys have made it much easier to survey an entire population on campus. However, through the use of inferential statistics and probability sampling it is possible to collect data from a subgroup (that is, a sample) of your population and infer the results to the population.

It is not possible here to go into all the procedures and protocols for sampling methods that will allow you to generalize your results to the population identified. If this is your goal, then it would be helpful to hire a statistical consultant or identify a faculty or staff member who has expertise in sampling methods. This person can also help you to identify whether your assessment calls for random sampling procedures that support probability sampling or whether a convenience sample (nonprobability sampling) will work just as well in accomplishing your assessment goals. (For a more detailed explanation on selecting participants and sampling methods, see Chapter Four.)

With nonprobability sampling methods, you can only make conclusions about those who completed your survey. There are several nonprobability sampling methods: convenience sampling, purposive sampling, and snowball sampling. Convenience samples are based on those who are accessible at the time of data collection when not every person in the population has an equal chance of being selected for the sample. Consider this example. Suppose the assessment goal is to get information from first-year students about the admission process, and the researchers go into a general core course classroom on campus to collect data. Only those students who are in that class when the data are collected have the opportunity to be a part of the sample. It is cost effective to collect data in this manner, but the sampling technique reduces the generalizability of the results to only those who completed the survey. In some instances, however, these methods may be the best suited method for data collection. For instance, if you are conducting an assessment of services utilized through campus recreation you may want to purposefully select those students who have used those services. Sometimes it is difficult to identify sufficient members of a population from which to draw a random sample; for example, lesbian, gay, or bisexual students. In this instance, you might use a snowball sampling approach by identifying a few students at the start and then asking them to pass on the information to other students who also identify as gay, lesbian, or bisexual.

## Will This Survey Be Used at More Than One Time and Over the Course of Time (for Example, Longitudinal)?

Consideration should be given as to whether the survey instrument will be used for multiple data collection events over a period of time or for just a one-time event. If the intent is to use the survey or questionnaire over a period of time, or with multiple groups, it is important to review the questions in the survey instrument, taking note of those that might be too specific for multiple uses. For example, questions that ask participants about a time-specific event or a specific group can be reworded as a more general question that allows for multiple uses. Table 3.2 illustrates a few examples. The wording of the first question under Specific Questions limits the survey to a one-time use. However, when it is reworded to a more general format, as shown under General Questions, the survey then can be used on multiple occasions (for example, at the start of every semester). An additional demographic question on the survey could ascertain when the student was admitted, thus allowing for multiple uses as well as a number of comparative analyses based on time of admission.

Now consider the second question, which asks about campus recreation activities. The question as phrased under the Specific Questions column limits the types of participants who can answer

#### Table 3.2  Examples of Specific and General Questions

| Specific Questions | General Questions |
|---|---|
| Do you think the fall 2007 admissions process for incoming freshmen students was easy to navigate? | Do you think the admissions process for incoming freshmen students was easy to navigate? |
| As a freshmen student, were there many opportunities to become involved in campus recreation activities? | As a student, were there many opportunities to become involved in campus recreation activities this year? |

it. However, the question as reworded under the General Questions column can be answered by various groups. Furthermore, by adding a demographic question on class year and utilizing a simple cross-tab analysis (see Chapter Six), responses from this same question could yield results for all four undergraduate class categories (freshmen, sophomore, junior, and senior), as well as graduate students.

## What Type of Instrument Will Be Used? Published or Locally Developed?

Deciding on which type of instrument best serves the purpose of the assessment is an important component in planning and implementing the data collection process. The different types of instruments (published versus locally developed), as well as advantages and challenges to using each, are discussed in detail in Chapter Five.

## How Will the Survey Be Pilot Tested?

Regardless of whether the instrument you choose is published or locally developed, it is important to pilot test the instrument with a test group prior to launching the authentic data collection event (perhaps even more so with a locally developed instrument). Colton and Covert (2007, pp. 140–141) list a number of questions to address when piloting your survey or questionnaire:

- Were the directions clear?
- Were there any spelling or grammatical problems? Were any items difficult to read because of sentence length, choice of words, or special terminology?
- How did reviewers interpret each item? What did each question mean to them?
- Did reviewers experience problems with the item formats?
- Were the response alternatives appropriate to each item?

- What problems did reviewers encounter as a result of the organization of the instrument, such as how items flowed?
- On average, how long did it take to complete? What was the longest time and what was the shortest time it took to complete the instrument?
- For Web-based instruments, did the respondents encounter any problems accessing the instrument from a computer or navigating the instrument once it was accessed?
- Did any of the reviewers express concern about the length of the instrument?
- What was the reviewers' overall reaction to the questionnaire?
- Did they have any concerns about confidentiality or how the questionnaire would be used?
- Did they have any other concerns?
- What suggestions do they have for making the questionnaire or individual items easier to understand and complete?

An additional suggestion not covered by Colton and Convert (2007) is whether any reviewers identified questionable or biased language toward stigmatized or underrepresented populations.

Upon gathering and synthesizing the reviews from the pilot test, the next step is to consider how to address the reviewers' comments. It is possible that you might not remedy every comment or concern of the reviewers. (See Chapter Five for additional information on pilot testing instruments.)

## What Is the Time Line for Collecting Data?

The schedule and steps for your data collection should be established ahead of time to uncover as many conflicts as possible in the data collection plan. For example, if the goal is to launch a Web-based survey on December 1, but a review of the calendar shows that December 1 falls on a Friday, a readjustment of the launch date might ensure a higher response rate. A typical plan for survey data collection involves four contacts with participants. The first contact is a letter or e-mail describing the survey and when the participant is likely to receive the survey. The second e-mail or letter includes the survey or the access link (or access instructions) for Web-based surveys. The remaining two contacts are reminders. The first reminder (third contact) follows the invitation letter or e-mail by one week; this is followed by the second reminder (fourth contact) letter or e-mail a week later. The majority of responses will occur when the participants have their first contact with the survey, with considerably smaller response rates for the reminders (third and fourth contacts). For Web-based surveys, it is a good idea to plan on sending the survey invitation e-mail at the beginning of a week, either on Monday or Tuesday.

For in-person data collection by survey or questionnaire, it is good practice to vary collection dates and the times of day during which the data will be collected. Maximizing the number of data collection opportunities ensures maximum variation in the data collection sample, as well as the number of participants, unless a particular time or date is essential to the data being collected for the assessment.

## How Will the Survey Be Implemented (for Example, Web-Based or Paper and Pencil)?

Access, cost, and time are all factors to take into account when deciding how the survey data collection will be implemented. Most often the choice is between a Web-based survey and a paper-and-pencil instrument (relatively few colleges and universities do phone-based surveys for assessments). Participant access is crucial in determining whether you will have a high response rate or one that fails to draw enough participants. When deciding on a Web-based survey it is important to review whether participants have (1) adequate access to the Internet and (2) adequate skills to navigate and use the Internet. Even with the ever-increasing capabilities of technology and the expanded use of the Internet, there are still individuals who prefer paper surveys over Web-based surveys. Some researchers find it effective to offer both a Web-based and a paper-and-pencil version of the survey during data collection.

Cost is another factor to consider when deciding upon an implementation plan for data collection. With Web-based surveys, costs include either the use of an in-house server to store the software and survey results or an Internet survey software provider. Surveymonkey and PsychData are two commonly used survey software providers that are easy to use; both of these companies offer free trial accounts with some limitations. Costs involved with paper surveys include the cost of printing, the costs of hiring one or multiple facilitators to aid the data collection process, and the costs for transferring the data collected to a data management software package (for example, SPSS, Excel, STATA).

Time is also a factor to bear in mind when considering the data collection method. If the data need to be collected and analyzed quickly, it is likely that a Web-based survey will be more efficient than a paper-and-pencil format. Transferring data from the paper copies to a data management software package is considerably more time intensive than transferring data from a Web-based survey software package.

One final thought to consider when choosing a data collection method involves being sensitive to the population you are surveying. In the case of dealing with stigmatized populations (for example, lesbian, gay, bisexual) or with sensitive topics (for example, drug use, sexual behaviors), Web-based surveys may provide a level of distance and anonymity not afforded with an in-person data collection method.

## Will Participants Be Compensated? If So, How?

Compensation and incentives can take many forms from nonmonetary enticements—such as copies of the survey results or appeals to the participants' sense of making a difference through their involvement in the project—to monetary items such as cash, gift certificates, clothing, and food.

When contemplating the use of incentives, it might be helpful to take into account two important concerns with incentives: "first, can you afford the motivator, and second, could the existence of the motivator bias the responses?" (Colton & Covert, 2007, p. 285). For example, if you are assessing the use of campus dining facilities for both on- and off-campus students, and you offer a gift certificate for an on-campus dining facility, your sample may be skewed toward those who live on campus.

Another issue is that many institutions require some form of documentation (for example, receipt) when using cash as an incentive. Policies such as this may have some level of impact on recruiting participants who may be from stigmatized and marginalized populations (for example, lesbian, gay, bisexual, or transgender individuals). (See Chapter Four for a more detailed discussion on incentives and participant compensation.)

## Interviews—Individual and Group

Interviews can be conducted in a one-to-one format (for example, individual interview) or in a group interview format (for example, focus group). There are many different types of interview formats, each with a purpose that guides the exchange between the interviewer and the interviewee(s). Interviews are commonly divided into three categories: structured, semi-structured, and unstructured. This section discusses the data collection methods for individual interviews and focus groups. Chapter Five explains the data collection tools (for example, interview protocols) for these data collection methods in greater detail.

## Structured Interviews

Interviews, for the most part, do not limit the researcher to set questions like those found on a survey except in the structured interview format. Structured interviews typically follow a controlled format with preestablished questions and no room for deviation from the interview protocol. Most of the questions tend to be close-ended. This type of interview is most associated with survey research (for example, telephone, product marketing). If you have ever answered a telemarketing phone call, more than likely you have experienced a structured interview.

Fontana and Prokos (2007, p. 20) suggest the following guidelines for conducting structured interviews:

- Never get involved in long explanations of the study; use the standard explanation provided in the protocol.
- Never deviate from the study introduction, sequence of questions, or question wording.
- Never let another person interrupt the interview; do not let another person answer for the respondent or offer his or her opinion on the question.
- Never suggest an answer or agree or disagree with an answer. Do not give the respondent any idea of your personal views on the topic of the question or survey.
- Never interpret the meaning of a question; just repeat the question.
- Never improvise, such as by adding answer categories or making wording changes.

The intent of structured interviews is to control the data collection process and environment as much as possible; however, in this controlled exchange there is an opportunity to miss a great deal of information (that is, what is left unsaid).

## Semistructured Interviews

With semistructured interviews the format is less rigid or controlled. This type of interview format is also referred to as an in-depth interview. Questions in a semistructured interview are not nearly as "fixed" as those in a structured interview. In a structured interview, the interviewer is directed from point A to point B and response categories for participants are typically prescribed, whereas in a semistructured interview, the interviewer has a guide (with topic areas and questions) to provide some structure to the interview but there is freedom to vary the course of the interview based on the participant's answers and the flow of the interview. Esterberg (2002) notes that the goal of the semistructured interview "is to explore a topic more openly and to allow interviewees to express their opinions and ideas in their own words" (p. 87). An interview protocol (see Chapter Five) helps guide the course of the semistructured interview.

## Unstructured Interviews

Unstructured interviews are the "least planned" interview format and tend to take place in a field setting and, in most instances, during a field observation (Esterberg, 2002). Interview questions are generated from experience and observation with little pre-planning of questions. For example, if you were observing a student activism event on campus and you wanted to find out more about the views of the students involved in the event, you might ask them questions about their opinions during the event.

# Individual Interviews

There is an art and science to interviewing with a host of texts discussing a variety of techniques, issues, and suggestions for conducting a successful interview (see, for example, Holstein & Gubrium, 1995; Seidman, 2006; Rubin & Rubin, 2004).

Figure 3.1 provides a review of items that if taken into consideration will result in a successful interview experience for the interviewer and interviewee.

A number of protocols exist that suggest guidelines for the number of the interviews one should conduct when collecting data via an interview method. Many of these may depend upon a number of issues: the type of interview (structured, semistructured, unstructured), access to participants, costs, and project timeline, to name a few. One approach that is often followed in qualitative inquiries is Seidman's (2006) three-interview protocol. Whereas the first interview serves to introduce the project and disseminate information, the second interview focuses on data collection (that is, questions) and the third interview offers a chance for clarification and follow-up.

## Figure 3.1 Suggestions and Considerations for the Successful Interview

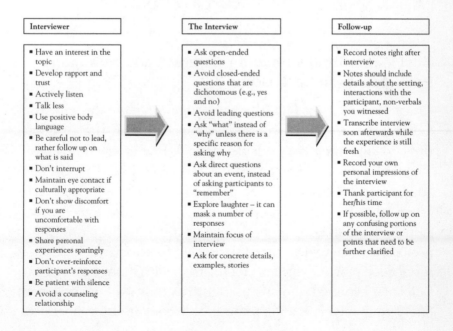

One other point of consideration is how many participants should be interviewed. Seidman (2006) recommends two criteria for assessing the number of participants needed: "sufficiency" and "saturation." For sufficiency, Seidman asks, "Are there sufficient numbers to reflect the range of participants and sites that make up the population so that others outside the sample might have a chance to connect to the experiences of those in it?" (p. 55). Saturation is reached when the interviewer (researcher) is not hearing or learning anything new in the interviews and the same information is being repeated.

## Focus Groups Interviews

Krueger and Casey (2000) identify five characteristics of a focus group: a focus group is "(1) people who (2) possess certain characteristics and (3) provide qualitative data (4) in a focused discussion (5) to help understand the topic of interest" (p. 10). They also provide a very helpful list of when to use and when not to use focus group interviews (see Table 3.3).

### How Many Groups Should I Conduct and How Many Participants in Each Group?

Krueger and Casey (2000) suggest planning for three or four focus groups for each type of participant group (for example, three to four groups for students, three to four groups for faculty). This helps ensure that enough data are collected to conduct analyses across groups. When considering the size of your focus group (that is, how many participants) there are some general guidelines. Marketing groups suggest ten to twelve participants; noncommercial topics suggest six to eight participants. Overall, it is not good practice to plan a focus group with more than ten participants. Having too many participants limits the involvement of all group members and promotes side conversations unrelated

## Table 3.3  When and When Not to Use a Focus Group Interview

| *When to Use* | *When Not to Use* |
| --- | --- |
| You are looking for a range of ideas that individuals have about a topic. | You want individuals to come to a consensus. |
| You are trying to understand differences in perspectives between groups or categories of people. | You want to educate people. |
| The purpose is to uncover factors that influence opinions, behaviors, or motivation. | You don't intend to use the results but instead want to give the appearance of listening. |
| You want ideas to emerge from the group. | You are asking for sensitive information that should not be shared in a group or could be harmful to someone if it is shared in a group. |
| You want to pilot test ideas, materials, plans, or policies. | The environment is emotionally charged, and a group discussion is likely to intensify the conflict. |
| You need information to design a large-scale quantitative study. | The researcher has lost control over critical aspects of the study. |
| You need more information to help shed light on quantitative data already collected. | Other data collection methods can produce better information. |
| The clients or intended audience places high value on capturing the comments or language used by the target audience. | Other data collection methods can produce the same quality information more economically. |
| | You can't ensure the confidentiality of the participants. |

Source: Adapted from Krueger and Casey (2000).

to the facilitated discussion. Krueger and Casey note that small focus groups (four to six participants) are becoming increasingly popular because of the relative ease of recruiting and hosting the group, as well as a higher comfort level for participants. The drawback is in limiting the range of experiences, which is one of the quality features of a focus group interview.

## How Do I Get Participants to Attend the Focus Group?

The first step is to select meeting dates, times, and locations, then make personal contact with potential participants. This can be done through e-mails, personal letters, phone calls, flyers, or word-of-mouth. If using multiple recruiting methods, it is important to ask participants to RSVP or have enough facilitators and equipment to conduct multiple groups. (Note: if conducting multiple groups, make sure that your location has the space available.) You will also want to consider whether you are going to use incentives for participation (see Chapter Four on participant incentives).

## How Should I Conduct the Focus Group?

For a detailed explanation of facilitating and moderating a focus group, as well as how to develop a focus group protocol (for example, types of questions to ask), see Chapter Five. See Appendix One for an example of a focus group protocol.

# Observations

The field observation is another method for collecting qualitative data. This may seem like a fairly easy and intuitive task for data collection, but you may be surprised at how much more you see when you are focused on the act of observing. A protocol designed for conducting field observations can help you in this process (see Chapter Five). Observing is not easy, and the more you train yourself to observe the more you will see and remember. The objective of the observation is to collect data in a "natural setting." As with most qualitative data collection methods, the individual identified as the observer is the instrument for the data collection. The observer role can be categorized in one of four ways depending upon the level of participation (involvement)

## Table 3.4  Role of the Observer

| Observer Role | Description |
| --- | --- |
| Complete observer (nonparticipant observer) | Not involved in the setting or with the participants. The observer is not seen or noticed. |
| Observer as participant | Observes the setting and individuals for brief periods. The observer is seen, but not involved with those being researched. |
| Participant as observer | Observer (researcher) takes part in the activity being studied or observed. Seeks to gain insider status without participating in the core activities that would change the outcome. |
| Complete participant | Highest level of involvement. Observers study scenes that they are already a part of or they become members of the group being observed during the course of the research. The experience is one of total immersion. |

Sources: Based on Gold (1958) and Spradley (1980).

the observer has with the event. With some variation, these four categories can be described as seen in Table 3.4.

Whether the observer is a nonparticipant or complete participant, there are a number of factors to take into account when designing a data collection plan that includes field observations. Following is a list of suggestions to consider when designing a field observation data collection plan:

- Does the location fit with your assessment purposes? Why?
- What are the parameters surrounding the site? Will you want to observe from multiple locations or stay in one location?
- How do you (for example, the observer) relate to this site? What is your positionality in relation to the observation site?

- Will there be access issues? Is it a public location or private?
- Are there risks?
- What are the ethical concerns with observing in this location?
- When, where, and how will you write field notes?

## Writing Field Notes

What to focus on and thus write about in the observation can be a daunting and often overwhelming task, particularly for novice observers. A well-defined field observation protocol (see Chapter Five) will help guide this process. Here, two helpful frameworks for observations and writing field notes are referenced.

Esterberg (2002) makes the following suggestions in what to write about:

- Record what people say and do.
- Record what you observe, think, and feel.
- Record what the place looks like—in detail.
- Record initial impressions.
- Note dates, times, locations, and people.
- Use quotation marks for direct quotes.
- There is no such thing as too much detail!

As well as what not to write about:

- Try to avoid generalizations (for example, "so and so always...").
- Try to avoid judgment statements (for example, "so and so eats a lot").

Spradley (1980) notes nine dimensions of data collection that are helpful to consider when focusing the field observations:

1. Space: the physical space
2. Actors: the people involved in the situation
3. Activities: the various activities the people are doing in the setting
4. Objects: the physical elements present in the setting
5. Acts: actions of individuals
6. Events: related activities that individuals carry out in the setting
7. Time: the time sequence in the setting
8. Goals: the activities, things people are attempting to accomplish in the setting
9. Feelings: emotions expressed in the setting

Emerson, Fretz, and Shaw (1995) also provide a detailed guide for writing field notes that is commonly used and referenced in qualitative inquiry.

## Document Review

The last data collection method discussed in this chapter is the review of documents and records. Because student affairs professionals have access to a wide range of documents from which to collect data in an assessment, this method can be particularly productive and beneficial. It might be helpful to draw a distinction between two different types of written or recorded texts—public records and documents. *Public records* are materials and records produced for an official purpose. On-campus examples would include official transcripts, immunization records, and admissions applications. *Documents* (and private papers) are items of a personal nature, such as e-mails and journals; analyzing such documents requires more interpretation on the part of the analyzer than do public records.

Some advantages of using the document review method for collecting data include (1) no coordination is necessary between the researcher and participants because access for the most part is based on the researcher's schedule, (2) data already have been transcribed, and (3) data collection is unobtrusive. Some disadvantages of this method include (1) access issues—documents may be protected (for example, private documents) or access may be limited for a variety of reasons (for example, confidentiality of transcripts), (2) documents may be coded and difficult to understand without insider knowledge, and (3) documents may be incomplete (that is, missing information) or inaccurate.

Technology has also increased the efficiency of using document review, thus making it a valuable and primary method of data collection or as a supporting method of data collection. When using this method it is important to establish a document review protocol for the data collection process (see Chapter Five).

## Conclusion

This chapter has reviewed primary methods used for data collection in student affairs assessment; specifically, surveys and questionnaires, interviews (both individual and group), field observations, and document review. Suggestions were provided that direct, support, and enhance the data collection process for each of the above-mentioned methods. Most of all it is important that you make a plan that addresses as many aspects of the data collection process as possible prior to collecting data. Using the questions outlined in this chapter as a guide will help ensure that you are prepared for the process of data collection.

# References

Colton, D., & Covert, R. W. (2007). *Designing and construction instruments for social research and evaluation*. San Francisco: Jossey-Bass.

Esterberg, K. G. (2002). *Qualitative methods in social science research*. Boston, MA: McGraw-Hill.

Emerson, R. M., Fretz, R. I., & Shaw, L. L. (1995). *Writing ethnographic fieldnotes*. Chicago, IL: University of Chicago Press.

Fontana, A. F., & Prokos, A. H. (2007). *The interview from formal to postmodern*. Walnut Creek, CA: Left Coast.

Gold, R. (1958). Roles in sociological field observations. *Social Forces, 36*, 217–223.

Holstein, J. A., & Gubrium, J. F. (1995). *The active interview*. Thousand Oaks, CA: Sage.

Krueger, R. A., & Casey, M. A. (2000). *Focus groups: A practical guide for applied research* (3rd ed.). Thousand Oaks, CA: Sage.

Nardi, P. M. (2003). *Doing survey research: A guide to quantitative methods*. Boston, MA: Pearson.

Rubin, H. J., & Rubin, I. (2004). Qualitative interviewing: The art of hearing data (2nd ed.). Thousand Oaks, CA: Sage.

Seidman, I. (2006). *Interviewing as qualitative research: A guide for researchers in education and the social sciences* (3rd ed.). Williston, VT: Teachers College Press.

Spradley, J. P. (1980). *Participant observation*. New York: Holt, Rinehart, & Winston.

# 4

# SELECTING, SAMPLING, AND SOLICITING SUBJECTS

Ann M. Gansemer-Topf and Darin R.
Wohlgemuth

During a mid-year meeting the staff in the Office of Institutional Research at a small, residential college compiled a list of the various surveys that were to be administered over the next sixteen weeks of the semester.

As a part of the college's promotion and tenure process, a sample of students would be surveyed to rate the teaching and advising effectiveness of selected faculty members. The college was involved in a longitudinal study of student writing in which faculty members assessed the writing of a randomly selected group of students. For the longitudinal study to be successful, data needed to be collected each semester. Every ten years, academic departments are asked to undergo a self-study and external review. This spring, three departments were involved in this process and were planning on conducting surveys of their current students.

The Office of Student Affairs was scheduled to administer a student health survey to all students to fulfill its commitment to assess students every three years. To coincide with the student survey, the Committee on Wellness, whose focus is on the health and wellness of its employees, was also planning to administer a wellness survey to faculty and staff. The college had hired a new director for its library, and with discussions about the potential for expanding staff, services, and space, the library personnel were reluctant to embark on any planning without first receiving input from the students, faculty, and staff of the college. Thus, a library survey was scheduled for the spring semester.

Each student class was also slated to participate in a unique survey. First-year students would be participating in two surveys as a part of a national study on the first-year student experience. Focus groups were scheduled to be conducted with second-year students to fulfill the college's goal to better understand and support the second-year experience. A significant number of juniors would be completing surveys as a part of their study abroad program, and seniors, prior to graduating, would be receiving an exit survey to gather information about their college experience and future plans.

As the list of surveys and assessment projects continued to grow, the staff in the Office of Institutional Research began to get nervous. The current list, already long, did not account for the other more informal surveys that would be conducted by students or faculty wanting to do their own research. To add to this concern, a newly approved strategic plan and an approaching re-accreditation visit were providing more pressure on departments on campus to engage in additional assessment activities.

All of these projects were related to the mission of the college and would provide valuable information about the institution and its students, faculty, and staff. But would all of these surveys be too much? As the number of surveys increased, response rates decreased. Would these assessment activities provide any value if the students stopped participating?

As public demands for accountability have increased, accreditation standards have been revised, and classroom effectiveness has focused on student learning rather than teaching, assessment activities have dramatically increased on college campuses (Priddy & Keiser, 2007). Today it is only the very rare institution that has not engaged, at least somewhat, in the process of assessment. But as assessment activities continue to increase, the campus population can soon become overwhelmed with surveys, opinion polls, or offers of "focus group" pizza. The best-developed assessment plans can easily disintegrate if few students participate. The well-known movie line, "If you build it, they will come," does not apply to assessment. Neither the most ingenious assessment plan nor the best-developed instruments will be helpful if the individuals do not participate. This chapter focuses on identifying students for an assessment study, increasing student participation through incentives and rewards, and minimizing survey fatigue.

## What Is Sampling and Why Is It Important?

Sampling provides a means for gathering data without surveying all individuals in a targeted population (Salant & Dillman, 1994). Whereas a *population* is the entire unit of people, a *sample* is a subset of this population that is chosen so that the results can be generalized to the population (Salant & Dillman, 1994). Sampling is used in many instances because it is not feasible to survey the entire population. Administrators at a large metropolitan hospital, for instance, will not have the resources or contact information to survey all individuals who may use their services. Through sampling, administrators can still gain valuable information about their organization by selecting participants who, as a group, mirror the larger resident population.

Even when campuses have the ability to survey all students, sampling can be used to prevent students from being exposed to too many surveys. In turn, this strategy can increase response rates (Salant & Dillman, 1994) and ultimately improve the effectiveness of all campus assessment efforts. The following section outlines three steps for developing a sample and describes sampling techniques that can be used for quantitative and qualitative studies.

### Developing Your Sample

The best-developed assessment plans can fail if the sample is poorly selected. Low response rates, underrepresented subgroups, or biased respondents can alter the assessment results significantly. For example, the director of the Academic Success Center has developed a tutoring program for students enrolled in Economics 101. In her initial assessment of the program she did a random sample of students, and since most of the students were enrolled in the College of Business, the sample consisted primarily of business majors. The results of this assessment found that, on average, students enrolled in tutoring had significantly higher grades than students who did not enroll in tutoring. In a subsequent assessment of the program, the director decided to conduct a stratified random sample, which resulted in students with more diversified majors. The results from this assessment were more nuanced: students in the College of Business who enrolled in tutoring did do significantly better than students who did not enroll in tutoring, but students in other majors within the liberal arts and sciences did not perform better than their counterparts who did not participate in the tutoring program. The sampling method in this assessment led to different conclusions about the success of the tutoring program.

Understanding the context within which you do assessment is also important. At some institutions, different groups of students may have different patterns of response rates. At Urban Institution, for instance, half of the students reside on campus and the other half are commuter students. On average, on-campus students have a response rate of 50 percent whereas commuter students' response rate is 25 percent. Thus, if administrators at Urban Institution would like to receive a total of 500 responses that are equally representative of their campus population (250 responses from on-campus students; 250 responses from commuter students), they would need to adjust their sampling strategies accordingly. To reach their response goal (and assuming all surveys would be completed thoroughly and accurately) they would need to choose a sample of 500 on-campus students and 1000 off campus students. The context and goals of the assessment need to be considered in developing sampling methods.

In addition, assessment planners must abide by all Human Subject Guidelines prior to engaging in any assessment project. Although most assessment projects will involve little risk to participants, legal and ethical practices dictate that these procedures be followed. With adequate advance planning the burden of obtaining Human Subjects approval is not significant. In Chapter Eight, John Schuh discusses this topic more in depth. For the purposes of this chapter, we reiterate the importance of following ethical guidelines for Human Subjects prior to implementing any sampling techniques or employing the use of incentives and rewards.

## Steps in Sampling

Salant and Dillman (1994) outline three steps to developing an effective sample: (1) identifying target population, (2) finding a list of the target population, and (3) selecting the sample.

*Identify Target Population* Except for large-scale surveys, the target population for campus assessment activities is not the entire student body. A targeted population must be finite (potentially one could count them), observable, and have time restrictions (Groves et al., 2004). While identifying the target population, be as specific as possible. For instance, if you are interested in examining the impact of first to second year retention at a community college, will you study all students or will you include only those students who had six or more credits? What about those students who may have taken one or more classes prior to attending full-time? Are you interested in commuters compared with students who may live in college-owned apartments? Should you focus on traditionally aged or adult students? The population must be clearly defined, such as all traditional age students (age < = 24 at the time of enrollment) who are first-year (not previously enrolled as degree seeking at any institution) full-time (registered for more than twelve credits), new, directly from high school (graduated from high school within one year of the fall term) freshmen (have not accumulated more than thirty credit hours). Clearly defining the population is an important step in the design of the assessment.

*Get a List of the Target Population* Having identified the target population, gather the list of names of those in the targeted population. Do not underestimate the complexity of this task. Different offices store and can access types of data. As is discussed in Chapter Two, the necessary data may reside in databases in various campus offices. The admissions office will have data on the precollege traits such as transfer credits and high school performance, but it may not have student financial aid information. The registrar's office will have data on course selection, grades, and scheduling. Housing offices will keep track of students in university-sponsored housing. However, many campuses have limited ability to integrate data from a variety of sources; instead of being able to access one list, you may get three. There are policies that govern how data are to be retrieved and can be used, and a cost may be associated with receiving these data.

Clearly understanding how to link student level data from each source is critical. In many cases, the university identification number may be sufficient to link data from various sources, but it would be important to verify this with the data steward in the planning stage. In some cases, certain offices may not be able to identify all of the constraints of your population. In those cases, the data they provide must have a less restrictive selection criteria. For example, only the registrar may have all necessary data elements to identify your sample. The housing office may not collect data on the number of credits the student has accumulated or when the student first enrolled. In this case, one may ask for all students in university sponsored housing and create the match with the target population identified from registrar's data.

Review the list of names when you receive them to ensure that all students may be eligible participants. Through this process you will identify the survey population—the actual population from which participants will be selected (Groves et al., 2004). Students who are on off-campus study, medical leave, or have requested that they not be contacted can be taken off the list. It can be embarrassing to have a student reply to your request with, "I apologize for not being available to participate in your focus group but the class I am taking in Rome, Italy makes it difficult for me to arrive in time."

*Select the Sample* There are a variety of approaches to sample selection. The following section outlines some of the most commonly used techniques.

## Sampling Techniques for Quantitative Studies

Several techniques are appropriate for quantitative studies. They are discussed briefly in this section.

*Probability Sampling* Probability sampling is a technique in which each student in the target population has a non-zero chance of being selected (Groves et al., 2004). Pure random sampling would assign the same probability to each student in the sample. In most cases selecting the sample from the population will be done with a computer and a random number generator. Appendix Two lists the procedures for doing this task. It is not required, however, that students have the same chance but only that the chance is greater than zero. If the population includes students who have attended a series of lectures, it is possible that some students may have attended more than once. Suppose that attendance is taken by asking students to write their names on index cards. The cards could be shuffled and every fifth card that is selected could be included in the sample. If the same student is selected twice, another name should be drawn from the pile. This eliminates the data entry of the population of students.

The following is an example of a project at a large public institution that changed its policy on smoking. The change increased the distance from a building entrance or window in which smoking was prohibited from fifteen feet to twenty-five feet. A question was raised as to whether this more restrictive smoking policy would have any impact on enrollment. On one hand, students who do smoke may be less likely to enroll under the new policy. Conversely, students who do not smoke may be more likely to enroll as a result of the more restrictive policy. To answer these questions both smokers and nonsmokers would need to be contacted. A key constraint to this question is the assumption (and at this institution, the fact) that no one on campus systematically collects data on the smoking habits of students.

Although the specific question focused on future enrolling students, it was determined that high school students would be reluctant to reveal that they smoked (they are below legal age), especially in front of their parents when they visited campus. The next best alternative would be to survey currently enrolled students, knowing that students who enrolled previously would allow some inference on the future students and enrollment patterns.

To gather student feedback on this issue a random sample of students was drawn. First, the population was defined as all students who were enrolled on campus (excluding distance education and off-campus-only students) in the spring term. The population identified over 23,000 students. Administrators wanted responses from at least 500 students. Responses rates for previous surveys were approximately 25 percent. Therefore, to achieve 500 responses, a sample of 2000 was selected. Using a list of the student population, a random sample of every nth person could be selected.

This random sample will allow the survey responses to be inferred on the entire on-campus student body. For example, if the survey finds that 5 percent of those surveyed self-report smoking, then it would be reasonable to infer that 5 percent of the campus population smokes. These data might be confirmed or compared with the campus health survey or national studies of college students mentioned in the introduction of this chapter.

*Stratified Random Sampling* Stratified random sampling is a method that is used when you need to have sufficient representation of two or more groups within the population. The strata (classification, gender, full-time, part-time, on or off-campus) need to be mutually exclusive (Salant & Dillman, 1998). After this is done, you can randomly sample within each group.

This technique could be applied to the smoking policy example. If, for instance, students from two countries were known to smoke at higher rates than the general student population, but the number of students from these countries was relatively small, a pure random sample would be likely to capture only a few of these students. Therefore, a stratified random sample could ensure that more students were included in the study. If administrators wanted at least thirty students out of a total sample of 500 and the average response was 25 percent, 120 students from these two countries could first be randomly selected, then a random sample from the larger student population could be randomly selected.

Computer software programs can be used to develop random samples via relatively simple procedures. Appendix Three provides instructions for how to conduct random sampling and stratified random sampling procedures with Microsoft Excel.

*Nonprobability Sampling* Nonprobability sampling methods mean some members of the population have zero probability of being selected (Groves et al., 2004). Suppose the director of Residential Life wants information from students in residence halls, but only has resources to work with two of four university housing complexes, say 1 and 4. In this case, the probability of someone who lives in either complex 2 or 3 being selected is zero. However, if there is random assignment of students to a complex, then the survey results may still be reflective of all four residence areas.

Convenience sampling is a frequently used nonprobability sampling technique (Salant & Dillman, 1994). A student government leader may decide to survey all students who walk through the campus dining union or a residence life coordinator may interview students studying in a lounge. In other words, students were not picked using any specific set of criteria except that they happened to be in a certain place at a specific time.

Using the previous smoking policy example, suppose that this campus has four residence hall units. The first two of these units are for "nonsmoking" students, the third allows students who smoke to live in the hall but does not allow smoking inside the building, and the fourth housing unit allows students to smoke in the rooms. Convenience sampling may gather data from all students who live in the fourth housing complex and all students who live in first residence hall complex (that restricts to nonsmoking students).

*Cluster Sampling* Cluster sampling differs from stratified sampling in that random selection occurs with the cluster but all in the cluster can be surveyed (Salant & Dillman, 1994). For example, in a large residence hall system, the list of all residence hall floors could be developed. The floors could be randomly selected but then everyone on that residence hall would be surveyed. This could be appropriate if a residence hall system had different types of housing options (apartments, suites, traditional double occupancy rooms, etc.) and one was interested in the differences in responses among residents in various housing options.

## Sampling Bias

Surveys generally are conducted so that the resulting statistics can be used to describe groups as opposed to individual respondents. A good survey methodology allows one to take these statistics and infer to a larger population. To be able to infer, one needs to minimize sampling errors. Sampling error can occur because of sampling variance or sampling bias (Groves et al., 2004). Sampling variance (also known as margin of error) is the degree to which the sample means vary across all samples. So, for instance, if 64 percent of the residence hall student sample favored expanding the nonsmoking area and there was a ±4 sampling variance, you would conclude that the mean sample for the overall population was between 60 and 68%.

Sample bias results from systematically excluding one group of the population by the survey technique, timing, or method. A biased sample results from systematically excluding some segment of the target population from the sample by the method of sampling (Groves et al., 2004).

For example, student affairs professionals at a large, urban university were interested in studying the off-campus work habits of students. They decided to use a telephone survey and contact students between 7:00 and 9:00 pm on weeknights. The target population was carefully defined and a random sample of undergraduate full-time students was drawn. Suppose the results indicate students work less than what was found in previous studies and that the students who are working are working fewer hours. Although the results may be interesting, they are probably a result of sample bias. The calls were made during times when those students who do work are often working, thus excluding them from potentially participating in the survey. In this case, it would be better to administer this survey by multiple modes, including Web or paper, so that students can participate at their convenience.

## Sampling Strategies for Focus Groups

In addition to quantitative approaches to assessment, qualitative methodologies are useful tools for assessment (Palomba & Banta, 1999). Unlike quantitative methods that seek to generalize to the larger population, the goal of qualitative methods is to explore a topic in depth. This difference in purpose also affects sampling strategies for qualitative methods. Whereas a quantitative research sample involves choosing people to survey, a qualitative research sample involves decisions "about settings, events, and social processes" (Miles & Huberman, 1984, p. 37). It is not just the students who are identified but also the context surrounding their experiences.

Qualitative methods use purposive sampling—choosing respondents who can best answer the research question(s) (Guba & Lincoln, 1985; Miles & Huberman, 1984). As Guba and Lincoln state, "the object of the game [in qualitative research] is not to focus on the similarities that can be developed into generalizations, but to detail the many specifics that give the context its flavor" (1985, p. 201). The sample, in qualitative research, also may change throughout the duration of the project as new information becomes available and new directions need to be explored (Guba & Lincoln, 1985).

There are many qualitative methods that could be used for assessment—the case study, document analysis, observation—but this chapter discusses focus groups, since sampling procedures are more relevant to this technique. This is not to stay that other qualitative methods (e.g., individual interviews) do not need to be concerned with sampling but, rather, many of the strategies used in developing a sample for focus groups can be applied to these methods.

The focus group, according to Morgan's (1997) broad definition, is a "research technique that collects data through group interaction" (p. 6). The goal of the focus group is to elicit ideas, attitudes, feelings, or perceptions about a particular topic (Vaughn, Shay Schumm, & Sinagub, 1996). Although the goals of focus groups do not need to mirror the general population, sampling methods may be useful in choosing the focus group members. For instance, if one were interested in examining the overall perception of a new student orientation program, it may not be necessary to invite all first-year students. In this case, assuming you are not interested in differences among members (i.e., as they relate to race, gender, etc.) of the group, simple random sampling could be used to identify the students who should be invited to participate. Simple random sampling can be used to eliminate bias—such as inviting people that you know would speak favorably about your program or staff to participate.

In addition to simple random sampling, Patton (1990) provides a complete description of the various sampling techniques used for qualitative studies. By way of an example, we highlight a few of the most common techniques but encourage readers to review Patton's list for a more complete description.

The director of Residential Life is interested in understanding the experiences of students who live in the residence halls. The results of previous surveys suggested that first-year students were very happy about their residence hall experience, but in the past three years the number of students who returned to the residence halls in the second year had declined. To understand more fully why students were not returning to the residence halls after their first year of studies, the director wanted to conduct focus groups of current students.

*Typical Case Method* This method of selection includes participants who represent the "average" first-year student as defined by the Residential Life department. The typical case method requires the assessment coordinator to understand the demographics and characteristics of the residents in order to choose the "typical" student. For this study, the typical student may be broadly defined as an incoming, full-time, traditionally aged, degree-seeking student living in a double-occupancy room.

*Extreme or Deviant Case Sampling or Intensity Sampling* Assuming a "typical" student can be defined, there may also be the "atypical" student. The difference between extreme or deviant case sampling and intensity sampling is the matter of degree. Whereas the extreme or deviant case sampling represents—as the name implies—students who have experiences that are vastly different from the typical student, intensity sampling "seeks excellent or rich examples of the phenomenon of interest, but not unusual cases" (Patton, 1990, p. 171). It may be a nontraditional student who chooses to live in the residence halls or a senior who has chosen to stay in the residence hall four years. It may include students who do not choose to live in the residence halls at all or those who leave after the first year. The primary purpose of these approaches is to get input from students who have had experiences that are different from most other students. By focusing on these differences the Residential Life office may gain insight into how they can improve the living experience for all students.

**Stratified Purposeful Sampling** This method can be a synthesis of the previous methods. You seek to coordinate focus groups that represent the different categories of individuals (Patton, 1990). You may create one focus group that represents the "typical" case, one focus group that represents the "extreme" case, a group of students who moved out of the residence halls after their first year, and a group of students who chose to stay in the residence halls after their first year.

**Maximum Variation Sampling** This method is commonly used to capture general themes or patterns when a variety of experiences or opinions exists. If the Residence Life system is large and includes a diversity of people and programs, this sampling method may be useful. Any common patterns that would emerge despite the significant variation in students and their experiences would be of particular significance (Patton, 1990).

**Snowballing or Referral Method** These methods involve asking other individuals to recommend or refer other participants to you (Litoselliti, 2003; Patton, 1990). For instance, after each focus group you may ask students to recommend other students who may be able to provide you with critical information. You may also contact other students or professional staff in the buildings and ask them to recommend students.

*Convenience Sampling*  As its name suggests, this approach involves picking a group of students that are available at the right time or right place (Patton, 1990). This may include conducting focus groups of students who are studying in a residence hall lounge, or meeting with students gathered at a particular event. The benefit of this approach is that they may be easier to recruit and are more likely to attend.

## Number and Size of Groups

When sampling techniques have been determined, it is quite common to jump to the next logical or *logistical* steps: How many groups should we have? The number of groups depends on the diversity of the topic and the purpose of the assessment (Krueger & King, 1998). Using the example above, an institution could conduct hundreds of focus groups if it wished to cover all the types of cases.

As mentioned earlier, sampling in qualitative research is a continuous process, and qualitative researchers suggest that the sampling process continue until one meets the point of saturation (Merriam, 2002). Guba and Lincoln (1985) have termed this the "point of redundancy" (p. 202). Morgan (1998) also refers to this technique as saturation. Focus groups are discontinued when the research questions(s) are addressed and no new information is discovered. In general, you want to select a sufficient number of groups so that findings become repetitive but still reflect the range of participants needed to understand the topic (Vaughn, Shay Shumm, & Sinagub, 1996).

How many people should we have in each group? Qualitative researchers acknowledge that groups may range in size from two to twelve but that ideally focus groups should have between six and ten individuals (Morgan, 1998). This number provides for enough conversation while yet allowing ample time for individuals to express their opinions. A focus group that is too small will not encourage discussion sufficiently rich but if too large may be difficult to manage. When groups are too large, participants may also become frustrated if they do not have enough opportunity to fully discuss their opinions. Most focus groups last about one hour; although this may seem ample time, large focus groups make it difficult to adequately educe everyone's opinion, especially on emotional or controversial topics.

Focus group size should also factor in no-shows (Morgan, 1998). The number of people who agree to participate but who subsequently do not attend the focus group can vary by institution, characteristics of the target population, and by the topic itself. If attrition rates are relatively high, it may be helpful to overrecruit individuals. For instance, if you would like a focus group of about eight to ten students and expect a 20 percent attrition rate, you may want to select twelve participants with the assumption that two or three students may not show up.

## Group Characteristics

In addition to determining the number of groups and people within the groups, it is helpful to determine each of the group's characteristics. Most research has shown that groups with similar characteristics tend to work better than do heterogeneous groups (Morgan, 1998; Litoselliti, 2003). The goal in choosing groups is to gather individuals who have opinions that are diverse without being divisive or that limit conversation. We can all think of topics on our campus about which opinions and emotions are so strong on opposing sides that bringing people together may not be productive. The purpose of the focus group is to explore people's perceptions and feelings; it is not an arena for debate or a platform for determining which opinions are "right" or "wrong."

In selecting groups, care needs to be given to understanding differences in status or power as they relate to the topic at hand. For instance, it is rarely advisable to mix students and faculty in a focus group. When conducting focus groups with faculty members, it may be important to separate the tenured professors from nontenured professors, and for staff it may be necessary to separate supervisors from those they supervise. On many campuses it is not usually necessary to differentiate between males and females but on some topics, perhaps issues such as sexual assault and awareness programming, this approach is advisable.

The assessment coordinator should consider campus culture and the topic of assessment when selecting participants. For example, in assessing the effectiveness of a career development office, it may not be necessary to separate domestic and international students. However, if one is interested in understanding how experiences differ between domestic and international students, international students may feel more comfortable discussing their experiences with other international students. Nonetheless, despite careful planning, the nature of the focus group method still leaves much to chance. As Bloor, Frankland, Thomas, and Robson (2001) concede, the reality is that "often the exact composition of the groups will reflect circumstance rather than planning" (p. 26).

## Survey Fatigue

The example at the beginning of the chapter highlights an increasing problem with assessment on many campuses: survey fatigue. Student response rates for institutional surveys have been consistently declining (Porter, Whitcomb, & Weitzer, 2004). Two factors contribute to this decline: (1) the increased need and interest in assessment that has led to more surveys, and (2) the increased ease in conducting surveys.

### Paper Versus Web Surveys

Technology has removed many of the barriers that may have once minimized survey use and distribution on campus (Porter, 2004). Most campuses have access to technological resources that allow them to develop online surveys, distribute these surveys to large numbers of people, and collect and analyze responses with relatively little work or cost (Umbach, 2004). Most Web surveys require only a working e-mail address, so assuming that you have accurate e-mail addresses, you are able to send hundreds of surveys cost effectively. A significant advantage in using online instruments is that it often eliminates keying data manually from paper to electronic format for analysis. This significantly reduces the cost of the project and will eliminate errors in data entry (although there may be errors when students enter the response) (Umbach, 2004).

Accompanying these advantages are a few disadvantages, however. First, as online surveys become easier to create and disseminate, the number of surveys on campuses may continue to increase. Second, it may also be difficult to ensure anonymity of the respondents in using an online survey (Porter, 2004). The pros and cons of Web versus paper surveys must be considered as a part of the survey development process.

With the increased use of online surveys, researchers have begun to study differences in response rate between paper and online surveys. The results of these studies have been mixed. Porter (2004) found that the response rate for Web surveys is generally higher than for paper surveys but cautioned, "The end result is that Web survey response rates will depend very much on the institutional context as well as on the ability of the researcher to conduct a well-designed electronic survey" (p. 10). In comparing paper-only, Web-only, and paper and Web distribution, Sax, Gilmartin, and Bryant (2003) found that Web-only surveys elicited the lowest response rate. The highest response rates were from students who were given a paper survey in the mail with the opportunity to complete the survey online.

Do students who complete surveys online differ from students who choose the paper method? Do students who choose not to participate in online surveys differ from students who choose not to participate in paper surveys? Although the research that has examined these issues is not conclusive, some findings are noteworthy. Carini, Hayek, Kuh, Kennedy and Ouimet (2003) found that students from institutions that devoted more time to technological resources used the Web more than paper surveys. Therefore, on campuses that may not have the technological resources to effectively administer online surveys or whose students are not technologically savvy, the paper mode may be more effective.

Carini et al. (2003) also point out the need to "evaluate issues of sampling, nonrespondent bias, and measurement error when interpreting the findings from Web and paper surveys" (p. 12). Sax et al. (2003) noted that for each type of survey (paper versus Web), females have higher response rates than males and white students have higher response rates than ethnic minorities. These differences can have a significant impact on how assessment results can be interpreted and applied.

As demands for surveys increase while response rates decrease, it is important to consider the problem of survey fatigue (Porter, 2004). Here are a few suggestions for combating survey fatigue:

1. *Coordinate assessment activities.* Designate a person(s) or office(s) within departments on campus who can collect information about assessment activities. The function may or may not need to be the gatekeeper or policymaker but primarily can serve as a resource person. The designee may be able to advise offices on what other surveys are occurring, who is the targeted audience, and what time of the semester may be best to distribute a survey. As Porter et al. (2004) found, survey fatigue can be reduced if the timing of the survey is changed. Most people are amenable to changing their time line if it would ensure higher response rates. In some instances, surveys can be developed in conjunction with one another. Salant & Dillman (1994) found that the length of the survey does not usually have an impact on response rates as much as the number of surveys does. In other words, once participants have begun completing the survey, they are likely to complete all of it. Therefore, if the Career Planning Center and a

Student Activities Center were interested in surveying the same group of students, they may be able to coordinate their efforts and disseminate one longer survey rather than two shorter surveys.

2. *Use a variety of sampling techniques.* As already mentioned, technology has made it easier to disseminate a survey to an entire population of students. However, it is not always a good idea to survey everyone simply because you have the ability to do so, as this approach will quickly lead to survey fatigue. Sampling allows you to limit the number of times students, faculty, or staff are asked to complete a survey, with the intent that response rates for all surveys will be improved.

3. *Use a variety of delivery methods.* When online surveys first appeared, response rates for this mode of delivery were higher than for the traditional paper survey (Umbach, 2004). As the novelty of this technology has worn off and students receive more online surveys, response rates continue to decrease. In this electronic environment, a personal phone call or letter may help increase response rates. At Iowa State University, for example, students are hired to conduct telephone surveys. With more students using cell phones, it may be more effective to contact students with the telephone. It may also be helpful to use e-mail, a telephone call, and a paper invitation to encourage participation.

4. *Provide feedback.* Too often students are asked to complete a survey but never see the results of their efforts. People are more likely to participate if they feel that their responses will make a difference (Porter & Whitcomb, 2003; Salant & Dillman, 1994). For instance, if your institution participates in an annual survey, it may be helpful to share the results of the previous year's survey prior to distributing the new survey. Before administering the National Survey of Student Engagement (NSSE), we spoke at a student government meeting about the results of the last survey, discussed what the college had done with these results, and asked for participation and support for the upcoming survey. In other online surveys, participants are able to receive instant

feedback about their responses, including how their responses compare to others, how many others have responded, and so on. Releasing the survey results to the campus newspaper or posting the results on the institution's primary Web page are other means of sharing the results. Providing feedback can help participants feel as though their responses are important.

## Overcoming Survey Fatigue in a Longitudinal Study

Survey fatigue can also be a factor in assessment methods that require tracking students through college. When St. Olaf College agreed to participate in a longitudinal study to assess students' critical thinking, it was faced with a significant challenge: encouraging first-year students to commit to participating in a three-hour, computer-based survey and then enticing them to do it again in their second year. The faculty and staff developed a variety of strategies to recruit students for this task: e-mails, phone calls, letters, incentives, and prizes (J. Beld, personal communication, August 31, 2007).

Through this process the college found that the most effective strategies were of a psychological rather than monetary nature. At St. Olaf, a third of the students are involved in at least one musical organization. The director of the assessment project, with the musical groups' permission, attended rehearsals to discuss the assessment project and recruit participants. Faculty members in students' first-year writing courses were also asked to encourage students to participate. When asked why they chose to participate again, the two most mentioned responses were "I had promised that I would do this again and I wanted to fulfill my promise" and "I wanted to see if I had improved from last year" (J. Beld, personal communication, August 31, 2007).

Other longitudinal assessment projects can encourage participation by offering an educational benefit for students. For example, Grinnell College is beginning a portfolio project that will require a small group of students to submit writing samples throughout their college experience. Students are provided a stipend for participating in this project but, in addition, they also meet with the writing staff to discuss their writing. Not only are the students compensated financially but they will also receive feedback about their writing in an informal environment, and although their work is evaluated, it is not graded. In the midst of doing our assessment tasks, we sometimes forget that one purpose of assessment is to educate. When assessment methods can be used to educate students during the process, it is a win-win situation for the student and the institution.

## Incentives and Rewards

What do we offer them? As a way to increase response rates and reduce survey fatigue, it has become common practice to offer incentives for participants. Response rates, according to Dillman (2000), are based on three things: reward, cost, and trust. Incentives are a way to increase the perceived reward, minimize the perceived cost, and increase the trust.

Many survey methods use incentives as a way to increase response rates (Porter & Whitcomb, 2003). Most of these incentives are given after completion of the survey: if a student participates, then the student receives a reward. Another incentive is the lottery incentive in which students, after completion of a survey, will be entered into a drawing for a prize. Porter and Whitcomb concluded that this type of incentive does not work: "the expected benefit is not the monetary amount of the incentive but the amount of the incentive multiplied by the probability that the respondent will be selected a winner of the lottery" (p. 392). Lottery incentives also require that the students trust that the process for selecting individuals will occur and will be run fairly (Porter & Whitcomb, 2003).

Porter and Whitcomb (2003) also examined the impact of offering incentives of different amounts. The authors distributed surveys to high school seniors; one group received no incentive for completing the survey, and other groups received amounts ranging from $25 to $100. They found that offering an incentive raised response rates slightly but that offering the smaller amount was as effective as offering a large amount. A study using National Household Education Surveys produced similar results. Respondents were sent the same survey; one group of respondents received no incentive, a second group received a $2 incentive, and a third group received a $5 incentive. Participants that received an incentive were more likely to complete the survey than those who did not. Response rates for the subgroup receiving the $5 survey were slightly higher but the difference in response rates did not justify the additional $3 cost (Brick, Hagedorn, Montaquila, Brock Roth, & Chapman, 2006).

Instead of spending a large amount of money for a big prize, a better strategy would be to send a smaller prize to all students. The most effective incentives (see, for example, James & Bolstein, 1990) are those that offer a reward upfront. Sending a small token upfront—either monetary, a pencil from the bookstore, a coupon or discount at the campus snack bar—has been found to be more effective than rewards offered after the survey is completed.

For departments on tight budgets, rewards and incentives do not need to cost a great deal of money to be valuable. The director of Institutional Research (IR) at Cornell College, Iowa, partnered with other offices to offer incentives. At her institution, first year students usually were the last group of students to choose their residence hall for the following year. The IR worked with the Department of Residence who was willing to offer a high-priority status as one of the incentives for participation. The Parking Office also offered parking passes for the upcoming year. In return, the IR director, by conducting the survey, would provide these offices with valuable information about student life to these offices (B. Elkins, personal communication, August 24, 2007).

Dillman (2000) recommends other psychological incentives. Some campuses have an established culture of a "norm of reciprocity" in which students, as members of a community, are expected to participate with or without a reward. Another approach, complying with a legitimate authority, can increase response rates if students feel a certain obligation to a person or an office. For instance, when campuses use national surveys from an outside entity, they often include a letter from an on-campus representative. A student is more likely to assume the survey is legitimate and therefore respond to it upon receiving a letter from someone affiliated with the student's institution.

"Survey sponsorship" can be a valuable way to increase response rates. At our decentralized institutions, influence does not always come with a specific title. In residence halls, for example, a letter from a student staff member asking his or her peers to participate may be more effective than a letter from a top administrator. A request from a well-respected or popular faculty member may be more effective than a letter from the chief academic officer. However, for a faculty survey, it would be critical for the chief academic officer to demonstrate support.

In addition to offering rewards, other techniques have been shown to increase response rates:

1. *Prepare your participants.* Before you ask them to complete anything, it can be helpful to apprise students of an impending survey. This prenotification (Salant & Dillman, 1994) can explain the purpose of the survey, discuss the timing of the survey, alert students to watch for the survey, and encourage their participation.

2. *Follow up with nonrespondents.* As a general rule, the more contacts you have with participants, the higher the response rate (Porter & Whitcomb, 2004). Plan for two to three follow-ups or reminders to participants.

3. *Develop a "professional" looking survey*—whether it is a hard copy or online. Poorly designed surveys can reduce response rate. Web surveys, too, must be designed simply (Umbach, 2004). Surveys with spelling or grammatical errors or that are printed on plain white paper minimize students' trust in the value of the

survey. It may be helpful to use smaller fonts in order to make the survey appear shorter, but if it looks overwhelming, students will not complete it. The length of the survey has minimal effect on students' completion rate (Porter, 2004). Once students begin a survey, it is likely they will complete it. It is worthwhile to spend time focusing on the aesthetic elements of the survey design and layout.

4. *Know your audience.* "Incentive" is in the eye of the beholder. Understand your participants and what they want. One coordinator found that offering a prize of an iPod was not much of an incentive because many students already had these devices. Instead, students suggested that a set of speakers to use with the iPod would be a more desirable incentive. Another institution offered to provide a cap and gown for their graduating seniors who participated in a survey. Although this approach can be expensive, it was effective in recruiting students.

5. *Minimize disincentives.* Each institution has periods when their students may be less willing or less able to participate in a survey or focus groups. Most institutions will avoid conducting surveys during final exam week but may be unaware of other important campus events or student activities. On one campus, for example, focus groups could not be conducted successfully during one hour on a Thursday evening because it conflicted with a popular television program.

6. *Be sensitive to students' time and commitments.* Understand and acknowledge that your audience is busy and that they are giving up their time to complete the survey. Recognizing the costs as measured in student time of completing the survey shows that the institution understands students' schedules and the demand for their time. Explaining the benefits of the completed results increases the value of the completing the instrument, even if it will only benefit future students. When inviting students to participate it is important to clearly communicate why participating is worth their time.

## Conclusion

A significant amount of time and energy is devoted to creating and implementing an effective survey or focus group. Yet despite the best developed methods, the ultimate success of the assessment rests upon the participants. Surveys, and the assessment goals that inspire them, will fail if no one participates. Securing effective response rates will become more challenging as students, faculty, and staff are asked to participate more often. Assessment coordinators need to weigh the benefits of receiving new information from more surveys with the drawbacks of decreased response rates. What can be done?

To reiterate a theme found often in this book: plan ahead. Discussions regarding data collection and instrumentation should also consider factors related to sampling. Problems such as access to student names, low response rates, or survey fatigue can be minimized with careful planning. To assist in this planning, we have created a checklist that can be used to guide discussions of sampling methods, the use of incentives, and survey fatigue (see Exhibit 4.1).

---

**Exhibit 4.1    Checklist for Developing a Sample**

☐ Finalize data collection design, methods, and survey tools and techniques to be used.

☐ Identify the target population to be studied.

☐ Secure the list of the target population.

☐ Describe the characteristics for the sample.

Does the sample need to include individuals with certain characteristics such as academic skills, motivation, demographics, and so forth?

Would it be feasible and beneficial to survey the entire population? If so, there is no need to develop a sample.

---

☐ Determine the sampling technique that will produce the desired sample.

☐ Outline how you will contact the participants for the sample.

☐ Consider factors that may enhance or detract from a person's ability to participate and revise sample criteria based on this.

Time of year the survey is administered.

Length, accessibility, and ease of survey instrument.

Survey fatigue—has the person been asked to participate in a variety of other similar survey?

Do certain subpopulations participate at higher or lower rates?

Why would students want to participate? Would incentives increase participation?

Focus groups—convenient time and location, non-threatening environment, little impact on time.

☐ Select your sample.

☐ Invite members to participate.

☐ Send reminders to increase participation.

☐ Thank members for their participation.

As the example at the beginning of the chapter illustrates, even though assessment activities are seen as important, these activities also place a burden on students, faculty, and staff. Using effective sampling methods can minimize this burden. Although campus leaders may be juggling dozens of surveys, sampling techniques can ensure that students are invited to participate in one or two of these surveys.

Another option may be to condense, as well as possible, the timing of surveys to a specific part of the semester. An institution may, for example, designate a week of assessment during which most of the information used for assessment is gathered. This event can help illustrate the importance of assessment activities on campus, and the synergy from these efforts may help improve responses rates for all surveys. Students may also be more willing to participate if it means they will be solicited less often during the semester.

Our purpose in writing this chapter was to describe methods for effectively selecting participants for quantitative surveys and focus groups, suggest ways to recruit participants, and offer ideas for minimizing survey fatigue. There are a variety of ways to select your participants. We encourage you to use assessments to understand your campus culture and to use assessment methods and approaches that will be most effective on your campus.

## References

Bloor, M., Frankland, J., Thomas, M., & Robson, K. (2001). *Focus groups in social research*. Thousand Oaks, CA: Sage.

Brick, J. M., Hagedorn, M. C., Montaquila, J., Brock Roth, S., & Chapman, C. (2006). *Impact of monetary incentives and mailing procedures: An experiment in a federally sponsored telephone survey* (NCES 2006–066). U.S. Department of Education. Washington, DC: National Center for Education Statistics.

Carini, R. M., Hayek, J. C., Kuh, G. D. Kennedy, J. M., & Ouimet, J. A. (2003). College student responses to web and paper surveys: Does mode matter? *Research in Higher Education, 44*, 1–19.

Dillman, D. (2000). *Mail and internet surveys*. New York: Wiley.

Groves, R. M., Fowler, F. J. Jr., Couper, M. P., Lepkowski, J. M., Singer, E., & Tourangeau, R. (2004). *Survey methodology*. Hoboken, NJ: Wiley.

Guba, E. G., & Lincoln, Y. S. (1985). *Naturalistic inquiry*. Thousand Oaks: Sage.

James, J., & Bolstein, R. (1990). The effect of monetary incentives and follow-up mailings on the response rate and response quality in mail surveys. *Public Opinion Quarterly, 54*, 346–361.

Krueger, R. A., & King, J. A. (1998). *Involving community members in focus groups*. Thousand Oaks, CA: Sage.

Litoselliti, L. (2003). *Using focus groups in research*. New York: Continuum.

Merriam, S. B. (1998). *Qualitative research and case study applications in education: Revised and expanded from case study research in education*. San Francisco: Jossey-Bass.

Miles, M. B., & Huberman, A. M. (1984). *Qualitative data analysis: A sourcebook of new methods*. Beverly Hills, CA: Sage.

Morgan, D.L. (1997). *Focus groups as qualitative research: Qualitative research methods series* (2nd ed.). Thousand Oaks, CA: Sage.

Morgan, D. L. (1998). *The focus group guidebook. Focus group kit 2.* Thousand Oaks, CA: Sage.

Palomba, C. A., & Banta, T. W. (1999). *Assessment essentials: Planning, implementing, and improving assessment in higher education.* San Francisco: Jossey-Bass.

Patton, M. (1990). *Qualitative evaluation and research methods* (2nd ed.) Newbury Park, CA: Sage.

Porter, S. R. (2004). Raising response rates: What works? In S. R. Porter (Ed.), *Overcoming survey research problems* (pp. 5–21). New Directions for Institutional Research, no. 121. San Francisco: Jossey-Bass.

Porter, S. R., & Whitcomb, M. E. (2003). The impact of lottery incentives on student survey response rates. *Research in Higher Education, 44,* 389–407.

Porter, S. R., & Whitcomb, M. E., & Weitzer, W. H. (2004). Multiple surveys of students and student fatigue. In S.R. Porter (Ed.), *Overcoming survey research problems* (pp. 63–73). New Directions for Institutional Research, no. 121. San Francisco: Jossey-Bass.

Priddy, L., & Keiser, J. (2007, April). *The commission's commitment to student learning: Hallmarks, trends, and challenges.* Paper presented at the Higher Learning Commission Annual Meeting, Chicago, IL.

Salant, P., & Dillman, D. A. (1994). *How to conduct your own survey.* New York: Wiley.

Sax, L. J., Gilmartin, S.K., & Bryant, A.N. (2003). Assessing response rates and nonresponse bias in web and paper surveys. *Research in Higher Education, 44,* 409–432.

Umbach, P. (2004) Web surveys: Best practices. In S. R. Porter (Ed.), *Overcoming survey research problems* (pp. 23–38). New Directions for Institutional Research, no. 121. San Francisco: Jossey-Bass.

Upcraft, M.L., & Schuh, J. H. (1996). Using qualitative methods. In M. L. Upcraft & J. H. Schuh (Eds.), *Assessment in student affairs* (pp. 52–83). San Francisco: Jossey-Bass.

Vaughn, S., Shay Schumm, J. S., & Sinagub, J. (1996). *Focus group interviews in education and psychology.* Thousand Oaks, CA: Sage.

# 5

# INSTRUMENTATION

## Kevin Saunders and R. M. Cooper

Institutions face a range of ever changing challenges that require information to assist with the decision-making process to meet these challenges. We imagine that the case studies presented in this book are common to many campuses and that a frequent first response to these cases is the statement, "We need more information so we need to do a survey," or "A focus group would help us gain some insights." This chapter provides information about the decisions student affairs practitioners will need to make when developing or selecting instruments to gather information. Using the case study presented in this chapter, we identify essential questions that guide instrumentation decisions. We then offer details about different types of instruments, including survey instruments for quantitative studies and various types of qualitative instruments (for example, protocols for interviews, focus groups, observations, or document review) for data collection. We outline several promising practices in instrumentation as they relate to student affairs assessment and offer resources that can be helpful in selecting instruments that best address the needs of the student affairs practitioner.

## Retention at Midwest State University

Chapter One identifies retention as one of the factors that contribute to the press for increased assessment efforts. Previous research indicates that certain college experiences, such as peer relationships, extracurricular involvement, and interactions with faculty, enhance educational attainment (Pascarella & Terenzini, 2005). Student affairs consistently affirms its important role in promoting student growth and development in ways that help enhance retention and graduation. Many institutions, however, find it challenging to identify specific factors that either positively or negatively influence retention rates. While acknowledging that student retention decisions are complex, following the small steps concept in the first chapter, the information discussed in this chapter offers some small steps to aid institutions in gathering additional information about factors that contribute to student retention and graduation. It is particularly important for individual institutions to engage in this assessment because although there is a vast literature considering the topic, student experiences and institutional contexts are unique.

Similar to most institutions, Midwest State University (MSU) is concerned with student retention. The issue is particularly important because of a projected future decline in the number of high school graduates in the state who represent the majority of new incoming students to the institution. The Institutional Research office recently provided a summary of the retention and graduation trends, which highlighted a decline in the first-year to sophomore one-year retention rate at the institution. Although it is unclear whether the one-year decline will continue, the president has asked a task force to develop a strategy for assessing various factors that contribute to student retention at Midwest State University. As the student affairs representative on the task force, you've been asked to consider how the institution might develop a systematic way to collect information about the impact of student experiences at the institution on student satisfaction and engagement.

## Creating a Plan

The initial planning stages for an assessment project represent an essential component in order to generate high-quality data that support decision-making efforts. It is important that the development and selection of instruments align with the purpose of the assessment project in a way that provides useful information. The task force will want to consider several questions to assist with their instrument development and selection.

1. What is the objective of data collection? Is the focus on student satisfaction with campus activities and services? Should the task force concentrate on the difference between entering student expectations and perceptions of their first-year experience? Are there specific student populations that need to be considered (for example, underrepresented students)? Defining the objective during the planning stages helps identify the necessary information to collect and helps eliminate questions that will not provide useful information (Suskie, 2004). For more information on planning for and implementing data collection see Chapter Three.

2. What information would be useful in understanding the objective (for example, student satisfaction and engagement at MSU)? Periodically returning to this question is important because sometimes further review reveals information that may be interesting but is not particularly useful in providing actionable data for decision making. For example, the task force may decide it would be helpful to compare student perceptions of the campus environment based on whether or not they live on campus during their first year. Without further defining what information would be useful, the comparative data may simply be a reflection of different use patterns of campus services from the two student populations without any detail about how the data connects to student engagement within and connection to the institution.

3. What literature is available regarding the objective for data collection? This can either inform instrument development or offer examples of existing data collection tools.

The plans should be designed in a way that will yield dividends—useful information that can help improve student satisfaction and engagement at MSU. A focused assessment that considers a few key areas will help gather information that is both high quality and useful. An effort should be made to maximize the use of existing information rather than invest in the purchase of new tools or spending time duplicating efforts. It also is helpful to limit the volume of assessment information. In considering a topic as complex as student retention decisions, it would be easy for the task force to branch out into a variety of different assessment efforts. However, attention that focuses on assessment strategies that provide the greatest dividends and developing staggered assessment efforts can help to maintain cost effectiveness.

## Selecting Quantitative or Qualitative Instruments

Creswell (2005) identified several steps in conducting studies that will help determine whether quantitative, qualitative, or a mixed-methods approach will most benefit the assessment.

1. Determine the feasibility of conducting the assessment. This is a function of the level of expertise within the team and the availability of time and resources. If these items are not adequate, the likelihood of successful implementation of the assessment is reduced, as well as limiting the utility of the assessment.

2. Identify the rationale. If you are unable to clearly articulate the rationale for selecting a quantitative or qualitative instrument, the purpose of the assessment may still be unclear.

3. Determine the design, type of data, and data collection strategy. Design decisions are shaped by the purpose of the assessment. For example, if the task force wants to gather exploratory information, a qualitative approach may prove more beneficial. In contrast, if the purpose

is to develop an explanatory model of factors related to student retention, a quantitative approach would be appropriate. Some assessment efforts wish to provide a triangulation of information in order to understand a question from multiple perspectives, thus suggesting a mixed-methods approach that would include elements of both qualitative and quantitative data.

4. Determine what type of data will best answer the specified research questions.

Attention to these framing questions in the planning process will help guide the assessment and focus attention on the basic principles of data collection design.

## What Type of Quantitative Instrument Is Best

Once the retention task force has developed an initial plan for the assessment, the selection of data collecting instruments will follow. This section of the chapter discusses the benefits and drawbacks of using published and local instruments, how to find potential instruments, strategies for developing a local instrument, and issues to consider that help determine the quality of collected data.

Published instruments are developed and published by an organization. Often, they require a fee to use them and are copyrighted. Many of the standardized national instruments described in this section are used at multiple institutions, allowing institutions to receive comparative data to students at other institutions.

There are several benefits associated with the use of a published instrument. The availability of comparative data from other participating institutions can offer a valuable perspective, often described as benchmarking. Published instruments may be perceived as more legitimate, in part because of efforts to document the quality of the instrument. Publishers often consult with field experts to design and test questions, and good-quality questions result. Sometimes, instruments are designed in a way that allows comparison of change over time. Finally, published instruments can be easier to implement, considering the time and expertise required to draft, refine, pretest, and revise a locally designed instrument (Suskie, 2004). Because organizations devote technical and financial resources to development, national surveys can be a cost-effective way to gather information. One potential limitation of published instruments is that comparative benchmarking may not be available either because the information is not provided or comparable institutions do not participate in the survey. In addition, if comparative data are available, these data may not be available at disaggregate levels (Borden & Zak Owens, 2001). Also, you will need to consider whether scoring of the instrument can be done by your institution or whether the publisher will require or offer to score the instrument.

Locally designed instruments may be more appropriate for institutions under certain circumstances. At times, the goals or interests of an assessment do not match the contents of the published instrument. For example, the Midwest State University retention task force may elect not to use a published instrument designed to consider incoming student expectations because they are interested in focusing on current student experiences at the institution. Alternatively, the MSU task force may decide that a locally designed instrument would allow a more nuanced understanding of institution-specific programs (for example, first-year student seminars, new student orientation) rather than the global measures considered in a published instrument. One of the drawbacks associated with published instruments is that the wording of items is already designated and there may not be an opportunity to add additional questions, which can be alleviated through a locally designed instrument that focuses attention on the areas of interest. Often local assessments offer information that is more directly applicable to the institutional context and information needs. Locally designed instruments are sometimes seen as a more cost-effective strategy when financial resources are limited but the institution has faculty and staff who have the expertise and desire to support instrument design. Others, however, assert that quality local instruments typically cost more than published instruments (Borden & Zak Owens, 2001).

It may be helpful to note here that assessment efforts require additional institutional commitment beyond participation (published) or development (local) costs. Campus staff may be involved in generating a sample, administering the instrument, developing subsequent analysis of processed data, and reporting results. In other words, the direct cost of participation is only part of the resources required for the assessment effort. In addition, the cost of conducting the assessment can be small in comparison to the costs of improving programs or services based on the results of data collection efforts.

When institutions are making decisions regarding the use of published or locally designed instruments, collaboration with faculty and staff contributes to the quality of the decision, successful deployment of the instrument, and effective use of the results (Suskie, 2004). It may be especially helpful to involve staff from the institutional research or assessment offices in order to review current initiatives at the institution. Several campuses find that the proliferation of assessment instruments at all levels is beginning to have an impact on student responsiveness and the quality of responses (see Chapter Four). In addition to expertise in selecting instruments, these offices can help manage the overall assessment load at the institution to reduce survey fatigue.

## Identifying Published Instruments

Once the purpose of the assessment is clarified, several resources can help to identify published instruments that may be useful.

*The Mental Measurements Yearbook* published by the Buros Institute offers information about instruments that assess mental traits and offers critical reviews by scholars. Copies of the yearbook are often available in campus libraries. The Buros Web site offers additional information. The Buros Institute also publishes *Tests in Print*, which "includes test purpose, test publisher, in-print status, price, test acronym, intended test population, administration times, publication date(s), and test author(s)" (n.p.).

The Policy Center on the First Year of College offers information about several instruments available to assess first-year students' experiences and learning goals. Their Web site also provides information regarding a monograph entitled *Proving and Improving: Strategies for Assessing the First College Year* (Swing, 2003) that gives an overview of first-year assessment instruments in addition to ideas for assessment activities. The document includes a typology of commonly used instruments that is cross-referenced with articles in the monograph that describe the instruments in more depth.

Another useful resource for selecting instruments is a copublication of the Association for Institutional Research and the American Council on Education entitled, *Measuring Quality: Choosing Among Surveys and Other Assessments of College Quality* (Borden & Zak Owens, 2001). The guide describes twenty-seven major national surveys and assessments and offers criteria that campus leaders can use to determine the usefulness of an instrument. Information about the publication can be found at the Association for Institutional Research Web site. The document includes tables that outline information such as the purpose of the instruments, use of data, history, information collected, target samples, participation rates, administration procedure, time line, reporting, comparison data availability, and costs. In addition, the guide offers a summary of the instruments based on their different uses (for example, profiles of entering students, experiences of enrolled undergraduates, student learning outcomes, alumni status and achievement, and changes in student attitudes and behaviors).

**Table 5.1  Resources for Selecting Published Instruments**

| Resource | Location | Information |
|---|---|---|
| *Mental Measurements Yearbook* | Campus library | Information about instruments and critical scholarly reviews |
| Buros Institute | Buros Institute Web site | *Tests in Print:* information about various tests, price, population, etc. |
| Policy Center on the First Year of College | www.firstyear.org | Instruments available to assess first-year experiences, ideas for assessment activities, monograph *Proving and Improving: Strategies for Assessing the First College Year* |
| *Measuring Quality: Choosing Among Surveys and Other Assessments of College Quality* | www.airweb.org | Describes twenty-seven major national surveys and assessments, with criteria to determine usefulness of instrument |

A summary of resources for selecting instruments is provided in Table 5.1. In addition, Appendix Three includes a table that describes several national surveys and assessments used in higher education based on Borden and Zak Owens (2001).

Once institutions have identified potential published instruments, a copy of the instrument will be helpful in determining how the items align with the purpose of the assessment. The publisher should also provide technical information about the development and quality (validity and reliability) of the instrument. Before final selection, details such as the administration procedures, costs, and reporting format should be reviewed. In the case of exploring retention at MSU, the task force may consider reviewing several instruments that are administered to currently enrolled undergraduates for the purpose of gathering information about students' experiences at the institution.

An effective next strategy for the committee would be to gather available information on the instruments and to discuss which instrument would be most useful in meeting their assessment needs. Suskie (2004) offers sound advice when reviewing the information available from data collection results. If an instrument does not give useful feedback on students, does not tell what is going right and wrong, and does not identify problem areas that need to be addressed, the instrument probably will not assist with making decisions. For several of the instruments discussed in Appendix 3, the publisher's Web site offers information about how institutions are using the data. This information can be an extremely valuable resource for thinking about how the instrument can align with other efforts at an institution. For example, the National Survey of Student Engagement (NSSE) annual report frequently lists participating campuses and how these institutions are using the survey in an annual report (see NSSE's Web site).

Overall, the use of published instruments can contribute to assessment efforts at various institutions. Borden & Zak Owens (2001) indicate that well-developed assessment programs typically use a variety of assessment instruments, including published instruments. They also suggest that published instruments may serve as an important catalyst at institutions that are beginning to develop assessment programs.

## Developing Local Instruments

Institutions may decide that there are compelling reasons for developing a local instrument, such as the desire to have greater attention to local issues that require results that are directly applicable to the institutional context (Borden & Zak Owens, 2001). We turn now to Umbach's (2005) three suggestions for reducing error associated with instrument construction: define a clear objective, pay close attention to question wording, and evaluate the instrument before administration.

Let us suppose that the task force at MSU already has spent considerable time gathering local faculty, staff, and students to discuss both the objective of the assessment and the availability of local expertise to assist with instrument development (for example, faculty from various departments, including education, psychology, and statistics; institutional research or assessment staff; and faculty and staff with program evaluation expertise). The next step is to carefully craft questions that will provide useful information that directly relates to the purpose of the assessment. Dillman (2007) offers several principles for writing questions that will be useful to the development of local instruments. Here we present several selected principles that are most salient for instrument construction in various student affairs assessment contexts. Interested readers may want to consult the full text for the entire set of recommendations. For a step-by-step, detailed guide on developing instruments we recommend Colton and Covert's *Designing and Constructing Instruments for Social Research and Evaluation* (2007).

## Phrasing Questions

Think about synonyms to replace long words and about using combinations of shorter words to simplify specialized words. An initial question posed by the committee asked individuals to rate how the institution supported their "adjustment to academic expectations or challenges." A revised question might ask about support for the student's "adjustment to academic demands." This revision also supports a different principle: choose as few words as possible to pose the question. Dillman (2007) explains that people try to be efficient when reading questions, sometimes resulting in the reader missing important words. Shorter questions maintain the respondent's attention and are less likely to create confusion. However, the instrument should use complete sentences to ask questions in an effort to reduce confusion.

The committee will also want to consider how respondents will interpret the words. For example, the committee may want to ask questions about the impact of specific programs such as learning communities, first-year seminars, service learning projects, or leadership development programs. The tendency of the committee will be to overestimate the level of shared understanding for terms commonly used for these programs. Involving students in the construction of the items or pretesting the questions with actual respondents will help identify areas where students interpret items differently.

It is important that questions be technically accurate (Dillman, 2007). Beyond efforts to correct misspelling and incorrect information, the committee will want to review questions to ensure accuracy. For example, the committee may create a question regarding students' level of satisfaction with information presented on academic support services during summer orientation. It would be important for the committee to share the question with summer orientation and academic support services staff to make sure that the question is aligned with the actual activities students experienced.

Two other recommendations for wording questions are to avoid double-negatives and avoid double-barreled questions. Let's say that Midwest State University is considering the elimination of a common reading program that is currently part of new student orientation. If we ask students, "Do you favor or oppose not having the common reading program," some students may find it confusing to sort out the meaning of each response or may misinterpret the question if they do not notice the word "not." The second recommendation, avoiding double-barreled questions, addresses questions that represent a combination of two different questions. For example, if the committee asks, "Please rate the extent to which you agree or disagree that you have had the opportunity to interact closely with faculty and staff," respondents may be unsure how to answer if they have had different opportunities with faculty in comparison to staff. The solution to the problem could include separating the two categories into individual questions (one for faculty and one for staff) or developing potential responses for various combinations of the two.

## Developing Response Scales

After developing question items, developers will need to put some thought into the types of responses available to individuals who are answering the questions. Dillman (2007) cautions developers to avoid vague quantifiers when more precise estimates can be obtained. The committee may be interested in learning about the frequency that students participate in various types of activities at the institution such as intramurals, cultural activities, theater performances, campus speakers, or student organization meetings. If the options for responses include "never, rarely, occasionally, regularly," the results will only support a vague interpretation because students will have different definitions of what "regular participation" means. A revision to the question could include more precise estimate categories such as "not at all, a few times, about once a month, two to three times a month, once a week, more than once a week."

The committee will want to be aware that the categories chosen for the responses require careful attention because the available options may influence how individuals respond. For example, one study asked students, "How many hours per day do you typically study?" but used two samples with two response scales. One scale had low categories (more than 2.5 hours was the high end) whereas the other scale had high categories (less than 2.5 hours was the low end). The different response scales resulted in 23 percent of respondents indicating they studied more than 2.5 hours per day in the low categories with 69 percent indicating the same in the high set (Dillman, 2007). The point here is that the categories defined in the response scales can have an impact on the resulting data. In our experiences in developing instruments, this important step is often overlooked.

In constructing the categories for the response set, it is also important to think about the periods used for reported behaviors. One challenge presented to developers is that memory tends to fade with time, making it difficult to provide a precise response. For example, whereas it may be hard for students to think about their entire experience at an institution, it may be easier to respond to questions that ask about their behaviors or attitudes regarding the current semester. Another challenge is trying to estimate time spent on regular activities. One solution to this problem for the studying example above would be to ask students for a general estimate "for the last three days" or "on an average week." A final problem related to time references and instrument development is that some responses will be different depending on the time the survey is administered. For example, if students are asked about the frequency of contact with their academic advisor during the current semester, student responses may differ based on whether the question is asked during the fall or spring semester. It may be that students are more likely to meet with advisors during the fall semester, so asking students to think about the entire academic year may be a more useful question.

Dillman (2007) also recommends using equal numbers of positive and negative categories for scalar questions. If a response scale includes three levels of satisfaction (somewhat, mostly, and completely satisfied) and only one level of dissatisfaction (dissatisfied) in the categories, then the neutral or midpoint of the scale would be "somewhat satisfied." The resulting data from this type of question would be suspect. When developing response scales, the committee will also want to think about distinguishing undecided from neutral response categories by placing undecided categories at the end of the scale. For example, the committee might want to ask students "To what extent do you agree or disagree with this statement: 'I have had the opportunity to interact closely with staff members.'" It may be useful to provide a "neither agree nor disagree" statement as a neutral category in the middle of the scale while providing a "no opinion" option at the end of the scale to identify students who have given little or no thought to an item. The committee may want to review its attitudinal questions where it would be useful to identify individuals who have no opinion.

Once the scale has been identified for the response categories, the question stem or introduction should indicate both sides of the scale. For example, instead of asking students to indicate their level of satisfaction with the social activities at the campus, the question might ask students to indicate the extent they are satisfied or dissatisfied with social activities. This change conveys to the student that the scale has a greater range and that dissatisfaction is an acceptable response. This strategy also offers a cue to readers when the response scale changes between questions (Dillman, 2007).

Sometimes instrument developers create questions that ask students to consider a large number of options or activities and to select "all that apply." Dillman (2007) recommends that developers eliminate these question formats because respondents may tend to review and check answers until they feel satisfied and then move on without considering all of the options. In addition, we have found that these questions present additional difficulties in recording, analyzing, and interpreting the data. It may be far more effective to isolate the specific information needs and areas of interest and then create individual questions that will offer useful results.

Once the questions for an instrument are developed, several additional issues remain, including the instrument design, the order of questions, the use of visual elements to support navigation, and the delivery mode (for example, paper, Internet). These issues are beyond the scope of this chapter. However, one important activity facing the committee after developing initial questions is determining whether the instrument will provide useful information that will match the objectives of the assessment. The next section offers strategies for this step.

## Determining Quality for Quantitative Instruments

Several technical issues should be considered in order to understand how well an assessment instrument reflects student experiences on our campuses. The retention task force at MSU will want to know whether survey participants are representative of the campus population. This includes attention to both the response rate (number of participants) and a possible response bias (type of participants). For example, the task force at MSU may elect to oversample underrepresented students in an effort to make sure that there is representative data from this population. The task force may also consider how decisions about the administration (format or timing) may potentially bias responses. For example, it may be that students with certain demographic characteristics are overrepresented in respondents to the survey.

The credibility of an assessment depends, in part, on the quality of the measurement instrument. In this section we describe two technical characteristics of measurement used to judge quality and appropriateness of instruments—validity and reliability.

### Validity

Borden and Zak Owens (2001) describe validity (does an instrument actually measure what it claims to measure?) as the thorniest issue in determining quality. Issues that influence validity include, among others, the complexity of what is being measured (for example, student engagement), how well students recall actual experiences (for example, satisfaction), and how institutions interpret results. Assessment instruments often try to gather information about characteristics that are presumed to exist but are difficult to measure directly (for example, engagement or self-esteem).

Here we consider various types of evidence that show that the intended interpretation of scores is appropriate and reasonable and offer ideas for how to develop this evidence. McMillan (2008) describes evidence based on test content that examines the extent to which items in an instrument are representative of a domain or construct. This type of evidence is usually gathered by having experts examine the content of the instrument and indicate the degree to which the items measure the criteria or objectives. This is often described as *face validity*. Validity is established through the presentation of evidence that demonstrates inferences are appropriate. A review by experts (or sometimes colleagues) will help determine whether individual items appear to measure what they purport to measure. Individuals with expertise can determine whether there are missing questions or if certain questions should be eliminated. Including analysts in the discussion can help identify questions that may seem interesting but will not offer information that will be useful.

A second type of evidence that supports validity is evidence based on the internal structure of an instrument. This indicates how items within the instrument relate to one another. Evidence of a valid instrument is provided when the relationships between items or parts in the instrument are consistent with the theory or intended use of the scores (McMillan, 2008). One process used to explore the internal structure of an instrument is factor analysis, which is a process used to determine which variables "cluster" together. Each factor is a grouping of variables that measure a common entity or construct. Student affairs practitioners may consult faculty or researchers on their campus on how to conduct an exploratory factor analysis of resulting data. The student affairs practitioner can then assist in seeing whether the resulting clusters or factors align with the underlying theory. See Mertler & Vannatta (2001) for additional information on how to conduct and analyze a factor analysis. (Chapter Six of this text also provides a brief description of factor analysis.)

One of the most common ways to establish validity of interpretation is by demonstrating how scores from a measure relate to similar and different traits. For example, if scores on an instrument correlate highly with measures of the same trait on a different instrument, there is convergent evidence. In contrast, discriminant analysis exists when scores do not correlate highly with measures of a different trait (McMillan, 2008). If possible, practitioners would want to explore whether measures on an instrument correlate with similar measures from other instruments.

For a more advanced technical resource, Colton and Covert (2007) recommend Baker's *The Basics of Item Response Theory* (2001), which they note is available for free download on the Internet.

## Reliability

The task force will also want to know whether the instrument is reliable, meaning the extent to which participant scores are free from error (McMillan, 2008). Here we identify several estimates of reliability, including stability, internal consistency, and agreement.

A stability estimate of reliability is determined by administering an instrument to a group, waiting a period, and then administering the same instrument again to the same group. The correlation between the scores offers a test-retest reliability score. The chief concern with this reliability estimate is with the waiting time between re-administering the instrument. If the period is too brief respondents may answer based on their memory of how they answered questions on the first instrument. If the period is too long between the initial administering of the instrument and the re-take, something might have happened that would influence a different response on items.

Internal consistency indicates the degree to which participants' answers to items measuring the same trait are consistent. Developers can calculate a reliability coefficient (for example, Cronbach Alpha) that determines whether several items measure the same trait. The benefit to this type of reliability estimate is the use of only one administration of the instrument. Note, however, that this type of reliability estimate works only when items are assumed to measure the same construct.

An estimate of agreement refers to a correlation or percentage of agreement. Although this evidence is typical for comparing ratings (for example, scores between two raters), it can be used when pilot testing an instrument with a small number of individuals. After the instrument is given to the same group of individuals twice, the percentage of responses that are the same represent agreement (rather than a correlation coefficient).

## Strategies for Enhancing the Quality of Quantitative Instruments

We close this section with some practical strategies for enhancing the quality of quantitative instruments. First, interviews with potential respondents to the instrument can offer important insight. There are various techniques for gathering this information, including an invitation for the respondent to "think aloud" while completing the instrument or asking the respondent to complete the entire instrument and then respond to specific questions. These techniques allow developers to see whether the words are understood, the questions are interpreted similarly among respondents, and respondents are likely to read and answer each question (Dillman, 2007).

Another recommendation is to conduct a small pilot study designed to see whether the parts of the instrument work as intended. This allows a review of distribution of responses on a scale, questions that may have a high nonresponse rate, questions that are redundant, and the usefulness of open-ended questions. In short, a pilot test allows the assessment team to examine whether the instrument is providing useful information.

The last strategy is to conduct a final check from a few people not involved with the assessment. They will take the instrument and review items to identify remaining issues. A fresh review is very helpful at this final stage in catching mistakes that are often missed by developers who lose the ability to detect obvious problems (Dillman, 2007).

Combining the discussion of validity, reliability, and pretesting together, we offer the following checklist for enhancing the quality of an instrument:

1. Have experts review the instrument.

2. Identify "clusters" of items that respondents respond to similarly and examine the relationship between these clusters and theory.

3. Explore correlation with scores on similar items on a different instrument.

4. Check test-retest reliability by administering the instrument to the same group at different times.

5. Examine the internal consistency (i.e., consistency of responses to similar items within the instrument).

6. Interview potential respondents, inviting them to "think aloud" and respond to the instrument.

7. Conduct a small pilot study.

8. Have a final independent review of the instrument using individuals who are not associated with the assessment project.

## Challenges to Selecting and Developing Quantitative Instruments

We close the discussion of quantitative instruments with some thoughts regarding the challenges of developing or selecting quantitative instruments. One clear challenge is the time required in designing useful instruments. Whether it is time required in reviewing literature and examining the properties of existing instruments, or time required to construct a local instrument and establish its validity and reliability, it is clear that this process is more involved than simply brainstorming some potentially useful questions. A second challenge is the availability of resources to support an initiative. It may be that the student affairs staff does not have the expertise or training in developing instruments. Or it may be that there are limited financial resources to support the purchase of a national instrument. A third challenge can be the limitations imposed by structured instruments. For example, if the task force selects an existing instrument for the assessment, the institution is limited by the specific questions within the instrument. It may be that the institution is interested in a particular subpopulation that is not identified through the demographic questions in the instrument. Understanding this limitation during the development and selection phase is important so that the assessment team can identify all the necessary pieces of information that an instrument must provide to adequately answer the assessment questions.

## Qualitative Approach

Up to this point, we have described instruments that will help the MSU task force collect data that are quantitative in nature. These instruments are typically administered either through the use of a paper and pencil medium or technology (for example, online surveys). Data also can be collected that are qualitative in nature. These data can be used to support and enhance quantitative data or as standalone data for exploring and addressing the assessment goal. Whereas both quantitative and qualitative approaches have their own unique advantages and challenges, they can be used to complement each other and to provide a more holistic approach to research, assessment, and evaluation projects. In this section, we describe some of the more commonly used qualitative instruments, the contexts in which these instruments might prove useful, and the challenges to using these types of instruments.

Why might the MSU task force be interested in collecting qualitative data to answer the question of the impact of student experiences at MSU on student satisfaction and engagement? One can envision the numerous complexities involved with exploring such a question. Although using a quantitative approach can most often be efficient and conducted in a narrow window of time, it may not provide data that will address the numerous dimensions of this question. When using a quantitative instrument we may not know the various contextual, environmental, or individual factors that influence individuals' responses. However, when a qualitative instrument is used, individuals have the opportunity to explain their answers and the practitioner has an opportunity to ask for clarification, more details, and follow-up questions. The data collected are often rich and robust (Jones, Torres, & Armino, 2006) in addressing the assessment question.

The qualitative methods used to collect data are discussed in greater detail in Chapter Three; however, the instruments that provide the data collection framework for these methods and the challenges of using a qualitative instrument are addressed here in the following sections.

## Qualitative Instruments

We revisit the case study at the beginning of this chapter and find that the MSU task force charged with determining the impact of students' experiences on student engagement and retention has decided to collect data in which the students' interpretations and perceptions are instrumental in understanding their experiences. By doing this, the task force has decided to collect data that are qualitative in nature; thus they will need a qualitative instrument based on the chosen data collection method. Here we suggest a number of qualitative instruments to achieve their goal. For more information on using the instruments described in the following sections in the data collection process, see Chapter Three.

## Open-Ended Questionnaires

Open-ended questionnaires provide a tool that researchers and assessment professionals can use to collect qualitative data from a large sample relative to other qualitative data collection methods (for example, focus groups, interviews). Open-ended questionnaires provide space for participants to describe and explain in detail their responses as opposed to predetermined response categories likely to be found in the quantitative survey instruments described earlier in this chapter. This type of instrument can be used through an online format or in person with paper and pencil. However, similar to some of the other qualitative methods used for data collection, the time required to analyze these data can be much lengthier when compared to the time required to analyze quantitative data. Coding is the method most often used for analysis of open-ended questionnaires. For more information on coding see Chapter Six on data analysis.

## Focus Group Protocols

To understand students' interpretations of their experiences, the MSU task force might chose to conduct focus groups or interviews with diverse student groups across campus, thus engaging students from all backgrounds in this qualitative investigation. Krueger and Casey (2000) note that focus group interviews are appropriate when "looking for a range of ideas or feelings that people have about something...trying to understand differences in perspectives between groups or categories of people...or [sic] the purpose is to uncover factors that influence opinions, behavior, or motivation" (p. 24). The qualitative instrument used in guiding focus groups is called the *focus group protocol*. The focus group protocol provides consistency between groups so that, when desired, the answers can be compared and contrasted with other groups. There are several steps in designing a focus group protocol; these include determining the questions that will be asked, the sequence of the questions, and the categories of questions (Krueger & Casey, 2000).

When determining the questions that will be asked it is important to consider the following guidelines suggested by Krueger and Casey (2000): specifically, good quality focus group questions are conversational; use words that are familiar to the participants, easy for the moderator to say, clear, usually short, usually open-ended, and usually one-dimensional; include clear, well-thought out directions. These characteristics are similar to those previously discussed when writing questions for quantitative instruments.

Sequencing of questions is another important consideration. Krueger and Casey (2000) refer to this as the questioning route and advise that a good questioning route has a beginning that starts with easy questions that everyone in the group can answer. The route should also be sequenced; in other words, it should flow from one question to the next. Questions should go from general to specific with attention paid to using time wisely. Novice focus group moderators often find managing the timing of the group to be one of the most difficult aspects of moderating the group. They get caught up in the discussion and the majority of time is spent on the beginning and general questions with little time left for the more specific questions that are of the greatest importance. There is an art and science to conducting effective focus groups, and one should consider the cost-effectiveness of hiring a trained moderator versus using a staff member with little or no experience in conducting focus groups.

Each type of question in the focus group protocol has a purpose, and different types of questions have different purposes in achieving the overall goal of the focus group. Krueger and Casey (2000) identify five categories of questions: opening questions, introductory questions, transition questions, key questions, and ending questions. Opening questions help break the ice and get everyone in the group talking, but Krueger and Casey caution against opening questions that draw attention to status and power (for example, education level, age) and those that emphasize differences in the group that may encourage some members to defer to others. In most instances, the results of these questions will not be analyzed.

Introductory questions give participants their first opportunity to think about the topic being discussed. With our MSU focus group, the moderator might ask the group to remember their first student activity that they participated in on campus and what comes to mind when they think about this.

Transition questions serve as a link between the opening and introductory questions and the key questions. The intent of transition questions is to take the participants to a deeper connection between their experiences, opinions, and attitudes than what was covered in the introductory questions. Leading into the key questions with the opening, introductory, and transition questions first will provide richer responses to these most important questions. An experienced moderator will make sure that there is adequate time to address these questions because they are the most important ones to analyze in the results. Whether the moderator is experienced with the topic or not, it is important to identify these key questions in the focus group protocol.

Ending questions bring the discussion to a conclusion and should include questions that provide an opportunity for participants to reflect on their prior answers as well as any additional information that they have not discussed that seems relevant to the discussion.

Krueger and Casey's (2000) process of developing questions for the focus group protocol starts with brainstorming, followed by attention to phrasing the questions, determining a sequence, estimating time for questions, getting feedback from others, and testing the questions. Protocols for focus groups vary from a formally structured narrative in which the moderator follows a strict narrative that includes an introductory statement, dialogue between questions, the list of questions, and a closing statement to protocols that are questions only that allow the moderator more flexibility. With novice moderators, we recommend a formally structured narrative.

For more information on planning and conducting focus groups we recommend Krueger and Casey's text *Focus Groups: A Practical Guide for Applied Research*, third edition (2000). See Appendix One for an example of a focus group protocol.

## Interview Guides

Rather than conducting focus groups, or in addition to the focus groups, perhaps the MSU task force would like to interview student leaders to supplement the results of a quantitative survey. There are several types of interview formats the task force could consider, including structured, semistructured, and unstructured. These types of interview formats and the purpose for each are discussed in Chapter Three. The most common of these formats and the one most likely to fit the needs of the MSU task force is the semistructured interview.

Regardless of the interview type, one of the first items to develop when conducting an interview is the *interview guide*. Esterberg (2002) explains that for semistructured interviews, the interview guide is not restrictive and rigid, but rather it helps the interviewer focus the interview while providing a medium of flexibility that adapts to the flow of the interview. The interview guide typically lists the main topics and wording of questions, as well as some suggestions for follow-up questions. Similar to many of the guidelines for the focus group protocol, the first step in preparing the interview guide is to determine what kinds of questions to ask. It is important to remember that not all questions will work in an interview. Participants can be asked questions about their experiences or behaviors, opinions or values, feelings, factual knowledge, sensory experiences, and personal background (Patton, 1990, as cited in Esterberg, 2002). However, most important is that the majority of questions are open-ended, since the purpose is to understand the participants' experiences and perceptions.

Esterberg provides some helpful hints to generating questions. Stay away from questions for which the answers are dichotomous (for example, yes or no), since these can bring a conversation to a standstill. Avoid leading questions that suggest a dichotomous response and deter participants from answering with their own perceptions and feelings. For example, the MSU task force would not want to ask the question, "Wouldn't you agree that participating in student activities has helped you engage in the campus environment?" This question is leading and can be answered with a dichotomous response. Rather, a more appropriate approach for asking this question would be, "What do you think about student activities and engagement in the campus environment?"

Esterberg (2002) also suggests asking both general and specific questions. A general question might ask the participant about student activities and engagement on all college campuses, and the specific version would direct participants to answer the question based on their college campus environment. Finally, Esterberg cautions against using "Why" type questions, stating that often participants don't know why they do or don't do something. Why questions can be particularly threatening when dealing with sensitive issues. For example, "Why did you take drugs before the test?" or "Why did you skip class on Friday?" can position the participant to be defensive. A less intimidating way to phrase the same questions above would be, "Can you talk a little bit about taking drugs before the test?" or "Can you talk a little bit about skipping class on Friday?"

Once questions have been brainstormed and determined, it is helpful to categorize the questions by topics and determine a sequence of the topics for an interview guide; doing this will help guide the flow and direction of the interview. The final step before conducting the interview is to pretest the interview guide. We have heard many stories from administrators and students about interviews that flopped because the questions were not conversational (i.e., the questions were all dichotomous and the interview was over in 10 minutes with very little data collected) or the participants didn't understand the questions being asked and the interviewer had a hard time trying to convey the meaning of the question. Both of these issues would probably be alleviated with a pretested interview guide. There is little doubt that an interviewer's skills improve with practice and over time, but a well-prepared and tested interview guide is an important tool that increases the probability of a successful interview that will yield quality data for both skilled and novice interviewers.

## Field Observation Protocols

Another approach that the MSU task force might consider with respect to understanding the impact of student experiences on student satisfaction and engagement would be to observe students on campus in variety of activities. Data from this method are collected through field observations and recorded in field notes. The data collection method for conducting field observations is discussed in greater detail in Chapter Three. In this chapter, we focus on a valuable instrumentation (i.e., protocol) tool for conducting a field observation. Emerson, Fretz, and Shaw (1995) provide a very thorough text on how to take and write up field notes that support field observations. Here, however, we discuss a generic field observation protocol and provide insights on how to focus the field observation by using a protocol.

A field observation protocol helps provide consistency and continuity between observations and the observers, especially if multiple observers are being used. The field observation protocol should identify the what, when, and where of the observation; in other words, the conditions under which data will be collected.

What should the observer focus on? The most difficult concept in conducting a field observation is determining what to focus on, and a field observation protocol will help ensure (as much as possible) that all observers are focusing on the same types of information. For example, the field observation protocol might ask observers to focus on what people are saying at the activity being observed, what they are doing or not doing, the layout of the activity (for example, how individuals negotiate the space), or what physical elements are present. The protocol may include a list of questions that help guide the observation. For example, "How are students interacting with the activity leader? With each other? With staff?"

Identifying when the observation will take place is a critical piece of the focus group protocol. Observations conducted at various times of the day or week or year may yield very different data. Depending on the goals of the assessment, it may be essential to ensure that data are collected at the same time each day or at different times and on different days. How long the observation should last is another point to determine before any field observations.

Finally, where the data collection will take place also should be addressed in the protocol. Similar to the parameters considered for "when" the observations take place, it may be important to set parameters that have data collected at the same location or multiple locations. Remember, even if a single location is used, it is important to consider that there are multiple vantage points from one location alone.

At the conclusion of the field observation, the protocol should also direct observers to record their own feelings and interpretations of the observation.

## Document Review

The final instrumentation tool that we discuss in this chapter is a protocol for reviewing documents. Suppose that the MSU task force would like to review official or unofficial records of student experiences as they relate to student engagement and satisfaction. For example, reviewing records that show how many students join a fraternity or sorority within the first semester of enrollment and continue on to graduate, or how many on-campus students compared with off-campus students participate in sports clubs on campus, might produce useful results. Are there clubs or activities that off-campus students are more likely to become involved with? Other examples of documents the MSU task force might review include the minutes from meetings that most student organization bylaws require or a review of articles in the student newspaper that address specific facets of students' experiences.

Once documents are chosen for review, a systematic method (i.e., protocol) should be determined for reviewing and recording data from these documents. The protocol should include (1) what documents are being reviewed, the type and source of the document (for example, local newspaper, minutes of meetings, student admission records), (2) the specific steps to review the document (i.e., what is the reviewer looking for), the questions to be asked regarding the document, (3) when were the documents produced (for example, copyright, meeting date and approval date for minutes), and (4) whether the documents are private and confidential or public. A systematically designed protocol for document review will allow for multiple reviewers to follow the same route for data collection. It can be beneficial to have multiple reviewers review the same document and compare results or divide the documents that are to be reviewed among multiple reviewers.

## Challenges to Using Qualitative Instruments

We have discussed the instrumentation tools for some of the more common methods used in collecting qualitative data: open-ended questionnaires, focus group protocols, interview guides, observation protocols, and document review protocols. Regardless of which qualitative approach is used, there are some common challenges that should be acknowledged when using qualitative inquiry to collect data. Contrary to quantitative methods that often secure data collection through indirect contact with the participants (for example, surveys) and analyzed by using statistical software packages (for example, SPSS, SAS), qualitative data are gathered by the researcher's direct contact with participants; in other words, the researcher is the instrument used to collect and analyze the data. With this comes recognition that the researcher's positionality is a key piece to consider in the process of collecting qualitative data (Jones et al., 2006). Jones, Torres, and Armino (2006) explain positionality as the "relationship between the researcher and his or her participants and the researcher and his or her topic" (p. 31). Social identities and power relationships should be explored as a part of the researcher's positionality. For example, if a senior student affairs administrator and a student leader were to conduct interviews with students regarding their experiences on campus, it is likely that the responses would be very different even with the same set of questions. In some instances it might be more advantageous for a senior student affairs administrator to conduct the interview than for a student peer group member. For example, if the goal is to understand what changes could be made on campus to enhance student experiences, a student being interviewed might be more forthcoming with the administrator who is viewed with the power and financial resources to make those changes versus a student peer who has little power or access to the financial resources necessary to make changes. Or the opposite could take place and the student participant might be intimidated by the status of the senior student affairs administrator and answer that all is well on campus, while sharing a much different view point with a student peer interviewer.

A second challenge to consider when using a qualitative instrument relates to time issues. Although the challenge of time is not necessarily in the development of the instrument itself, but rather in (1) the time it takes to facilitate data collection via a qualitative instrument (for example, open-ended questionnaire, interview guide) compared to a quantitative instrument (for example, survey), and (2) the time it takes to analyze the data collected through using a qualitative instrument. Once data are entered into a dataset and cleaned, most statistical analyses can be run quickly with the current statistical packages on the market. Qualitative analyses, whether done by hand or by a qualitative software package (for example, Atlast/ti, Nud*ist, NVivo), take considerably more time (see Chapter Six). Although we recognize the issue of time as more of a methodological challenge, we believe it is important to revisit here in the discussion on using qualitative instruments. Despite the time necessary to collect and analyze qualitative data, the findings are contextually rich and robust in providing participants' relative interpretations and points of view to the question being explored.

## Conclusion

In this chapter, we described instrumentation tools used to collect qualitative and quantitative data, highlighting the most commonly used instruments in both approaches. We pointed out that when using a survey or questionnaire, one should consider the cost and benefits of whether to develop a local instrument or purchase a published one that has been psychometrically tested. The local instrument can be more time consuming to develop, but it can be tailored to fit the specific needs of the institution. The published instrument will have been tested for its reliability and validity, and in most cases the instrument has been used at other institutions and there is access to comparative data for benchmarking purposes.

For both quantitative and qualitative instrumentation, the types of questions and the sequencing of those questions are important concepts to address in the design of the instrument. And in conclusion, all instruments should be pretested with a sample audience and the contexts in which they will be used.

## References

Baker, F. (2001). *The basics of item response theory*. College Park, MD: ERIC Clearinghouse on Assessment and Evaluation. Retrieved May 7, 2008, from http://edres.org/irt.

Borden, V.M.H., & Zak Owens, J. L. (2001). *Measuring quality: Choosing among surveys and other assessments of college quality.*

Washington, DC: American Council on Education and Association for Institutional Research.

Colton, D., & Covert, R. W. (2007). *Designing and construction instruments for social research and evaluation*. San Francisco: Jossey-Bass.

Creswell, J. W. (2005). *Educational research: Planning, conducting, and evaluating quantitative and qualitative research* (2nd ed.). Upper Saddle River, NJ: Pearson.

Dillman, D. A. (2007) *Mail and internet surveys: The tailored design method* (2nd ed.). Hoboken, NJ: Wiley.

Emerson, R. M., Fretz, R. I., & Shaw, L. L. (1995). *Writing ethnographic fieldnotes*. Chicago, IL: University of Chicago Press.

Esterberg, K. G. (2002). *Qualitative methods in social research*. New York: McGraw Hill.

Jones, S.R, Torres, V., and Armino, J. (2006). *Negotiating the complexities of qualitative research in higher education*. New York: Routledge.

Krueger, R. A., & Casey, M. A. (2000). *Focus groups: A practical guide for applied research* (3rd ed.). Thousand Oaks, CA: Sage.

McMillan, J. H. (2008). *Educational research: Fundamentals for the consumer* (5th ed.). Boston: Pearson.

Mertler, C. A., & Vannatta, R. A. (2001). *Advanced and multivariate statistical methods: Practical application and interpretation*. Los Angeles, CA: Pyrczak.

Pascarella, E. T., & Terenzini, P. T. (2005). *How college affects students: A third decade of research*. San Francisco: Jossey-Bass.

Suskie, L. (2004). *Assessing student learning*. Bolton, MA: Anker.

Swing, R. (2003). *Proving and improving: Strategies for assessing the first college year* (2nd vol.). Columbia, SC: National Resource Center for The First-Year Experience and Students in Transition.

Umbach, P. D. (2005). Getting back to the basics of survey research. In P. D. Umbach (Ed.), *Survey research: Emerging issues*. New Directions for Institutional Research, no. 127. San Francisco: Jossey-Bass.

# 6

# DATA ANALYSIS

## R. M. Cooper and Mack C. Shelley, II

After data have been collected, they need to be analyzed. In quantitative studies, this usually means the use of statistical techniques. Which techniques are most appropriate for analyzing data for an audience of nonstatisticians while maintaining the integrity of the study? In qualitative assessments, how does one make sense of the data? How does one ensure rigor in data analysis? These issues and others will be considered in this chapter. Examples are provided throughout the chapter to illustrate how data can be used to answer questions related to student affairs practice.

## The Quantitative Path

The primary example employed throughout this discussion is undergraduate student retention through the use of learning communities, which use linked courses, residential housing proximity, and heightened contact between students and faculty to enhance student satisfaction, achievement, and, ultimately, retention and graduation.

## What Do We Do with the Data?

To pursue your research on a student affairs issue, you have collected quantitative data from a survey, institutional records, or some other sources. What do you do next?

With any luck, your data will have come to you already in machine-readable form—which means it would be in the form of an Excel spreadsheet or a dataset in a statistical package such as SPSS (Statistical Package for the Social Sciences) or SAS (the Statistical Analysis System). However, if the data have not yet been entered into a computer software package (for example, Excel, SPSS), that would be the next logical thing to do. Unless you are really good at data entry yourself, this is an opportunity to hire students or use existing staff to do that for you.

Whether the data came to you ready-made for computerized analysis or had to be entered into the computer directly from their raw format, you will have to make sure the data have been cleaned and coded properly. Data cleaning basically has to do with making sure that all the data values have been entered correctly, no "wild codes" (impossible values) have been entered inadvertently, and everything has been at least double-checked. Above all else, be sure to back up your data by maintaining several copies of the data, ideally on different storage media (hard drive, flash drive, Zip, CD, or DVD) and possibly in different software formats (Excel, SPSS, SAS, etc.). As friendly advice, it also would be a good idea to think about e-mailing the data to yourself as an attachment, so you can open the data file anywhere you can access e-mail.

Data coding (and recoding) is a high art form, and it is difficult to provide a template that will work for all situations. Nonetheless, here are a few pointers:

- Make sure that data values are consistent. For example, if some of your survey questions had choices ranging from 1 = strongly disagree to 5 = strongly agree and other questions had the opposite coding (1 = strongly agree and 5 = strongly disagree), you will want to reverse the coding on one set of items so any data value always has the same interpretation.

- Missing data will need to be coded consistently, and probably should be distinguished from answers that are blank or illogical. The basic objective is to use a missing value indicator that is distinctly different from legitimate data values for your variables. Good choices may be −1 (negative 1), or sometimes 9 or 0. However, you will want to be able to distinguish a missing answer (a respondent failed to fill in any response to an item) from a structurally impossible response. For example, if a screening question asks, "Have you ever been involved in a learning community?" students who said "No" could not respond to the follow-up question, "Did you think it was a good experience?"

- Maintain an electronic codebook that keeps track of all the decisions you made about coding and update the codebook as you make later decisions about the data when issues arise that could not be foreseen earlier.

- When you use computer software to implement your coding decisions, be sure to save the syntax (a listing of the computing steps that were followed) in both electronic and hard copy formats.

## Levels of Measurement

How we analyze data for student affairs assessment depends greatly on the properties of the variables that are involved in the analysis and whether they play the role of independent or dependent variables. The things we measure about student affairs may be qualitative—defined as nominal (that is, named categories; for example, whether a student comes from in-state or out-of-state)—or quantitative—defined as ordinal (with some inherent ranking, such as student classification measured as freshman, sophomore, junior, or senior), interval (with known and usually equally spaced distances between successive units, an example of which is SAT or ACT scores), or ratio (with a fixed and meaningful zero point, such as the number of dollars of parental financial contribution to a student's cost of attendance).

Quantitative variables can be either discrete (that is, "lumpy," such as the number of students enrolled in the fall 2007 semester) or continuous (that is, smooth, such as the size of the student affairs budget for the 2007–2008 academic year). The distinction between the interval and ratio levels of measurement usually is not important in practice; both are usually treated as continuous variables that in principle could be divided into infinitely small components, in contrast to discrete variables. Qualitative variables are discrete, by definition, and ordinal variables sometimes are treated as discrete and sometimes as continuous.

## Simple Descriptive Statistics

At whatever level they are measured, we can describe the characteristics of these variables in terms of their central tendency (that is, the most common, middle, or average value) and their dispersion (their spread or variation relative to the central tendency). The traditional ways to measure central tendency include the mode (the most frequently occurring values or values), the median (the value in the middle when the observations are ranked from smallest to largest), and the mean (the arithmetic average calculated by adding up all the data values and dividing that sum by the number of observations). In your study of learning communities, for example, you might find that the modal (most common) participant is a freshman, that the median (middle-ranked) high school graduation percentile is 35, and that the mean retention rate for students participating in learning communities over the last five years is 85 percent.

Dispersion is measured most commonly by the range (the maximum value minus the minimum value), the variance (the sum of the squared distances of each observation from their mean divided by the number of degrees of freedom, which is the number of independently varying differences and which equals the sample size minus one for a single variable), the standard deviation (the positive square root of the variance), and the coefficient of variation (the standard deviation divided by the mean, multiplied by 100, which permits more balanced comparisons of variables with substantially different units of measurement—such as number of students enrolled and number of tuition dollars). For example, the range of retention rates for learning community participants over the last five years may be from 82.5 to 89.4 percent, the variance of the retention rates might be 25 percentage points, and the standard deviation of the retention rates would be 5 percentage points (meaning that each year's retention rate differs on average by 5 percentage points from the mean retention rate). The coefficient of variation of retention rates then would be $(5/85) \times 100$ percent = 5.88 percent, which means that learning community retention rates vary from year to year by a bit less than 6 percent.

## What Kinds of Things Can We Do with Student Affairs Data?

Following are some of the forms of data analysis that are appropriate for student affairs data. This list is not comprehensive; rather, it suggests the wide array of alternatives that are available to apply to the scientific study of student affairs. The interested reader is referred to Agresti and Finlay (2009), Hinkle, Wiersma, and Jurs (2003), Howell (2002), and Tabachnick and Fidell (2001).

### Simple Linear Correlation and Regression

Bivariate correlation and regression evaluate the relationship between two continuous variables, such as students' high school class rank when they enroll and their grade point average (GPA) at the end of the first academic year. A bivariate correlation measures the association between two variables without assuming that one variable depends on the other. In contrast, bivariate regression predicts values of the dependent variable from values of the independent variable; for example, we could use incoming students' high school graduation rank to predict their college GPA. In general, you can use bivariate correlation and regression for the same variables, but regression analysis produces more useful information. For example, a regression analysis predicting the GPA of students in learning communities from the number of advanced mathematics courses each student had taken in high school would show the slope of the straight-line relationship between the two variables (that is, how much GPA changes, on average, for each additional advanced math class), the intercept for that relationship (measuring mean GPA for students who took zero advanced math courses in high school), the predicted values of the dependent variable, and the proportion of the variation in the dependent variable that is explained by the independent variable (often referred to as $R^2$, which ranges from zero to one; for example, $R^2 = .13$ would indicate that 13 percent of the variation in GPA from student to student is accounted for by the number of advanced math courses taken in high school).

## Multiple Linear Correlation and Regression

Multiple correlation assesses the extent to which a continuous variable is related to two or more other variables that also are usually continuous. For example, we could correlate students' first-year college GPA with their high school GPA, dollars of unmet financial need, and number of college credits attempted.

Multiple regression predicts the values of a dependent variable (let's say first-year college GPA, again) from the linear combination of high school GPA, dollars of unmet financial need, and number of college credits attempted. The predictive accuracy of a multiple regression can be measured either for the entire set of predictor variables all at the same time, or in order of importance determined by the researcher or by automated forms of sequential multiple regression by entering the independent variables one at a time (forward selection) or by eliminating the least important independent variables one at a time (backward elimination).

## Canonical Correlation and Multivariate Regression

We also could correlate one set of continuous variables with another set of continuous variables, which defines a canonical correlation. For example, we could correlate several measures of student finances (such as total budgeted need, gift aid, work-study funding, and loans) with various measures of student outcomes (for instance, first-semester GPA, cumulative first-year GPA, and number of credits earned). A multivariate regression would predict these student outcomes variables from the student finance variables.

## Frequency Tables and Logit Models

Two-way frequency tables are used to assess the relationship between discrete variables, particularly those measured at a nominal or ordinal level with a relatively small number of categories. Nonparametric measures of general association and nonparametric correlation coefficients measure relationships between these cross-classified variables. Such analyses can be extended to include three or more categorical variables, although that requires a big dataset because the analysis divides the total number of observations into a large number of "cells." An example of a three-way frequency table would examine the relationship between whether students participated in a learning community and whether they returned the next fall, controlling for their ethnicity.

A logit analysis, commonly expressed in the form of a log-linear model, is conducted when one of the cross-tabulated variables is treated as a dependent variable and the others are independent variables. Such models involve the logarithms of the odds ratios of the likelihood of one outcome of the dependent variable for different combinations of the categories of the independent variables. For example, we could predict whether a student is retained, defined by enrolling for the second fall semester, from whether the student participated in a learning community and the student's sex.

## Analysis of Variance and Related Methods

Analysis of variance (ANOVA) is appropriate when the goal is to compare mean levels of a continuous dependent variable across the levels of a "main effect" (a categorical variable). One-way ANOVA is an adaptation of a *t*-test to compare means between two groups. For example, we could compare first-year cumulative GPAs across academic departments to see whether students in some majors have higher grades than do students in other majors.

If one or more continuous predictor variables are is added to a one-way ANOVA, the result is a one-way Analysis of Covariance (ANCOVA). For example, we could add a measure of the difficulty of each major to the one-way ANOVA comparison of mean GPAs across academic departments. ANCOVA permits a more valid comparison of mean GPAs across departments, after adjusting for differences in the difficulty of each major.

Factorial ANOVA involves using more than one categorical main effect. For example, we could predict first-year cumulative GPA from both whether the student participated in a learning community and the student's sex. Factorial models also make it possible to measure the effect of interaction between the main effects—for example, to see whether there are differences in first-year GPA between male students in learning communities, male students not in learning communities, female students in learning communities, and female students not in learning communities. Factorial ANCOVA models also can be estimated by adding continuous predictor variables (for example, high school rank).

## Multivariate Analysis of Variance and Covariance

Multivariate forms of ANOVA and ANCOVA are appropriate when there are two or more continuous dependent variables (for example, each student's GPA and total number of credits earned) and one or more categorical main effects (such as whether the student participated in a learning community), taking into account correlations among the dependent variables (MANOVA), and adjusting for continuous covariates (MANCOVA) such as family financial contribution. Factorial MANOVA and factorial MANCOVA models also can be estimated to predict, for example, GPA and credits earned from whether the student participated in a learning community and the student's sex, possibly adjusting for family financial contribution.

Repeated measures is a special type of MANOVA in which the same thing is measured at different times or there are multiple measures of the same trait. The simplest form of repeated measures is a pretest-posttest comparison. For example, we could measure students' sense of being engaged with higher education both before and after they participate in a learning community experience. More elaborate repeated measures models can be estimated for more than two time periods; an example would be to track the pattern of student GPAs for every semester they remain enrolled. Main effects and covariates may be added to these purely within-subjects designs to produce between-subjects repeated measures MANOVA or MANCOVA models. An important condition that must be satisfied for repeated measures results to be satisfied, at least without appropriate adjustments, is sphericity, or constant correlations among values of the same variable measured repeatedly over time or among different measures of the same trait.

## Discriminant Analysis

If the goal is to predict correctly the category in which an observation belongs on a categorical outcome variable, and all the independent variables are continuous and normally distributed, then discriminant analysis is the appropriate procedure to use. For example, a discriminant analysis would use student cumulative GPA, unmet budgeted need, and number of credits earned to predict (that is, to discriminate between) whether that student returned or did not return the second fall semester. The validity of a discriminant analysis is determined by how well it predicts the correct classification overall, and for each of the outcome categories separately.

## Logistic Regression

As with discriminant analysis, logistic regression is used to produce models that correctly classify outcomes for a categorical dependent variable. Logistic regression is more appropriate when there is a combination of continuous (for example, cumulative GPA, unmet budgeted need, and number of credits earned) and categorical (for example, gender and learning community participation) predictor variables, and it is a better procedure when the dependent variable consists of an ordinal set of categorical outcomes (for instance, whether the student was retained in the university, within his or her entry college, or within his or her entry department).

## Factor Analysis

Factor analysis consists of a set of procedures to establish construct validity, which involves using the correlations among a set of variables to determine the number of composite variables (factors) that underlay a (usually large) number of continuous variables. For this reason, factor analysis often is referred to as a method of data reduction. Factor analysis involves two steps: (1) an appropriate number of factors, or latent variables, that do a good job of summarizing the correlations among those items are extracted, and (2) the factors are rotated to improve the fit of each item on each factor. The goal is "simple structure," in which each item has a strong correlation ("loading") with only one factor. For example, we could conduct factor analysis on the large number items in the annual Cooperative Institutional Research Program Freshman Survey on students' high school experiences to reduce the complexity and sharpen the focus to a smaller number (say, five) of factors that summarize the patterns of students' responses.

## Structural Equation Modeling

Structural equation models (SEM) combine aspects of factor analysis, canonical correlation, and multiple regression to estimate complex relationships among variables by estimating several equations simultaneously. SEM is most appropriate when a dependent variable in one equation is an independent variable in another equation. In its simplest form, path analysis, SEM uses observed variables (as opposed to composite factors) to estimate continuous dependent variables. SEM results are sensitive to problems with lack of normality, particularly kurtosis, in the dependent variables. The validity of SEM is assessed largely by the extent to which the simplified model accurately reproduces the patterns among the variables in the sample data. SEM is particularly important for its ability to estimate both direct relationships among variables, which also is done in linear regression, and indirect effects, in which other variables intervene between a predictor variable and a dependent variable and which cannot be estimated by other methods. For example, SEM could be used to estimate the relationship between college undergraduate students' ACT scores and their first-year cumulative GPAs, mediated by their high school GPAs and controlling for their demographic traits.

## Hierarchical Linear Models

Hierarchical linear models (HLM) are used when variables in a model are measured on two or more types of observational units. For example, an analysis of student performance in sixty sections of a freshman English class would use variables measuring individual student characteristics and performance and information about each section's instructors (gender, years of experience, whether English is their first language). Student-level data vary for students in the same section, but instructor-level variables are constant for those same students; this requires a nested, or mixed-model, HLM analysis.

## Time Series Analysis

Time series analysis is the appropriate method when a variable is measured repeatedly over long stretches of time, preferably at regular intervals. Particularly when there are fifty or more such repeated observations, it is possible to develop forecasting models to predict future values. An example would be using historical values of annual student enrollment head counts to forecast student enrollment for next fall. This can be done either as a univariate model, based solely on determining the patterns that exist over time among successive repeated enrollment values, or as a multivariate input-output model for one or more continuous predictor variables measured repeatedly over the same time interval (for example, size of the traditional-age population for first-year students) or a transfer function model with categorical input variables that measure the onset of an intervention and the extent of its intensity and duration (for example, consolidating departments or colleges).

## An Example: Cross-Tabulation Analysis for Learning Communities and Student Retention

Two-way frequency tables are used to assess the relationship between discrete variables, particularly those measured at a nominal or ordinal level with a relatively small number of categories. A large family of nonparametric measures of general association and correlation coefficients are used to measure the relationships between these cross-classified variables. These analyses can be extended to include three or more categorical variables, although doing so requires a large dataset because the analysis divides the total number of observations into "cells" at the intersection of all of the variables' categories.

The simplest, but still effective, method for analyzing the relationship between discrete variables is to formulate the analysis as a two-way crosstabulation, in which both the "predictor" variable and the "outcome" variable is a dichotomy or polytomy (i.e., multiple categories). In this configuration, the information of interest is whether the proportion of observations on the "outcome" variable varies across the categories of the "predictor" variable.

Table 6.1 summarizes the results from the two-way cross tabulation that relates students' learning community participation with whether they are retained to the second year. The individual cells within the table contain information on

- "Count"—or how many students fall into each combination of categories (for example, 350 students who did not participate in a learning community were not retained to the second fall)
- "% within fall2r"—67.3 percent, that is, 350 (67.3 percent) of the 520 students who were not retained to the second fall did not participate in a learning community and the other 32.7 percent, that is, 170 of 520, were in a learning community
- "% within learning community participation"—17.8 percent, that is, 350 of the 1,963 students who did not participate in learning communities, were not retained to the second fall, compared to 9.9 percent, or 170 of the 1,709 students, who did participate in a learning community

The general trend of the results suggests that students who participate in learning communities are more likely to be retained to the second year (90.1 percent) than are students who did not participate in learning communities (82.2 percent). The question

**Table 6.1  Crosstabulation of Student Learning Community Participation with Whether Student Is Retained from First Fall to Second Fall Semester**

| | | | Learning Community Participation | | |
| | | | No | Yes | Total |
|---|---|---|---|---|---|
| fall2r | Not retained | Count | 350 | 170 | 520 |
| | | % Within fall2r | 67.3% | 32.7% | 100.0% |
| | | % Within learning community participation | 17.8% | 9.9% | 14.2% |
| | Retained | Count | 1613 | 1539 | 3152 |
| | | % Within fall2r | 51.2% | 48.8% | 100.0% |
| | | % Within learning community participation | 82.2% | 90.1% | 85.8% |
| Total | | Count | 1963 | 1709 | 3672 |
| | | % Within fall2r | 53.5% | 46.5% | 100.0% |
| | | % Within learning community participation | 100.0% | 100.0% | 100.0% |

*Note:* The computer syntax code for this analysis can be found in Appendix Four.

here, however, is whether there is a statistically meaningful difference between the two groups of students—learning community participants and nonparticipants—in the rate at which they are retained to their second undergraduate year. If it can be shown that learning community participation is associated with (and possibly causally related to) higher rates of student retention, this is the kind of positive outcome—for the students, for their families, for everyone who invests in the students' education, for society at large, and for prospective future employers—and is likely to be rewarded by university administration and external funders of the university. First, though, we must be able to demonstrate beyond any reasonable doubt that there really is a payoff of higher student retention for the investment of resources to support learning communities on campus.

Whether this relationship exists may be determined by the use of different versions of the chi-square test statistic and other measures based on chi-square that can serve as correlation coefficients. Here, we only scratch the surface of what turns out to be a very large and diverse family of nonparametric measures of association. Readers interested in further information on other measures for relationships involving discrete data are referred to Agresti and Finlay (1997), Hinkle, Wiersma, and Jurs (2003), and Howell (2002). Our interest here is focused on the family of measures based on the chi-square statistic.

Several different versions of chi-square are presented in Table 6.2. The Pearson chi-square, named for Karl Pearson, is appropriate for discrete (categorical) variables and can measure any kind of association.

### Table 6.2  Chi-square Measures of Association Between Learning Community Participation and Undergraduate Student Retention

|  | Value | df | Asymp. Sig (2-sided) | Exact Sig (2-sided) | Exact Sig (1-sided) |
|---|---|---|---|---|---|
| Pearson Chi-Square | 46.699[b] | 1 | .000 | | |
| Continuity Correction[a] | 46.053 | 1 | .000 | | |
| Likelihood Ratio | 47.769 | 1 | .000 | | |
| Fisher's Exact Test | | | | .000 | .000 |
| N of Valid Cases | 3672 | | | | |

[a]Computed only for a 2x2 table

[b]0 cells (.0) have expected count less than 5. The minimum expected count is 242.02

The Pearson chi-square statistic is the easiest of these results to understand and is the version of chi-square that is used most commonly. However, the most useful of these measures probably is the likelihood ratio chi-square, because this is closely related to comparable statistics used in more advanced methods for predicting categorical outcomes. Here, the estimated likelihood ratio chi-square value of 47.769 would be compared against an appropriate critical value of chi-square with 1 degree of freedom (3.84 and 6.63 for Type I error levels of $\alpha=.05$ and $\alpha=.01$, respectively): The computed likelihood ratio chi-square value here exceeds these critical values, and the attained level of significance (that is, the probability that we are wrong in concluding that there is a relationship between learning community participation and student retention) is less than .001, although the SPSS default output shows this value inaccurately as .000 (the actual $p$-value is much smaller than .001). More detail about these computations is included in Appendix Five.

## Statistical Software

A wide array of computer software is available to assist with the analysis of quantitative data. Some of the leading packages are discussed here.

- Excel works very well for data entry and storage, spreadsheet calculations, and for many graphical applications, and it has some basic statistical data analysis functions. Many other packages can read Excel files, so Excel often is used as a form of "universal translator" for importing and exporting data across software.

- SPSS (the Statistical Package for the Social Sciences) is a full-purpose, commonly-used package focused on social statistics and education-related data analysis, particularly because its popular pull-down menus facilitate data analysis by not requiring knowledge in building program syntax. SPSS is particularly well-designed for the analysis of survey data, and is also very good for analyzing institutional records. It has procedures for exploratory data analysis and graphics, basic hypothesis testing, cross-tabulation tables, and simple correlation and regression relating two variables. It also has advanced procedures for multivariate data analysis, using procedures such as general linear models (multivariate analysis of variance and regression, and analysis of covariance), factor analysis, cluster analysis, discriminant analysis, logistic and probit regression, loglinear models, reliability, time series analysis, and survival analysis, as well as nonparametric tests.

- SAS (the Statistical Analysis System) provides nearly every conceivable technique for data analysis and hypothesis testing, and has powerful capabilities for merging and manipulating datasets. SAS has particularly useful procedures for general linear models, time series, multilevel models, correlations, discriminant analysis, geographic information systems data, categorical data analysis, complex survey data analysis, structural equations, econometrics, nonparametrics, canonical correlations, cluster analysis, correspondence analysis, survival analysis and life testing, failure-time analysis, logistic regression, and principal components and factor analysis.

- Stata offers a full range of data analysis options informed by its heritage from economics. Its capabilities include basic linear models, econometric procedures, multilevel models, logistic and related (for example, probit, tobit, Poisson) specialized forms of regression, panel data, nonparametric methods, balanced and unbalanced ANOVA designs (factorial, nested, and mixed), repeated measures ANOVA, factor analysis, principal components, discriminant analysis, multidimensional scaling, correspondence analysis, graphics, cluster analysis, resampling and simulation methods, advanced survey methods, survival analysis, epidemiological methods, and time series.

- JMP (pronounced "jump") features outstanding graphics and a wide array of statistical procedures, including descriptive statistics, simple and multiple regression, one-way analysis of variance, contingency tables, logistic regression, repeated measures ANOVA, response surface models, discriminant and canonical analysis, nonlinear models, classification and regression trees, neural nets, time series, cluster analysis, correlations, principal components, discriminant analysis, principal components and factor analysis, and survival and reliability analysis.

A large number of other general-purpose software packages, such as S-Plus and R, are used widely to analyze quantitative data. Other statistical packages are used for more specialized applications. For example, LIMDEP is used for advanced econometric analysis and particularly to produce appropriate results for models with limited dependent variables. Structural equation models are estimated commonly by software such as LISREL, AMOS, and M-PLUS. HLM software is used to estimate multilevel models. Other packages (for example, StatTransfer) are extremely helpful for moving data files (particularly with labels and missing value codes attached) across major packages.

## Qualitative Data Analysis

In the first half of this chapter, we discussed a number of methods for analyzing quantitative data, but suppose data were collected through qualitative methods (for example, focus groups, interviews, observations). How does one then analyze and make meaning of qualitative data to address the assessment, evaluation, or research questions? For some individuals, the mounds of interview and focus group transcripts, fieldnotes, and notes from document reviews can be overwhelming. In a quantitative analysis, all of the information is assembled in a dataset that can be less intimidating than the stacks of paper (e.g., transcripts from interviews, document reviews, fieldnotes) that must be synthesized and analyzed for qualitative data. In the remainder of this chapter, we provide a step-by-step process for analysis of qualitative data that may make the process less intimidating, as well as strategies for ensuring goodness and trustworthiness (comparable to validity and reliability in quantitative analysis) with qualitative inquiry.

Qualitative data can be analyzed by hand or through the use of a software package specifically designed for qualitative data analysis (for example, NVivo, Atlas.ti). In this chapter, we discuss the methods for qualitative data analysis that are not supported through a software package. Readers interested in further information on qualitative data analysis using a software package are referred to Lewins and Silver (2007) or Internet Web sites for Atlas.ti and NVivo.

## Getting Started

A number of different methods can be used for making sense of qualitative data. Within the framework of qualitative research, there are a number of methodological approaches that employ and direct more specific data analysis strategies that are consistent with the chosen methodology. For example, a grounded theory design would use methods of analysis that involve open coding (categorizing information), axial coding (identify one central category, identify relationships relative to central category), and selective coding (constructing a theory based on the relationships) (Charmaz, 2006; Strauss & Corbin, 1998). Regardless of the qualitative methodology used, Creswell (2003) notes "qualitative inquirers often convey a generic process of data analysis," and suggests that "an ideal situation is to blend the generic steps with the specific research design steps" (p. 191). In the remainder of this chapter, we identify and explain generic steps for qualitative data analysis. Creswell lists these as: (1) organize and prepare data, (2) read through all the data, (3) start analysis with a coding process, (4) describe participants, setting, and categories and themes, (5) determine how categories and themes will be represented, and (6) interpret and make meaning of the data; we add a final generic step (7) connect the categories and themes with the assessment objectives or research question to ensure that the analysis answers the question or objectives of the project.

## Organizing and Preparing Qualitative Data

The first step in a qualitative analysis is to make sure the data are prepared for analysis. Esterberg (2002) calls this "housekeeping." In the case of preparing interviews and focus groups, all audiotapes should be transcribed. When transcribing audiotapes, we strongly encourage using a transcribing machine. Transcribing is not an easy process; in general it usually takes an individual four hours to transcribe every one-hour of conversation. This is not to say that there are not individuals who can do this much more quickly. One option is to hire a person who is skilled in transcribing. Graduate colleges and many departments on campus will have a list of individuals who provide transcribing services. However, some researchers prefer to transcribe their own interviews and focus groups because they are able to review the data throughout the transcribing process. There are cost savings and benefits to transcribing one's own tapes, and it would be helpful to consider what will work best prior to the start of a project. In addition to transcribing interviews and focus group audiotapes, all notes from field observations and document reviews should be reviewed to ensure they are legible and as complete as possible. Some researchers prefer to have an electronic copy of these notes so that they can employ electronic methods in their analysis of the data. Therefore, we encourage researchers to transfer all notes to an electronic format (this also helps with storing data).

Once data are prepared for analysis, the next consideration is how to organize the data so that they are manageable. Esterberg

(2002, pp. 153–157) suggests the following items to consider in managing data:

- *Sort and separate different forms of data.* For example, all information relating to field observations is stored together and separate from all data pertinent to interviews, focus groups, and document reviews. Furthermore, within each of these different data collection methods, each data collection event is given its own storage space (for example, folder) and unique identifier. Each interview transcript is stored in a separate folder with any other information perti-nent to that interview, but all interview folders are stored together.

- *Store data in a chronological format.* Some researchers prefer to organize their data by topic or document type (as noted in the third bullet below). If this is a preferred method it is still important to make sure that some chronological for-mat or identifier is associated with the data (for example, interview conducted on the date of _____).

- *Organize data by topic or document type.*

- *Make and keep a logbook.* This is helpful in tracking your analysis and in providing an audit trail (Merriam, 2002), which helps ensure goodness and trustworthiness in a qualitative study. Examples of entries in the logbook could include dates of focus groups, who moderated the focus group, dates that the focus group audiotapes were transcribed, and who transcribed the audiotapes.

- *Choose between computer and hard copy.* Whether you choose to conduct your data analysis with a qualitative software program or a word pro-cessor, it is considered a best practice to keep and store a printed hard copy as a backup.

- *Keep multiple copies.* Anyone who has worked with a computer has probably encountered a lost or corrupted file. To ensure that the data will not be lost forever, it is vital to keep multiple copies and to store these copies in different secure locations.

## Read Through All the Data

Once the data are prepared and a system for managing the data is in place, the next step is to read through all of the data, a step otherwise referred to as immersing oneself in the data, or getting intimate with the data. During this step, the analyzer's goal is to focus on an overall sense of the data. It may be helpful to take a few notes regarding the data, but we recommend that you do not start analyzing the data in depth without reviewing them in their entirety.

## Start Analysis with a Coding Process

Coding provides the analyzer with a systematic process for organizing and categorizing the data so that meaning can be derived from the data to answer the research question. Coding is used in both quantitative and qualitative analyses. Typically with quantitative coding there are preestablished categories that are assigned codes and the researcher then analyzes the data to fit or match with these predetermined codes, whereas in qualitative analysis the codes are typically not predetermined but are used as a framework for determining categories and linking categories together. There are myriad formats, schemes, and methods for the coding process from coding themes that are specific to a research design such as the grounded theory coding scheme (open, axial, selective) described at the beginning of this section to more generic coding schemes.

We describe a generic systematic process for coding below. This process incorporates methods and suggestions from Charmaz

(2006), Creswell (2003), Esterberg (2002), and Tesch (1990), as well as lessons we have learned from conducting numerous qualitative research, evaluation, and assessment projects.

1. The first step in the coding process we have already discussed, and that is to read through all the information collected to gain an overall sense of the data.

2. Select a document (for example, an interview or focus group transcript) to review from one of the data collection methods. This may be one interview transcript, one focus group transcript, or a fieldnote. Read through the document to get a macro sense of what is going on, what stands out from the participants' words, and what is the overall meaning. Write notes in the margins, but do not get too focused on micro meanings at this point; rather, focus from a macro view. Do this for all documents.

3. Upon completing this task for all data collected, make a list of all the macro topics generated. Arrange similar macro topics together and create a coding scheme once you have decided on your macro topics.

4. Once you have an established coding scheme, go back through the data and identify these codes in the texts. There are numerous methods for coding schemes, and the key is to find what method works best for each individual analyst. What might work for one analyst may not work well for another. Some of the more common methods used are writing letters, numbers, or topic abbreviation codes in the margins of the texts that correspond with the macro topics identified. Using different colored highlighters to identify segments of the text that correspond to the macro topics is another method for coding; this approach also works in a word processing document such as Microsoft Word by using

the highlighting option on the Microsoft Word toolbar. Some individuals prefer a more physical approach to coding by using index cards or cut-out sections of transcripts to physically place data in categories.

5. After coding the document for the macro topics, read through the document again to see whether some macro topics may be combined to create a new macro topic or whether there are macro topics that may be micro topics (i.e., that would fit under a macro topic already identified), and finally be willing to consider other topics that might emerge through this process. Esterberg (2002) refers to this process as "focused coding."

6. Create categories or themes for your topics and identify relationships between these categories and themes. Creating a taxonomy is one method that is helpful in identifying and exploring relationships between the data, topics, and categories. Drawing maps or diagrams are other visual methods that can be used.

7. Assemble all data that support each category and theme together. Conduct an analysis to determine whether (a) the data support the theme as originally determined, (b) there are data that have been left out that support the theme, and (c), very important, whether the themes answer the original research question or assessment objective. Often novice analysts get so involved in dis-covering and generating themes and categories that they lose sight of whether the themes and categories answer the research questions or address the objectives of the assessment.

8. Finally, if a, b, and c (in item 7) are not adequately addressed and answered, it is time to reassess how the data were coded and start the process over.

## Generating Descriptions of Participants, Setting, and Themes

One of the many benefits of qualitative inquiry is the ability to study a phenomenon of interest within a context. Describing in rich detail the context and the key informants in the context is a critical piece to ensuring goodness and trustworthiness in a qualitative study (Merriam, 2002). Creswell (2003) notes that "description involves a detailed rendering of information about people, places, or events in the setting" (p. 193). Methods to describe and represent data are discussed in the next section.

## Determine How Categories and Themes Will Be Represented

Once themes and categories have been finalized, the question to address next is how they are represented in the findings of a paper or report, as well as how to describe the participants and settings used in the qualitative inquiry. One of the most common methods is to identify a theme or category that emerged from the data analysis and follow this with a discussion and interpretation of the theme or category, then to support the interpretations with exemplar quotes or narrative passages from the participants or fieldnotes. Sometimes this involves a main theme or category with several subthemes that interconnect with the main theme. In some instances multiple perspectives are drawn from and represented by the participants' words. These can also be used to compare and contrast views within a theme or category or across categories or themes.

Other techniques for representing data include visuals, figures, or tables. Drawings of settings help contextualize the setting for the reader. Using the participants' own words to develop a narrative passage that describes the participants can be particularly powerful for connecting the reader to the participants. For example, the following narrative is from a research study that focused on the social integration of students with disabilities in the college campus environment. The narrative was assembled through segments of interview transcripts.

> I'm [age] and I came back to school as an undergrad to get a double undergrad degree. I'm majoring in [major] and I plan to go to medical school. Family for me is pretty broad because our family is very big, but we are very, very close. I'm one of [number] siblings, and I'm the oldest. My mom is one of seven and her father is one of twelve and all of those people live within the same community. The only person that has moved outside of the community was me.
>
> I was diagnosed out of the blue. I had had no problems with my vision. I had great vision. I had glasses, but I had no problems reading, no nothing. It happened right after my [edit] year and they said it could have been magnified due to all the stress. Things just got blurry out of the blue. Signs that I could see the day before I couldn't see the next day and pretty much for me it was overnight. It never gets better it only gets worse.
>
> I was never a person who worried about anything. I had the future all planned out. This changed my whole outlook on how optimistic I was cause I went through that whole thing that once I was diagnosed I was the worst pessimist. The world was horrible and how could this have happened to me. I've always been a person who believes in a purpose and now how my life has turned out I definitely believe there was a method to the madness I guess at the time. It definitely changed me, but I'm not going to say that it changed me for the worse, I value and like who I am and that came from where I've been and what's happened.

Through this narrative we learn the participant's age (edited here), family background, a bit about the participant's disability, how the participant processed the diagnosis, and finally some insight into the participant's view of herself or himself. All of this information is presented in the participant's own words.

In some situations, there may not be enough space in a final report or manuscript or enough time in a presentation to include as detailed a description as the one above. In these cases, a table identifying selective descriptive traits (for example, age, income, race and ethnicity) of participants is useful as a technique for concisely describing information about participants.

## Interpreting and Making Meaning of the Data

"What do these data tell us?" "What have we learned?" "What is the 'so what?'" are all questions that can and should be considered at this point in the project. How one interprets the data and the connections made between categories may appear to be a daunting task. To help the analyst focus the connections between categories, Esterberg (2002, p. 167) suggests asking a number of questions about

- Events: What happened? Who was involved? How did the event begin? How did it end?
- Chronology: What happened first? Next? Then?
- The setting: What is this place like? What does it look like?
- People: Who are the people involved? What are they like?
- Processes: What are people trying to accomplish? How do they do this?
- Issues: What are the key issues for these people? What is important to them? How do they describe what is important? What language do they use?

Regardless of when, who, or what the analyst chooses to focus on with respect to the data analysis, the interpretations made by the analyst must all be grounded in the data; in other words, they must be supported by data.

As a final step in the interpretation process, the analyst might interpret the findings with relevance to existing literature or theories the findings deviate from or support. The analyst might also consider identifying future questions that have arisen as a result of the data collected and analyzed.

## Responding to the Assessment Objective(s) or Research Question(s)

Earlier in this section, we mentioned that one of the common faults made by novice analysts is to sift through the data, coding for commonalities that generate themes or categories without maintaining a focus on the objectives of the assessment or research question. To help ensure that the findings of the data analysis respond to the goals of the research or assessment, we find it helpful to list the assessment objectives or research questions and make explicit connections between the categories and themes generated for the reader or stakeholder.

## Ensuring Goodness, Trustworthiness, and Rigor in the Findings

When conducting qualitative inquiry there are criteria that, when addressed, will help ensure the goodness, trustworthiness, and rigor in the data collection and analysis processes. Several texts also provide excellent resources for promoting and attending to "goodness" in qualitative research. We recommend Merriam (2002), Jones et al. (2006), Esterberg (2002), and Creswell (2003), to name a few. Here we identify a few of the key strategies:

- Triangulation—using multiple sources of data, data collection methods, or both, and multiple investigators to collect data.

- Member checks—taking initial interpretations, findings, and descriptions back to the participants from whom they were derived to determine whether they are accurate from the participants' point of view.

- Positionality—making sure that the positionality (e.g., race, gender, class, sexual orientation, ableness) of all researchers in the study is addressed particularly as it relates to the topic being researched and the participants.

- Peer-debriefing—having someone who is not familiar with the study review findings and interpretations, as well as ask questions about the study.

- Audit trail—keeping detailed records of all assessment and research procedures, methods, and decisions made throughout the course of the project.

- Use of rich, thick descriptions—when conveying the setting, context, participants, and findings. This helps the reader determine whether the findings would be transferable in a similar situation.

## Conclusion

In this chapter, we identified some of the more commonly used methods of quantitative data analysis and the software used to conduct such analyses. Our purpose was to introduce assessment scenarios that could be addressed by various statistical procedures. We also provided a generic step-by-step data analysis guide to use with qualitative data that is appropriate for assessments. It is important to point out that in qualitative research inquiry, qualitative data analysis should be linked with a qualitative methodology (for example, phenomenology, ethnography, grounded theory) that drives the data collection methods and data analysis. Whether data analysis is quantitative or qualitative, the analyst must also address issues of reliability and validity (quantitative) or goodness and trustworthiness (qualitative).

# References

Agresti, A., & Finlay, B. (2009). *Statistical methods for the social sciences* (4th ed.). Upper Saddle River, NJ: Prentice-Hall.

Charmaz, K. (2006). *Constructing grounded theory: A practical guide through qualitative analysis.* Thousand Oaks, CA: Sage.

Creswell, J. W. (2003). *Research design: Qualitative, quantitative, and mixed methods approaches* (2nd ed.). Thousand Oaks, CA: Sage.

Esterberg, K. G. (2002). *Qualitative methods in social science research.* Boston, MA: McGraw-Hill.

Hinkle, D. E., Wiersma, W., & Jurs, S. G. (2003). *Applied statistics for the behavioral sciences* (5th ed.). Boston, MA: Houghton Mifflin.

Howell, D. C. (2002). *Statistical methods for psychology* (5th ed.). Pacific Grove, CA: Duxbury.

Jones, S. R, Torres, V., & Armino, J. (2006). *Negotiating the complexities of qualitative research in higher education.* New York: Routledge.

Lewins, A., & Silver, S. (2007). *Using software in qualitative research: A step-by-step guide.* Thousand Oaks, CA: Sage.

Merriam, S. B. (2002). Assessing and evaluating qualitative research. In S. B. Merriam (Ed.), *Qualitative research in practice: Examples for discussion and analysis* (pp. 18–33). San Francisco, CA: Jossey-Bass.

Strauss, A., & Corbin, J. (1998). *Basics of qualitative research: Grounded theory procedures and techniques* (2nd ed.). Thousand Oaks, CA: Sage.

Tabachnick, B. G., & Fidell, L. S. (2001). *Using multivariate statistics* (4th ed.). Boston: Allyn and Bacon.

Tesch, R. (1990). *Qualitative research: Analysis types and software tools.* New York: Falmer.

# 7

# WRITING REPORTS AND CONDUCTING BRIEFINGS

Once we get to the point of having an assessment project completed, what is left, and this is by no means an afterthought, is to make the findings available to various stakeholders, that is, people who are interested in the findings of the assessment and whose practice, thinking, or perspectives might be influenced by what has been found. Sharing the findings can be a pleasant task, but it is important to understand that the way the findings are presented or packaged can have a significant influence on how they are received. What is very important is that specific strategies can be employed so that the findings will reach a wide audience of people who will actually pay attention to them and use them as they consider the purpose of the assessment. In addition, accompanying the findings of the report should be recommendations for practice. "Recommendations, based on evaluation findings, can serve as a vehicle to insert evaluation data into the administrative apparatus of the organization, thus ensuring visibility and scrutiny of the evaluation report. Recommendations for change are an integral part of the evaluation—not an afterthought to conclusion of data collection and analysis" (Sonnichsen, 1994, p. 534).

In this chapter we discuss how to present findings in written form and through oral briefings. Our general purpose is to make sure that those who conduct assessments have the necessary tools to prepare documents that will capture the attention of readers and also conduct briefings that will have an impact on those in the audience. We provide a case study to help illustrate our approach. In this chapter the terms *assessor* and *evaluator* are be used synonymously. In either case they refer to a person, or persons, who conduct assessment studies or evaluation projects.

## Assessing Academic Advisor Effectiveness at Mid South University

Mid South University (MSU) is a regional, public institution that has academic programs in the health sciences, business, teacher preparation, and the liberal arts. It offers bachelor's and master's degrees. MSU has conducted a number of studies in the past ten years that have focused on student retention and in the past two years has administered the Survey of Academic Advising prepared by the American College Testing Program (ACT, 1990) to all first- and second-year students.

Professional advisors at MSU provide advising services to students until they reach their junior year. The advisors provide assistance to students who are planning their courses and other experiences in general education, but once students complete their general education requirements they are advised by faculty members in their academic department for the final years of their study at MSU.

Retention at MSU has been about what one might expect. That is, about three-quarters of the students who enroll at MSU return for their second year and ultimately about 58 percent graduate in six years. This is typical for MSU and its peers, but a new president came on board four years ago and wanted to identify what could be done to improve both the retention and graduation rates. One of the areas under consideration was trying to improve academic advising, although no one had any evidence that the quality of academic advising either contributed to or detracted from student experiences at MSU.

With this in mind the campus coordinator of academic advising, Sean Johnson, who reports to the assistant vice president for academic affairs, and the advising staff developed a series of experiences that were designed to improve the quality of advising.

The steps that were taken included in-service training for staff, the use of consultants, and an evaluation of the advising services through the use of the survey instrument referenced above.

After the first year of administering the survey it was determined that one element of the advising process needed attention. This had to do with helping students understand the financial aid process more clearly. Although financial aid counseling traditionally had been assigned to a different office on campus, when students needed additional information financial aid they tended to ask their academic advisors, since they had formed a relationship with them. The students really did not care how MSU was organized; they were comfortable with their academic advisors, and these were the people to whom they turned for advice.

The summer then was dedicated to providing workshops and other information to the academic advisors so that they would be ready for the students in the fall should they inquire about financial aid. Indeed, that is exactly what happened. This time the advisors were ready, and in their opinion they were much more effective in providing financial aid information to their advisees.

To determine whether the advisors' reactions were accurate, the instrument was administered at the beginning the second semester. The instrument was sent to first- and second-year students after the first month of classes in the second semester, and the data collection process was smooth. A very healthy response rate of 64 percent indicated a high level of student cooperation. Now that the data had been collected and analyzed, it is time for the assessment team to present the results. What might be the best way to do that?

## Preparing the Written Report

A traditional way of approaching the dissemination of results would be to prepare a research report and send it to the parties that are interested in the results of the assessment. Typically, the distribution list might include senior institutional leaders, academic deans and their staffs, department chairs, a handful of people in student affairs, and perhaps a student leader or two. The report would follow the standard format for a research report with a cover letter. That approach, in the twenty-first century, is obsolete. So, let us look at some principles for disseminating assessment reports.

## Specific Steps in Preparing Written Reports

A series of steps can be followed to develop written reports:

1. Identify the audience for the reports. Our assumption is that multiple audiences will be interested in the assessment, so it is likely that various audiences will seek more or less detail.

2. Develop appropriate formats for the reports. Some of the reports will provide extensive detail whereas others will focus just on recommendations. Hence, multiple forms of the findings will be required.

3. Identify the components of the reports. Some of the reports will provide more information about the context of the assessment; others will emphasis the changes sought as a result of the report.

4. Identify recommendations for practice. Reports need to emphasize action steps. A clear set of recommendations is essential for the report to stimulate conversations about organizational change.

Now let's take a look at some of the details related to the preparation of reports related to the assessment of academic advising at MSU.

## A Readable Report

Various stakeholders are interested in the report, and their interests are likely to vary considerably. For some of the stakeholders, simply finding out how well the advising process is working will be sufficient, but in the case of others, details about the technical aspects of the advising process will be important. Here are a few examples of what various stakeholders might be interested in learning from the report.

MSU has four general program areas: health sciences, business, education, and liberal arts. This academic organization can provide a format for the development of the report. Deans of these areas are likely to be quite interested in the results for their academic units, but very well may be less interested in the results for the other units on campus.

In addition, it is likely that senior administrators and the president will be interested in the findings, since the president has indicated that improving retention and graduation rates were on the institution's agenda. It is highly likely that the president will forward the report to members of the institution's governing board.

People who are responsible for the advising process also will be interested in the reading the report. Since they are responsible for the technical aspects of the advising process, their perspectives very well may be different from those of the senior administrators, deans, and members of the governing board. So it is likely that they will need more details. They also will want to learn whether the staff development activities of the summer between the two administrations of the instrument appeared to have an influence on the services provided.

All of this points to an inescapable conclusion: the report will have to take several forms. For the president and senior administrators, the report probably will have to take the form of an *executive summary*. Executive summaries should run a page or two. People in these roles have tremendous amounts of material to read, and one could assert, correctly in our view, that there is an inverse relationship to the length of the documents that these people receive and the likelihood that they will read the material. So a short report with an indication as to where they can find more details will be the most appropriate form of report to send to them.

The deans and their associates may be interested in the entire report, but their focus is likely to be on advising services in their specific college. For example, the dean of health sciences will be especially interested in the results from students in the health sciences and how these results compare with advising for the campus in the aggregate. It is likely that they will be less interested in the results for the other colleges. So for each of the colleges a *targeted report* might be prepared that would provide the results for the specific college and then provide comparison information provided for the entire institution. Again, they can be told where to find a copy of the entire report. What this means is that four targeted reports would be prepared, one for each college.

A third form of the report would focus on the needs of the advising staff. The purpose of the report is to give information so that the staff can determine the extent to which they have made progress toward their goal of improving advising services and also can sharpen their focus in terms of steps they might take to improve advising services in the future. This report might be thought of as an *operations report*. That is, it really focuses on the advising process, how well services are delivered, and how well the needs of clients are met. It provides information for staff about what they are doing well and what areas they might wish to address to improve their services. It could have to do with the organization of the office and how services are provided to clients.

A fourth type of report is the entire report. It would include data for all of the colleges and also should provide information related to comparing advising services from the first year to the second. It is likely that this report will be complex and it very well may not be distributed to anyone other than perhaps the director of advising services. That person can make copies available to anyone who seeks to read the entire report.

## Watch for Land Mines

Producing the written word can be challenging, particularly when one realizes that once a report is distributed, it cannot be recalled. The language of the report may be reviewed multiple times. The use of the wrong language, no matter what the writer's intention, can result in the language of the report becoming the focus of the readers' attention rather than the means by which the findings are conveyed.

At least two dimensions of the language of the report can become problematic. First, language, particularly as it refers to groups of people who historically have been unwelcome in higher education, needs to selected with care (Upcraft & Schuh, 1996). The history of higher education is full of examples in which people who were not members of the majority culture received a less than robust experience, even if they were welcome at all (Thelin, 2004). Hence, one needs to be careful in writing about members of historically underrepresented groups.

Second, assigning blame to a unit that receives a tepid evaluation or worse in an assessment project should be avoided. Suppose an evaluation of the residence hall environment is conducted, and the results are negative. The residents evaluate the food service, which is provided by a private contractor, very critically in this illustration. It would be convenient to blame the food service for everything that is wrong in the residence hall, but that may simply be a game of passing the blame to a convenient target. The reasons for the tepid evaluation may be a consequence of many other conditions, including poor building maintenance, inadequate staffing, poor supervision, and so on. Moreover, if the food service did not have a representative on the assessment team, it is unfair to the food service for "outsiders" to assign blame to it without the food service having an opportunity to provide an analysis of why the study generated unfavorable results.

Just as sloppy language can result in a variety of problems, all of which will detract from the message of the report, the use of italics, boldface, and underlining also should be approached with care. Bers and Seybert (1999) advise that these features be employed judiciously, and along the same lines, they recommend that white space be used strategically. They point out that white space "should be used by decision and not default" (p. 40).

## Emphasize Findings

People who have written a master's thesis or a doctoral dissertation understand that these documents can be cumbersome. They tend to state the problem many times and in many respects are redundant. Often they are very lengthy and quite appropriately emphasize the theory that has been explored in the research process. They also emphasize the methodology and methods that have been employed in the study. But this approach to preparing an assessment report is ill advised.

Typically, in assessment reports, readers are interested in findings. The question that is most important to them is simply this: What have we learned? The research methods and technical aspects of the process are of less interest to them, so in preparing an assessment report, focus the report on what was learned. In structuring the report, the bulk of it ought to report findings. What works well is that a paragraph or two at the most might be included to indicate how the data were collected, but after that a reference can be provided to an appendix that includes the details of the methodology or to a technical report that provides all relevant information related to the methods of the report that is available on request. Appendix Six includes a sample of what might be said about the methods used at MSU in the study of academic advising.

## Recommend Action Steps

One of our concerns is that assessment reports wind up on shelves collecting dust because they do nothing more than report results. Although the information may be useful, assessment reports have failed if they do not provide recommendations for practice. Accordingly, an assessment report without recommendations for practice is incomplete.

Most assessments identify areas for improvement. That is, a practice could be improved, a policy could be modified, the organization of a unit might be realigned. Along with the data, readers will either look for recommendations in the report for change or they will reach certain conclusions on their own about what might need to be done. Or they may review the recommendations and decide that different approaches should be taken to improving the situation.

Our view is that those conducting the assessment should offer suggestions for improvement rather than assuming that the readers will reach their own conclusions and the process will move from that point forward. In many cases the evaluators have more background and knowledge about their subject than the readers, regardless of how complete the report is, and they should set the agenda in terms of appropriate action steps to take. Sonnichsen adds this excellent advice: "Recommendations, properly conceived and given exposure in the decision-making memoranda, link the evaluation process with the decision-making process and help ensure that evaluation findings are debated in the organizational decision-making arena" (1994, p. 548)

Most assessments are conducted in an environment in which people hold different points of view, and assessors need to guard against radical conclusions that are based on the readers' hunches, biases, or uninformed opinions. Suppose that a group of faculty decide, based on reading the MSU report, that the advising office ought to be abolished and advising responsibilities be assumed by emeritus and emerita faculty members and take their recommendation to the Faculty Senate for study and potential action. On the surface this approach might make be worth exploring, since the emeriti and emeritae have substantial experience with MSU and understand the general education program very well, but such a plan is full of pitfalls. Although faculty could take this action regardless of any steps the assessors might take, setting the agenda and framing the conversation will serve the assessment process best.

Sonnichsen (1994) identifies several characteristics of well-written recommendations. The recommendations should be "timely, realistic, directed to the appropriate person or entity, comprehensible, and specific" (p. 543). He asserts that timeliness "has supremacy over the others" (p. 543). "Timely" recommendations have to do with when the decision is made. If the decision has been made too late, no matter how elegant the recommendation, it is irrelevant. Realistic recommendations are those that have a decent chance of being adopted and implemented. The recommendations need to be directed to a person or organization that has an opportunity to put them into effect. In the MSU academic advising example, recommending changes in the ways that advising services are delivered would make great sense, since the coordinator of academic advising is central in this assessment. The report also needs to be understandable by the readers. Jargon, technical language, acronyms, and so on may not be known by many of the readers of the report, particularly those who are not academic advisors. The report should be crafted in such a way that a layperson who is not an academic advisor will be able to understand the report. Finally, the report should include specific recommendations about how to improve. A comment about a commitment to excellence in academic advising might be an appropriate platitude, but it does not provide specific suggestions for the consumers of the report. A much better approach would be to recommend a series of specific steps in advisor professional development so that advisors can improve their skills in concrete aspects of their work.

Toward the end of the report recommendations for changing practice should be identified, including a process for considering and then implementing them. This approach helps set the agenda and provide a direction for organizational improvement. Without recommendations for change, the process could wind up going in a direction that was unanticipated by the evaluators, which could lead to unintended consequences.

## Acknowledge Limitations

This bit of advice has to do with preparing a frank report. That means that given the exigencies of the situation, the writers ought to acknowledge any limitations of the report. Doing assessment is not the same as conducting research studies for many reasons (Upcraft & Schuh, 2002). Among these are using a convenience sampling technique, preparing an instrument that has not undergone rigorous psychometric analysis, or providing a cursory analysis of the data. None of these approaches would stand the test of a serious research study. But assessments sometimes may be undertaken with significant time constraints, and the only way to produce a report on time is to cut corners.

Rather than wait for someone to point out methodological flaws, the best approach for the evaluators is to acknowledge, clearly, the limitations of the study. The general approach behind conducting such studies is to provide useful data for decision makers, and they should know that the study had certain inherent flaws.

## Use Creativity

Finally, we recommend that the report include a minimum of text and include charts, tables, and other graphics that catch the reader's eye. The days of gray text on a white sheet of paper are over. Newspapers have been in the vanguard of this trend, and the Internet also reinforces the concept that eye-catching reports are far more likely to capture the attention of readers rather than pages of text without interruption.

Technology allows those who prepare reports to use graphics, figures, and tables in ways that would have required graphic designers and highly sophisticated equipment years ago. Most computer programs have the capability of helping the writer produce a report that will be easy to follow, clear, and attractive.

If reports are produced in a series, as opposed to occasionally, those preparing them might want to consider developing a format for the reports, including a masthead, logo, cover, and other identifiable features so that readers know, upon picking up (or downloading) a copy of the report, who produced it.

## Samples of Reports

With the use of technology, the format and "look" of reports have the potential to vary widely from institution to institution. The following are examples of approaches that are possible in formatting and producing reports.

*Penn State Pulse* has been produced since 1995 and as of the time of this writing, 149 surveys have been completed (*Penn State Pulse*, n.d.). The reports are included on a Web site so that any person with access to the World Wide Web can review them. The reports tend to run two to four pages and incorporate many of the features identified above that make for very attractive products. The Web site of *Penn State Pulse* is http://www.sa.psu.edu/SARA/pulse.shtml

*The Orange Slice*©, prepared by the assessment arm of the department of residence life at Syracuse University, also provides useful information to the campus community through the use of assessment reports (*Assessment*, n.d.). According to its Web site, twenty-eight *Orange Slices*© have been produced since 1999. As is the case with *Penn State Pulse*, the *Orange Slice*© features colorful reports that are just a couple of pages in length. The findings are attractively presented and easy to understand. The web site for *Orange Slice*© is http://students.syr.edu/orl/assessment/.

## Accuracy

Finally, reports must be crafted as accurately as humanly possible. This means that numerical data should be checked and rechecked to make sure that they are accurate. Analyzing data twice is a good practice just to make sure that in each case the results are identical. In the case of preparing tables and figures in a report from computer-generated tables, authors should ensure that the tables and figures are identical with the source document.

Finally, writers need to make sure that the report is presented without typographical or other errors. Using the "spell check" feature of one's word processing program will root out most errors. But it will not point out if the report includes "form" when the author means "from." The names of people, their titles, and places need to be presented without error. All the pages need to be included in the report. If citations are included in the text, they should be listed in a reference section, and vice versa. One of the best ways to make sure that these errors are avoided is to have a disinterested third party with a careful eye review the report. This person has the potential to be very helpful in sorting out errors that will detract from the report.

## Preparing and Presenting the Oral Report

Not all reports will be presented in written form. At times the assessors will be asked to present their findings in oral form. They might be asked to present them to a staff meeting, a meeting of campus administrators, the faculty senate, or other, similar, bodies. Obviously one is not going to read the report to any of these groups, so a different approach to presenting the information must be developed. This section presents ideas about how to prepare and present an oral report.

Hendricks (1994) has developed a three-stage approach to presenting an effective oral report, a term that will be used synonymously with briefing in this section. His steps include preparing the materials, preparing for the briefing, and delivering the briefing.

## Preparing the Materials

Typically, one would use PowerPoint slides and handouts based on the slides at a briefing. But simply using PowerPoint does not ensure that the message will be communicated, nor will it ensure that the message will be received. The slides need to be attractive and apropos. Slides with balloons and the beach probably would not fit with an evaluation of a bursar's office, but they might be appropriate for a spring break trip sponsored by the student activities office. The slides should not detract from the text but, rather, provide an attractive visual image.

If PowerPoint is used, the size of the screen and the slides themselves must be large enough so that all members of the audience can see them. That generally would not be a problem if the briefing occurred at a staff meeting, but it might be a concern if one is using an auditorium to make a presentation to the faculty as a whole. The best way to determine whether the slides are visible is to go to the back of the room and have a colleague flash them on the screen. The font size should be such that the slides can be seen easily from every place the members of the audience might sit.

The amount of information on each slide should be kept to a minimum. Grob (2004) recommends placing not more than five lines of text on a slide. Dense text is hard to read even if the amount of text on each slide is kept to a minimum. Having just a few words on each slide makes much more sense rather than trying to jam too much text on each slide. Grob also advises that slides include cartoons or pictures, but only if the graphics are related to the content of the slide. Otherwise, in his view, the audience will focus on the graphics and not pay attention to the message that the presenter is trying to convey. Hendricks indicates that "One expert recommends that briefings use graphics twice as simple and four times as bold as those we use in our reports. Briefings are usually not the time for graphics requiring careful, detailed study" (1994, p. 571).

If one uses graphics such as tables or figures, they, too, need to be visible. If one has imported video, as is the case with graphics, the material needs to be visible from all parts of the room. Similarly, imported audio should be easy to understand and clear to all members of the audience.

The number of slides that one uses is crucial. In providing advice about briefing charts (the technology of the day), Hendricks (1994) recommends six to ten as an optimum number. Although there is no magic number in terms of the number of slides, without question fewer slides will work better than too many.

Finally, the issue of preparing a handout to supplement the slides ought to be addressed. Audiences typically receive a printed version of the slide show. The handout should list the Web site from which the complete report can be downloaded so members of the audience can secure the report if they desire to have a copy.

Grob (2004) recommends that the handouts be prepared in black and white (not the color version presented on the screen) but notes that printing on the front and back of the pages often results in errors. He observes: "If you print on both sides of the paper, odds are high that many readers will get a copy with every other page missing" (p. 624). To be safe, the handout should be printed on just one side of the page. With the presentation including just a few slides, the number of pages of the handout should be relatively few. It is important, however, to make sure that enough copies are made. Nothing can sour an audience like having an insufficient number of handouts.

## Preparing for the Briefing

In some respects, briefings are performances. That is, the audience will respond to the quality of the presentation in addition to the content of the briefing. So the briefing must be presented in such a way that the audience stays focused on the content of the briefing rather than on how it is presented. An excellent place to start the preparations for a briefing is for the presenter to identify a person who can serve as an assistant. This person can handle everything from distributing handouts to taking care of emergencies, such as an equipment failure. The assistant should be thoroughly familiar with the report and also have the technical skills to step in should the presenter be unavailable at the last moment. Suppose that the presenter is called away on an emergency, takes sick, has a family crisis, or is unable to present due to unforeseen circumstances. Rather than canceling the briefing, the assistant can step in and make the presentation.

In preparing for the briefing, the presenter should be completely familiar with all of the technical equipment that is to be used in the presentation. This includes the use of a liquid crystal display (LCD) projector, computer, microphone and other technical aids. Not all LCDs are alike, and certainly computers vary widely. Nothing can be worse than trying to make a presentation and master an unfamiliar computer simultaneously. The presenter and the assistant ought to practice with the equipment before the briefing. More than one briefing or presentation at a professional conference has been marred when the equipment did not behave the way the presenter had planned. The presenter should be entirely comfortable with the equipment and the software used in the presentation. A high-stakes presentation probably is not the time to try out new, sophisticated, and complex software. For such a presentation the presenter is better off using simpler software, software with which he or she is familiar and has confidence in how to use it.

If the presentation has links to Web sites, the presenter should make sure that the room has Internet capability or additional equipment will be necessary. Internet connections can be dramatic, but they also have the potential to fail at the worst possible moment, so a backup plan should be available if the connection does not work as planned.

In practicing the presentation, notice how long the dry run lasts. The presenter should make sure that an adequate amount of time is left for questions or observations from the audience. Hendricks (1994) identifies a ratio of about 1:2 in terms of the amount of time devoted to the formal presentation compared with the time left for questions, rebuttal, and so on. In a period of one hour set aside for a briefing, twenty minutes is not a great deal of time, so practice will be necessary to make sure that the presentation does not run over time and that questions and discussion receive a full 40 minutes.

## Delivering the Presentation

Finally, it is time to present the briefing. Hendricks (1994) advises the presenter to be informative and understandable, true to life, professional, and balanced. With practice and command of the information, all of these characteristics of a good presenter are possible. Some questions may be raised for which the presenter does not have the answer. In these cases the best thing for presenters to do is to acknowledge just that, and let the questioner know that the information will be provided just as soon as possible.

Whether questions ought to be postponed until the formal presentation has been completed or taken as they arise probably is a function of the size of the audience. In a small briefing, with, say, fewer than twenty participants, questions might be taken as they arise. But with a large audience, deferring questions until after the formal presentation has been completed makes good sense. This way the presenter will not lose track of the content and can stay focused on the message. If questions are taken in a briefing of a larger group, microphones ought to be available so that all members of the audience can hear the questions. If for some reason microphones are unavailable, or not working well, the presenter ought to be sure to repeat the questions so that all members of the audience can understand them.

The assistant can play a key role in the delivery of the briefing. This person can help with any technical malfunctions, make sure that the handouts are distributed, and provide a microphone to members of the audience during the question and answer period. Depending on the nature of the equipment, the assistant also might operate the equipment during the presentation to free up the presenter to concentrate on the message and maintaining rapport with the audience.

## Conclusion

Hendricks points out that the most important goal of reporting is to make sure that audiences "understand our results. . .see their many implications. . .realize what actions are needed, grasp the best ways to accomplish those actions. . .take action, and. . .follow up on the impacts of those actions" (1994, p. 573). This chapter has provided details about how to prepare written reports and deliver oral presentations. These suggestions, observations, and recommendations are designed to facilitate the assessment process. Properly applied, assessors will be able to convey their message in clear, succinct terms so that student affairs practice can be improved and student learning facilitated.

## References

Bers, T. H., & Seybert, J. A. (1999). *Effective reporting*. Tallahassee, FL: Association for Institutional Research.

Grob, G. F. (2004). Writing for impact. In J. S. Wholey, H. P. Hatry & K. E. Newcomer (Eds.), *Handbook of practical program evaluation* (Vol. 2) (pp.. 604–627). San Francisco: Jossey-Bass.

Hendricks, M. (1994). Making a splash: Reporting evaluation results effectively. In J. S. Wholey, H. P. Hatry, & K. E. Newcomer (Eds.), *Handbook of practical program evaluation* (pp. 549–575). San Francisco: Jossey-Bass.

Sonnichsen, R. C. (1994). Evaluators as change agents. In J. S. Wholey, H. P. Hatry & K. E. Newcomer (Eds.), *Handbook of practical program evaluation* (pp. 534–548). San Francisco: Jossey-Bass.

Thelin, J. (2004). *A history of American higher education.* Baltimore, MD: Johns Hopkins Press.

Upcraft, M. L., & Schuh, J. H. (1996). *Assessment in student affairs.* San Francisco: Jossey-Bass.

Upcraft, M. L., & Schuh, J. H. (2002). Assessment vs. research: Why we should care about the difference. *About Campus, 7 (1)*, 16–20.

## Web Sites

Penn State University. (n.d.). *Penn State Pulse.* Retrieved July 3, 2007 from http://www.sa.psu.edu/SARA/pulse.shtml

Syracuse University (n.d.). *Assessment.* Retrieved July 3, 2007 from http://students.syr.edu/orl/assessment/orangeslice.htm

# 8

# ETHICS

The ethical dimension of assessment is an element that is absolutely central to the overall process. To overlook or dismiss ethics as being unimportant in the assessment process is to make a grievous error that could have significant consequences for the investigators. Merriam described the situation this way:

> [T]he burden of producing a study that has been conducted and disseminated in an ethical manner lies with the individual investigator. No regulation can tell a researcher when the questioning of a respondent becomes coercive, when to intervene in abusive or illegal situations, or how to ensure that the study's findings will not be used to the detriment of those involved. The best a researcher can do is to be conscious of the ethical issues that pervade the research process and to examine his or her own philosophical orientation vis-à-vis these issues" (1998, p. 219).

Although no document or set of guidelines can anticipate every ethical exigency related to assessment, considerable guidance is available related to how studies can be conducted with the greatest care. Some of this information comes in the form of federal law and regulations that have been promulgated in recent years, whereas other advice has been available for a long time. Certainly, investigators are advised to refer to the ethical codes of their professional organizations for background information about to conduct studies ethically. Beyond that, we offer information in this chapter that should provide a framework for conducting studies in an ethical manner. However, we also urge those planning assessments to use resources available on campus, particularly the Institutional Review Board (IRB) for assistance in addressing puzzling or difficult situations.

This chapter provides a basic framework for conducting assessment studies ethically. It offers longstanding, background material on investigator ethics, and then addresses more contemporary topics, including federal guidelines for conducting projects involving human subjects. It concludes with several additional ethical dimensions that should be addressed as assessment projects are conceptualized.

## A Conceptual Framework for Thinking About Ethics in Assessment

Kitchener (1985) developed a wonderful conceptual framework several decades ago for applying ethics to student affairs practice, and her thinking has applicability in contemporary student affairs work. Her principles are timeless and have particular utility for assessment activities. The following discussion provides brief illustrations of these principles and how they apply to assessment.

### Respecting Autonomy

In the case of assessment, we interpret the notion of respecting autonomy to apply to assessment in the context of recruiting people without any form of coercion or pressure to participate in assessment projects and respecting their perspectives as they contribute data.

Obviously, assessment projects cannot be successful unless an adequate number of people participate in the project. Participation can range from a large number of people responding to survey instruments to a potentially smaller number of individuals participating in focus groups. Some people are more than willing to participate in assessment projects and will do so very willingly. Others need some information about the project and their role in it as respondents before they will participate, and it is appropriate to explain the benefits to them and the larger organization if they participate. Yet others have no interest in participating and will not do so under any circumstances.

In the latter case, coercing individuals to participate is a clear ethical problem, and it should not occur. In the case of random samples or people being selected more or less by chance, the opportunity to apply undue pressure on the potential respondent to participate is minimal. But students might feel as though they are being coerced into participating if a call comes from a staff member of the dean of students or the vice president's office stressing how important participation is and then the caller pressures the student to participate. Although one would hope this is an exceedingly rare situation, nonetheless, it is obvious that this tactic would create an ethical problem and should never be used.

Another dimension of this ethical principle occurs when potential respondents are invited to participate in focus groups. The identity of the participants is known in a data-gathering technique such as a focus group, and if the student also happens to be a departmental or institutional employee, excessive pressure could be applied. Thus, one has to be very clear in assuring resident assistants (RAs), for example, to participate in a project in which the RA role is being studied that their participation is voluntary and completely confidential. If certain RAs do not want to participate, that should be their business and no penalties, actual or implied, should be threatened in this circumstance.

## Doing No Harm

This principle has guided practice in the health professions for centuries. As applied to assessment projects, above all, no harm should result from participating. That means that anonymity must be protected, that special measures should be taken to protect opinions that do not reflect mainstream thinking or are critical of offices or individuals in positions of authority, that personal characteristics of the participants are not revealed, and that reports are carefully masked so that no person can be identified in them.

Let's suppose that an assessment is being conducted of the student activities office, and leaders of selected campus organizations have been invited to participate in a series of focus groups. The leaders are willing to participate, but in the course of the discussions, several are quite critical of the dean of students. Their philosophy and the dean's simply are antithetical. In the final report, the identities of these leaders need to be protected. They should be identified as nothing more than participants, and the content of their observations should be couched in terms such that they could not be traced to specific individuals. Although the dean may not be concerned about the level of criticism received, others may want to punish the leaders or their organizations. Clearly, assessment projects should never result in a person or group potentially being disadvantaged by the data that are revealed. Those responsible for conducting the assessment need to be sure that data can never be traced to specific individuals and that final reports are crafted in such a way that no one ever suffers from participating.

## Benefiting Others

A third principle has to do with benefiting others. Assessments are undertaken in many cases so that organizations can be more effective. That may have to do with the extent to which programs and services are cost effective, that learning experiences are consistent with the institution's mission, or that staff are responsive and thoughtful in their work with students. Hence, these projects have specific purposes related to organizational improvement.

An environment needs to be created so that assessments are not seen as ways to get rid of staff or programs or to retaliate against specific individuals. Sometimes assessment projects may result in reorganization, and it is possible that positions might be eliminated, but that should happen as a result of what the information reveals, not the reverse. In short, a culture of improvement needs to be created (see Kuh, Kinzie, Schuh & Whitt, 2005) in which data are sought for improvement and staff, students, and others are not fearful of the implications of the results of assessment projects. In an environment in which accountability is increasingly stressed in higher education (National Commission on Accountability in Higher Education, 2005), those conducting assessment projects need to reassure the units or programs being assessed that organizational improvement is the goal.

A corollary to this principle has to do with making the case to potential respondents as to why they should participate. In the letter of invitation, it is common for the writer to assert, sometimes overstate dramatically, that substantial benefits will accrue to those who participate. Suppose a random sample of students is invited to complete an online survey related to improving the institution's food service. Although the goal of this process has to do with providing a food service that better meets the needs of students who participate in one of the institution's food service plans, it is unlikely that the entire array of board plans will be jettisoned on the basis of the assessment and a brand new set of plans instituted. To claim that major changes could result from the assessment probably overstates the case. The benefit to each participant simply is that the board plan might be modified to better meet student needs in the future, but nothing more dramatic than that is likely to occur. Change is likely to be modest, and participation in the assessment should be conceptualized in those terms, that is, the plans may result in a modification of the food plans based on the results of the assessment.

## Being Just

In the case of assessment, being just is defined as being absolutely true to what is promised. If completing the questionnaire will take an average of 20 minutes based on a pilot study, then the invitation should indicate just that rather than use the fastest completion time of 15 minutes among participants in the pilot study. If a focus group is likely to take about an hour, then that should be the amount of time prospective participants should be told is their likely time commitment.

If certain prizes for participation are promised, they should be delivered. Although if prizes or compensation are offered for participation they should be made available to all participants rather than offering an expensive prize to one or two persons; even more important is that the prizes should be provided as soon as is practical to the participants. If each participant in a focus group is offered a discount coupon for a purchase at the campus bookstore, the coupon should be provided at the conclusion of the focus group. If a coupon is promised to each participant in an online survey, it should be sent to each participant who completes an online questionnaire immediately after the response has been submitted.

In years past when abstracts or summaries of the findings were promised to participants, they had to be mailed to them after the study was completed. That was done in response to a promise to provide findings to participants. With contemporary technology, this promise is easier to fulfill. Results do not have to be sent to each participant. Instead, the results can be posted on a Web site and an electronic message can be sent to all of the participants (assuming that they have an electronic mail address) when the findings are available with instructions as to how to access the material.

## Being Faithful

Finally, those conducting the assessment must be faithful to those who participate, those persons and programs being assessed, and to the data. Each of these dimensions of this principle should be discussed.

Those persons who agree to participate in an assessment are giving of their time, their experiences, and perceptions to the project. As a consequence, they have an investment in the project. Consequently, anything promised to them, as well as any other promise, implied or otherwise, needs to be fulfilled. These promises can range from the amount of time participation will require to compensation they might receive to protecting their anonymity. Anything less than full compliance with these promises will result in a serious ethical breach.

Those persons and programs being assessed may see their situation as being unsettled. If the institution does not have a culture of assessment or one in which routine organizational improvement is not the norm, it is possible for such people, their staffs, and their stakeholders to worry about the assessment. What will happen to us? Will we be outsourced? Will our program be eliminated? These questions are reasonable. Those conducting the assessment should do their best to reassure the unit as to the purposes of the assessment. However, if the unit's future is in jeopardy, then there is no point in being disingenuous; in such a case the person having the ultimate responsibility for the decision should discuss the purpose of the assessment, not those who are going to conduct the study and provide the results to the decision maker. If it is conceivable that the bookstore will be outsourced, that possibility should be discussed.

Finally, those conducting the assessment need to be faithful to the data. There is no point in engaging in "wordsmithing" so that the report is slanted in ways that are not supported by the data. If the services of the unit being assessed are not perceived very positively, then that needs to be presented. Now, there may be a variety of reasons as to why the data indicate what they do, but the fact is that if things are not going well, that conclusion needs to be reported and strategies for improvement should be developed. If the data do not point to a conclusion, alternative analyses can be developed and presented.

## Informed Consent

An obligation that is paramount for investigators is to obtain informed consent from persons who are willing to participate in assessment projects. If there is any concept that the reader should take away from this volume on assessment techniques, it is that informed consent must be obtained in working with human subjects. Failure to do so can have significant consequences for investigators as well as the institutions with which they are affiliated, so failing to obtain informed consent is *never* an option for an investigator. A corollary to this concept is that if the subjects are deemed to be incapable of rendering an informed judgment as to whether they will participate or not, such as people who have not reached the age of majority, the person or persons who are legally responsible for them must provide consent for them to participate. Details about selected compliance issues are available from the Department of Health and Human Services.

The Code of Federal Regulations, Title 45 (Public Welfare), as administered by the Department of Health and Human Services (DHHS) Part 46 (Protection of Human Subjects), includes information about the basic policy of the Department of Health and Human Services related to the protection of human subjects that is very useful in ensuring that the appropriate steps are taken to protect human subjects. Several basic elements are part of this process.

## Definition of Projects Covered by the Regulations

The DHHS policy defines research as "a systematic investigation, including research development, testing and evaluation, designed to develop or contribute to generalizable knowledge. Activities which meet this definition constitute research for purposes of this policy, whether or not they are conducted or supported under a program which is considered research for other purposes. For example, some demonstration and service programs may include research activities."

Assessment projects fit under this definition, since they are systematic investigations related to developing knowledge about effectiveness. In seeking approval from the campus institutional review board (which is described in the next paragraph) one should not engage in intellectual gymnastics designed to make the case that assessment projects do not fall under this definition. They do. One simply needs to move ahead and seek approval, which is the next step in the process.

## Institutional Review Boards

Colleges and universities, under these guidelines, are to develop an Institutional Review Board (IRB) that is designed to oversee proposals for research projects and to make sure that they fall within the guidelines established by the federal government. For the purpose of assessment projects, the campus IRB will review the procedures the investigator proposes to put in place to protect human subjects. Permission is needed from the IRB before subjects can be invited to participate in assessment projects. And IRB approval is necessary if the investigators plan to disseminate their work beyond the campus, such as through a program presentation at a conference or meeting, or if they plan to turn the final report into a manuscript and submit it for publication. When IRB approval has been secured, what this means, according to the DHHS guidelines, is "that the research has been reviewed and may be conducted at an institution within the constraints set forth by the IRB and by other institutional and federal requirements."

## Elements of Informed Consent

An informed consent checklist that provides excellent guidance as to what should be communicated to potential subjects in any assessment project is available on the Department's Web site (http://www.hhs.gov/ohrp/humansubjects/assurance/consentckls .htm). In the case of assessment projects, the basic elements need to be covered. The additional elements may or may not need to be covered depending on the project. Guidance from your campus Institutional Review Board can be helpful in determining the extent to which any of the additional elements needed to be included. A copy of the informed consent checklist is included as Appendix Seven.

## Expedited Review

Sometimes assessments may be eligible for expedited review by the IRB. *Expedited review* means just that: the review process may not require all the procedures that normally are associated with campus review according to the Department's guidelines.

> An IRB may use the expedited review procedure to review either or both of the following:
>
> 1. some or all of the research appearing on the list (of categories of research) and found by the reviewer(s) to involve no more than minimal risk,
> 2. minor changes in previously approved research during the period (of one year or less) for which approval is authorized.

Category 7 of this list of research categories includes the following: "Research on individual or group characteristics or behavior (including, but not limited to, research on perception, cognition, motivation, identity, language, communication, cultural beliefs or practices, and social behavior) or research employing survey, interview, oral history, focus group, program evaluation, human factors evaluation, or quality assurance methodologies." Program assessments typically fall within Category 7 of research studies and as a consequence may receive expedited review. The decision to conduct an expedited review will rest with the campus IRB. "An expedited review procedure consists of a review of research involving human subjects by the IRB chairperson or by one or more experienced reviewers designated by the chairperson from among members of the IRB in accordance with the requirements set forth in 45 CFR 46.110."

## Getting Started

An initial reaction to these guidelines is that they seem very cumbersome and almost appear to discourage research projects, including assessments. But as campuses have developed Institutional Review Boards and the boards have adjusted to what the desired outcomes of assessment projects are, the process of gaining approval has become smoother over time. Regardless of how difficult or bureaucratic this process appears to be, investigators must seek IRB approval before moving forward with their project. An early step that one might take is to schedule a meeting with the chair of the IRB and explain the goals of assessment projects. That can be helpful is educating the chair of the board, because most of the proposals that the board will be considering will be sponsored projects, faculty research, advanced graduate student research, and so on. In short, assessments in student affairs will not be the norm. So the chair and ultimately the board will need to be educated along the lines of how campus-based assessments in student affairs and related units are different from what is normally reviewed.

## Other Selected Issues Related to Ethics

Several additional issues related to the ethical dimensions of assessment projects need to be explored before undertaking projects. These issues are discussed now.

### Data Access

Suppose a person from one department agrees to lead an assessment project for another department on the same campus. An example of this situation could be the director of student orientation whose unit is in student affairs agrees to lead an assessment project for the advising unit of the College of Engineering (COE). This assessment hypothetically is designed to focus on the quality of academic advising provided both by the advising staff who advise first- and second-year students as well as by faculty members who serve as advisors to upper-class students. The plans for this assessment project include distributing the ACT Academic Advising Questionnaire (American College Testing Program, 2006) to all engineering majors and, based on the results from the questionnaire, some focus groups might be conducted to elicit additional data.

The director of orientation is highly skilled at conducting assessments and has a wonderful reputation on campus. She has collaborated with several other units on assessment in the past and is looking forward to working on this project. After the results from the Academic Advising Questionnaire have been tabulated, she receives a call from the dean of the College of Engineering who wants to see the raw data from the students who were advised by several faculty. The dean wants to know how well these faculty members were doing as advisors, because in the case of three of them they are being considered for tenure and promotion in the current academic year and a high level of advising skill is an essential element for promotion. The dean's assistant calls the director of orientation and asks whether the director would send the data over to the dean's office as soon as possible. The director of orientation is perplexed. Using the data in a promotion dossier was never discussed when the assessment was planned, and besides that, the students who participated by completing the questionnaires were not informed of this use of their responses. What should the director do?

This brief scenario illustrates the problems that can emerge when the issue of data access is not settled before the project is begun. In this case, the director should have worked out data access issues with College of Engineering staff, including representatives from the dean's office, and made it clear that the data were to be used in aggregate form as an assessment of the advising process, not an evaluation of specific faculty members in their role as academic advisors. This understanding should be confirmed in writing through a memorandum of understanding.

In this scenario, the director will have to inform the dean that the data are not available to be used in faculty evaluations and the chair of the IRB might be called in for support. In general, deans don't like to be told that they will have to back away from a request, but in this case, the data should not be shared.

## Data Ownership

The professional staff of residence life department at Western University (WU), a private comprehensive university, formed a committee of the whole and decided that they would implement an environmental assessment project focused on the quality of life in the residence halls at WU. All undergraduates are required to live in campus residence halls at WU, and their experiences are considered to be essential elements of their educational experience at WU. The staff really clicked, and they developed a questionnaire, collected data, analyzed them, and then made plans to implement changes in specific residence halls as soon as possible. By all accounts the process was successful.

After the data had been analyzed, one of the staff members received an electronic message about a drive-in one-day workshop that was being offered for residence hall staff members in the state. He called his closest colleague in the department and suggested that they prepare a program proposal for the workshop on the assessment project implemented at WU, since it had been so successful. The two of them then prepared a proposal and submitted it for review. A few days after that they mentioned at a professional staff meeting that they had submitted a proposal about the assessment project. Several other staff looked puzzled when they received this news. One asked why other members of the professional staff had not been invited to be listed on the proposal, since all of them had participated in the assessment project. Nonplussed, the two staff that had prepared the proposal simply said they did not realize that others might be interested in joining them in the proposal and they apologized. They said they would try to rectify their error.

This scenario illustrates a problem related to who owns assessment data and who can do what with it. These issues need to be settled in advance for several reasons. First, from an ethical point of view, credit for contributing to the project needs to given proportionally to the contributions individuals make to it. In this case everyone contributed about equally, so each person should be included in any additional work products from the process, such as conference presentations or journal articles. Second, from a human subjects point of view, the IRB would need to know that presentations or articles might emanate from the project. Accordingly, issues along the lines of who owns the data and how the data will be used other than for the project need to be settled in advance of beginning the project.

## Crediting Contributors

Closely related to data ownership is the matter of providing appropriate credit to those who contribute to the project. Roles in the project need to be delineated in advance of the project, and projected levels of credit should be determined before the project is undertaken. Is every person involved in the project listed on the title page of the report? Should a faculty member who is an expert on the development of instruments and consults with a draft of questionnaire be a coauthor of the report? What if the report evolves into a manuscript submitted for publication? Is every person listed as a coauthor? Appropriately attributing and recognizing roles in the project need to resolved in advance of the project. Failure to do so can result in an ethical breach and beyond that, hard feelings on the part of those who feel as though they have not been recognized appropriately.

## Obligations Beyond Ethical Issues

There may be times when investigators, particularly if they are conducting assessments in the field, will encounter circumstances in which their obligations will extend far beyond the bounds of ethical codes. Examples of these circumstances include observing violations of the law. What do investigators do if they observe underage drinking? Drug use and abuse? Child abuse? Misuse of institutional funds? These issues and perhaps others place the investigator in an incredibly awkward position and also require some form of response. For example, in the evaluation of a child care center, what if child abuse in the form of an adult supervisor spanking a child is observed? Does this need to be reported to proper authorities immediately?

In circumstances such as these, the investigator as a witness may have certain legal obligations to report what has been observed and he or she may have to call off the project or at least postpone future data gathering activities until the situation is addressed and resolved. In the spanking example, university counsel should be contacted immediately for advice related to next steps, since it is possible that the person engaged in spanking a child has violated laws.

## Additional Help

On campus, other sources of assistance with ethical issues typically are available to those conducting assessment projects. When ethical issues arise, investigators should feel as though they have someone to turn to for advice. Among resources that are available on many campuses include the following:

*IRB chair.* This person should be familiar with the very latest guidelines from the federal government related to human subjects issues. The chair can be very helpful in sorting out issues related to the review of assessment proposals and how best to protect the rights of human subjects.

*Legal counsel.* In circumstances that could result in legal exposure, the institution's office of legal counsel can provide assistance about how to handle unanticipated situations as described above.

*Senior faculty.* Senior faculty who are well known on campus for their perspectives and insights can be contacted for advice of an unofficial nature. Sticky questions such as who should be credited with contributing to a project can be directed to such individuals.

*Judicial affairs.* This office is responsible for administering the institution's code of student conduct and can provide advice related to student behavior. The office also might be assigned responsibilities related to academic misconduct of students, and should a problem along those lines arise, this office can be very helpful.

*Office of human resources.* Staff is this area can provide help when issues related to employee conduct might arise. Hiring practices, sexual harassment, discrimination against institutional members, and other, similar issues may be uncovered in an assessment. If these problems are uncovered, assistance from this office should be sought.

## Codes of Ethics

Various professional organizations have published codes of ethics that speak to conducting research projects. These codes tend to be quite consistent in the information they provide in that the approaches outlined in the codes are remarkably similar. The Web sites of those that provide excellent guidance for individuals conducting assessment projects are included in Appendix Seven.

One other very useful resource is the American Evaluation Association's *Guiding Principles for Evaluators*. The complete text of the principles can be found at the association's Web site. We recommend these principles to the reader. The general categories of these principles include the following:

- Evaluators conduct systematic, data-based inquires about whatever is being evaluated.

- Evaluators provide competent performance to stakeholders.

- Evaluators display honesty and integrity in their own behavior, and ensure the honesty and integrity of the entire evaluation process.

- Evaluators respect the security, dignity and self worth of the respondents, program participants, clients, and other evaluation stakeholders.

- Evaluators articulate and take into account the diversity of general and public interests and values that may be related to the evaluation.

The complete text of these principles provides excellent detail in terms of how evaluators should approach their professional practice (American Evaluation Association, 2006).

## Conclusion

The ethical dimensions of an assessment project are central to the project's success and can be encountered at virtually any stage of the project (Morris, 2008). One cannot understate the importance of being true to the ethical dimensions of assessment projects. Failure to handle all the ethical aspects of a project in keeping with federal law, institutional guidelines, ethical codes, and so on will result in failure of the project. As many ethical issues as possible should be anticipated as the project is being conceptualized. As the project unfolds, if ethical problems arise, help should be sought so that the problems can be resolved in the best way possible.

## References

Kitchener, K. S. (1985). Ethical principles and ethical decisions in student affairs. In H. J. Canon & R. D. Brown (Eds.), *Applied ethics in student services*. New Directions for Student Services, no. 30 (pp. 17–29). San Francisco: Jossey-Bass.

Kuh, G. D., Kinzie, J., Schuh, J. H., & Whitt, E. J. (2005). *Student success in college*. San Francisco: Jossey-Bass.

Merriam, S. B. (1998). *Qualitative research and case study applications in education*. San Francisco: Jossey-Bass.

Morris, M. (Ed.). (2008). *Evaluation ethics for best practice: Cases and commentaries*. New York: Guilford.

National Commission on Accountability in Higher Education. (2005). *Accountability for better results: A national imperative for higher education*. Denver, CO: State Higher Education Executive Officers.

## Web Sites

American College Testing Program. (2006). *Survey of academic advising*. Retrieved June 12, 2006 from http://www.act.org/ess/fouryear.html

American Evaluation Association. (2006). *Guiding principles for evaluators*. Retrieved from http://www.eval.org/Publications/GuidingPrinciples-Printable.asp, March 5, 2008

Code of Federal Regulations. (2005). *Protection of human subjects*. Washington, DC: Department of Health and Human Survives. Retrieved July 12, 2006 from http://www.hhs.gov/ohrp/humansubjects/guidance/45cfr46.htm#46.101

Department of Health and Human Services (2005). *Expedited review* §46.110. Retrieved July 12, 2006 from http://www.hhs.gov/ohrp/humansubjects/guidance/45cfr46.htm#46.110

Department of Health and Human Services (2005). *Definitions.* §46.102. Retrieved July 12, 2006 from http://www.hhs.gov/ohrp/humansubjects/guidance/45cfr46.htm#46.102

Department of Health and Human Services (2005). *Categories of research that may be reviewed by the Institutional Review Board (IRB) through an expedited review procedure.* Retrieved July 12, 2006 from http://www.hhs.gov/ohrp/humansubjects/guidance/expedited98.htm

Department of Health and Human Services (2005). Expedited review procedures §46.110. Retrieved July 12, 2006 from http://www.hhs.gov/ohrp/humansubjects/guidance/45cfr46.htm#46.110

Department of Health and Human Services (2005). *Informed consenty checklist.* § 46.116. Retrieved July 12, 2006 from http://www.hhs.gov/ohrp/humansubjects/assurance/consentckls.htm

Department of Health and Human Services (2005). *IRB approval.* §46.102. Retrieved July 12, 2006 from http://www.hhs.gov/ohrp/humansubjects/guidance/45cfr46.htm#46.102

Department of Health and Human Services (2005). *Institutional review boards.* §46.102. Retrieved July 12, 2006 from http://www.hhs.gov/ohrp/humansubjects/guidance/45cfr46.htm#46.102

# 9

# USING A MIXED METHODOLOGICAL APPROACH TO ASSESSMENT

## A Case Study

Over the years some methodologists who are oriented toward quantitative or qualitative studies have asserted that their approach to research methods is more appropriate, more precise, conceptually superior, or simply better. Rossi, Freeman, and Lipsey (1999) observed the following: "The relative advantages and disadvantages of the two types of data have been debated at length in the social science literature" (p. 271) (citing Cook & Reichardt, 1979; Guba & Lincoln, 1994). For some studies, using quantitative methods is more appropriate than qualitative methods, but for others, the reverse is true. On the one hand, qualitative studies do not lend themselves very well to situations in which the consumers of the research want statistical data so that the results from the research site can be compared with like data from other institutions or national norms. On the other hand, it is a very difficult task to ask respondents how they made meaning of a situation, why they chose option A over option B, or how they arrived at a particular perspective using quantitative methods. Therefore, the goals and purposes of a study ought to dictate the kinds of methodology that the investigator uses. Taylor and Trumbull (2000) viewed qualitative and quantitative approaches to research as having similarities and differences. But they added that "they are more similar in that problems are defined in both approaches; research questions or hypotheses are stated, methods and procedures and analysis of data are developed" (p. 171). Taylor also observed, "In many instances, the researcher may wish to combine the two approaches" (p. 197). Mark, Henry, and Julnes (2000, p. 313) added, "the combination of group interviews and survey techniques, when feasible, is often the desirable option for representing stakeholder and public values."

It is important to remember that the underlying assumptions of the two methodologies are dramatically different. Taylor and Trumbull (2000) pointed out, "Quantitative research is designed to provide objective descriptions of phenomena and to demonstrate how phenomena can be controlled through specific treatments. On the other hand, qualitative research is designed to develop understanding of individuals in their natural environment that cannot be objectively verified" (p. 171). Caudle (1994, p. 70) added, "the evaluator literally becomes the primary measurement instrument in the investigative process, in contrast to quantitative research where the researcher tries to stay removed from the process" (citing Kidder & Fine, 1987; Tesch, 1990). Our assertion is that both methods have great value, depending on the research question, and combined with institutional databases provide a splendid repertoire for those planning to conduct assessments. Moreover, in some studies, using both methodologies can result in a powerful design that will result in extremely useful data. Taylor and Trumbull appear to agree. They concluded, "The skilled researcher can draw the best from both approaches and combine them. Researchers should not assume that one approach is superior to the other, or that qualitative data are easier to use" (p. 176).

We also believe preliminary data that can be retrieved and analyzed for many studies are available in various databases (see Chapter Two for more information about using databases), including institutional databases, federal sources such as The Integrated Post Secondary Data System (IPEDS) or private sources (for example, *College Results Online*, The Education Trust, 2006). We think investigators too often try to build their own database when the information already is available. The following question provides an example: How does our institution's six-year cohort graduation rate compare with that of our peer institutions? One way to find out is to call the institutional research offices of our peers, or we can visit the Web sites of our peers. Or the fastest, easiest way to find the answer to this question is to visit IPEDS, use the Executive Peer Tool, and get the answer in a matter of just a few minutes. This brief example illustrates how easy it is to find data by using existing databases. Nonetheless, we fear that the simple, accurate approach too often is overlooked when investigators are trying to answer questions raised on their campuses. But, of course, just having information from databases does not answer a host of questions that then must be addressed by additional quantitative and qualitative studies.

This chapter discusses how to conduct assessments by using databases, quantitative methods, and qualitative methods. We illustrate our approach by using a case study. As the case study evolves, and research questions arise, our investigators in the case will have to use different methodologies because the questions raised simply demand one approach rather than another. We hope that through this case study, and our explanation of why certain methods were used rather than others, it will become clear that using several methodologies is appropriate, given how the research questions evolve and build on each other.

## Alumni Development at Easternmost College: Background Information

Easternmost College (EMC) is a regional, state-assisted institution that has a long history of serving the state and the surrounding states in the areas of teacher education, business, and nursing. The college has a wonderful reputation among its constituents. The focus of the institution for years has been on undergraduate education, and the general sense of institutional leaders was that as long as EMC provided top-notch educational experiences for its students, state funding would be steady, if not spectacular. And that is what occurred for years. EMC did its job, the state was supportive but never lavish, and the institution enjoyed years of success.

In the past few years the support of the state has waned. This is not because the state's leaders have had any particular concerns with EMC, but rather because the state's economic base has been eroding and economic development plans have not generated the kind of results that everyone associated with the economic development plans had anticipated. In short, the money has not been available to support EMC as had been the case in the past, and as a consequence EMC has experienced ongoing fiscal difficulties. Tuition has been raised faster than anyone would like, and senior administrators and budget managers have begun to feel quite uneasy about the economic future of EMC.

In the past year the long-standing director of the EMC Alumni Association retired. The director was an EMC graduate, had been with EMC for years, and was very popular on campus and in the region. The director had focused on sustaining relationships with those people who had graduated about the same time he had, but the impression on campus was that he had not developed close relationships with more recent graduates. Those who had graduated from EMC in the past fifteen years really did not feel a connection through the alumni association, and a manifestation of this was that few of these graduates joined the alumni association or attended alumni association events in their cities. EMC graduates tended to stay in the region, usually somewhere within 750 miles of the university. Attendance at alumni association events had tapered off in the past few years.

In looking at the fiscal situation of the institution, it became clear that the only way that EMC could keep its fiscal house in order was to begin a transition for many units that had been funded wholly or to a large part by the institution's general fund (tuition and state appropriation) to more of a self-supporting approach. This transition had occurred for many of the units in student affairs. Student health had moved to a student fee and fee-for-service approach to securing the necessary funding to balance its budget; student counseling and campus recreation also were moving toward this approach. Institutional leaders began to look at other units that also could be weaned from the general fund, and the alumni association appeared to be the next in line.

Through a long-standing tradition, the alumni association was a unit in the Division of Student Affairs. Decades ago when the alumni association was founded, the EMC president at the time was not quite sure where to place the unit in the organizational scheme of the institution, and it was decided that the best place for the alumni association to be assigned was the Division of Student Affairs, since student affairs had a good relationship with student leaders and, in general, was well thought of by students on campus. Student leaders often became engaged with the alumni association and over the years volunteered for many significant roles in the association. Even though this arrangement was a bit unusual by national standards, it worked very nicely at EMC. In terms of the current situation, no one thought that moving the alumni association to another administrative unit on campus was a good idea. But the Alumni Association was going to have to change its approach to securing resources just as the long-standing director was going to retire. Major changes potentially were just around the corner for the alumni association.

## A New Approach at the Alumni Association

So the previous director retired, a search was conducted, and a new director, Sean Cunningham, was hired. Sean was a graduate of EMC but had been working in alumni affairs for nearly twenty years at other colleges and universities between returning to EMC. Sean was surprised at the state of affairs at the EMC Alumni Association. The level of technological sophistication of the association was far behind the contemporary standards for similar organizations at EMC's peers. Record keeping was a mess, the revenues realized by the association through annual dues and other events were far below what Sean thought was possible, and the quality of the program was substandard. But before tackling some of these issues, Sean decided that a profile of who was a member of the alumni association and, as important, who was not was necessary.

The place Sean started in revitalizing the alumni association was to try to determine the characteristics of EMC graduates who became members of the alumni association and the characteristics of those who were not members. This meant learning about them, what they had done as students, and why they had joined the association. People who had attended EMC were the primary members of the association, logically enough, but some townspeople and some members of the EMC faculty and staff who were not EMC graduates also held memberships. The records in the alumni association office were incomplete so Sean turned to Alex Johnson, the director of Institutional Research (IR) at EMC, for help. The information in Alex's databases was crucial to developing a profile of the members of the association.

Sean knew who the members of the alumni association were, based on a check of the association's records, but there were many things Sean did not know. Before trying to develop some strategies to bring the association up to contemporary standards he needed more information. The alumni association had current addresses and other contact information for current members. Other than when the members had either graduated or left EMC, the association did not know the following information about its members:

- What were their degrees?
- What were their majors?
- Had they received any academic awards or honors?
- Had they made contributions to the institution's annual fund?

This information was essential in developing a profile of members. Were business majors more likely to become members of the alumni association than liberal arts majors? Were people who earned undergraduate degrees more likely to join than people who earned graduate degrees? This information was crucial if organizing clubs and developing special programming for association members was to occur in the future.

This information could have been gathered by mailing questionnaires to each of the association's members or even by conducting a massive telephone campaign, but the surest, fastest way to collect the data was through the institutional database. Without question this process would require effort on the part of the Office of Institutional Research (IR). The most complete, most accurate information was available in IR databases, and it made much more sense for the alumni association to provide support for the office rather than to develop its own survey of members.

The second general area of information that the alumni association required also involved the Office of Institutional Research. The association could identify who its members were, but what needed to be known were the names of the persons who had attended EMC for the previous fifty years who were not members of the association. As was the case with the members, once these people could be identified, a profile of them could be developed, including the following information:

- When had they left EMC? This could be determined by their last term of enrollment.
- Did they earn a degree at EMC? If so, what was their major?
- Had they received any academic awards or honors?

Again, this information was available from the Office of Institutional Research. The IR used the same approach to securing these data as it had to answer the first set of questions. It examined the records of EMC for the previous fifty years and deleted all those individuals who were members of the alumni association. The amount of information developed was extensive, but by going through this process, the alumni association had two sets of data:

- A profile of those people who were members of the alumni association
- A profile of those people who were eligible to join the alumni association but had not become members

Basic data retrieved from the institution's database allowed for a comparison of these people. Were those in certain majors more likely to join? Were those who had graduated during certain periods more likely to join than others? Sean had many more questions about members and nonmembers of the alumni association that could not be answered through the institutional database, but what was provided made for a good start.

## Commentary

The process followed in the first step of trying to revitalize the alumni association illustrates how useful an institutional database can be. As was pointed out in the case, a questionnaire could be sent to all the members of the association that asked them to provide the same information that was sought through the database but that would be slower and perhaps less accurate than using the data on file. Without question this process required additional work for the Institutional Research office, but there is no question that conducting a mail campaign and ultimately having to analyze and produce reports of the findings also would be an expensive, labor intensive process for the alumni association, and, given how poor response rates can be to questionnaires distributed through the mail (see Dey, 1997; Porter, 2004), the association could be more confident that the IR data would be accurate and serve as a starting point for other studies. There may be a few people for whom IR did not have the data (such as persons who had changed their names but had not notified EMC of the change), but these cases would not detract substantially from the value of the IR data. In any event, using the IR files made the most sense in this problem.

Taken further, IR records can be used for all kinds of inquiries about issues that arise in student affairs. What is a profile of students who live in campus residence halls? Well, the housing department can easily provide that, but when these data are published, a counterpart profile of students who live off campus also ought to be published for comparison purposes. Student health could publish a profile of the students who use the services of the department, but similarly a profile can be developed of those students who do not use student health. Are there differences in the characteristics (for example, gender, race, class standing, financial aid status) of students who use a campus service compared with those who do not? This information can be very useful in developing marketing strategies for various services and programs. We do not know the extent to which those engaged in assessment use the services of IR offices regularly, but what we are certain of is that IR can be a wonderful institutional resource for those trying to provide a foundation for their assessment activities.

## Learning More About EMC Alumns: A Quantitative Study

The next major challenge for Sean was to develop an understanding of the experiences of the members of the alumni association while at EMC and similarly to learn more about the experiences of the graduates of EMC who were not members of the alumni association. The general approach that Sean elected to use was a mailed survey questionnaire that would explore the experiences of EMC graduates while they were students and also some of their experiences after they graduated. The survey instrument that Sean decided to use was the Alumni Outcomes Questions questionnaire, published by the American College Testing program (2006). Commercially prepared questionnaires have advantages and disadvantages. Among the advantages are that commercially prepared instruments from reputable sources have

- Psychometric properties that have been developed on the basis on a large number of respondents.
- The opportunity to compare the results from a local administration with national norms, or in this case, the results from EMC could be compared with the norms for this instrument.
- A very professional-looking instrument that communicates that the EMC Alumni Association is taking this survey very seriously.

On the other hand, a commercial instrument may not provide the exact information that Sean needs.

- The cost of purchasing instruments can be costly.
- Analysis may take some time since the instruments have to be collected and shipped back to the company.

In any event, Sean and the leaders of the alumni association decided that using this instrument was a better option than working with people at EMC to develop their own instrument. Approval from the campus Institutional Review Board (IRB) was secured before any instruments were distributed. More information about the role of the campus IRB in conducting studies is included in Chapter Eight.

This particular instrument has a feature whereby the campus administering the instrument can provide up to thirty items in addition to the items already on the instrument. These items can be tailored to specific information that the local campus needs. Sean and the leaders of the alumni association prepared some items and worked with the company to conduct the survey.

The decision was made that because the alumni association had approximately 8000 members, a random sample of 2000 of them would be drawn, and these people would receive the questionnaire by mail. The process was put in motion and the hope was that maybe half would complete the questionnaire and return it to the EMC Alumni Association.

A more difficult problem had to do with identifying the current addresses of the people who were not members of the alumni association. The best estimate was that potentially 40,000 people had graduated from EMC in the past forty years who were not members of the alumni association. This was gleaned from the institutional records in the study done with the institution's database, referenced above. Sean knew of an organization that provides services in locating people, so this process was put in motion. After a couple of months, it became clear that around 20,000 of the 40,000 potential respondents had been located with what looked to be accurate address information. The general feeling was that a sample of these people would be less likely to complete the survey than a sample of those who were members, so the decision was made to sample a larger percentage of nonmembers than members of the alumni association. Even though it would be expensive, the decision was made to select 4,000 people from this group, and survey instruments were sent to them. The hope was that 15 percent of this group ultimately would reply.

A few months went by and the results began to come in. From the survey of association members, the participation esti- mate underestimated the results. A total of 1100 people returned completed, usable questionnaires, for a response rate of 55 per- cent, which was gratifying. The results for the nonmembers of the EMC Alumni Association were less encouraging. First, 1000 of the instruments were returned as being not deliverable—the addresses of the persons were incorrect. Then, the response rate of the original sample was just 10 percent, or a total of 400. This was disappointing, but not unexpected. It is hard to secure the participation of people who are not engaged with an organization that wants their time. Still, Sean figured that this was enough of a response to learn some valuable information.

In each case a profile of respondents was developed to determine how closely the characteristics of the respondents matched the characteristics of the nonrespondents. These characteristics had been developed in the study by using the institutional database and such items as race, sex, major, when the student had graduated, and so on. In the case of alumni association members, the characteristics were close to those of the entire group. In the case of the nonmembers, those who completed the surveys were more recent graduates, were more likely to be female and white and had majored in professional programs rather than the liberal arts. Members of the association had been more engaged in the life of the institution as undergraduates, meaning that more commonly they had participated in activities, had held paraprofessional jobs on campus as resident assistants or student employees on campus, and lived closer to EMC after graduating. These data were useful as Sean began to develop strategies to revitalize the alumni association.

## Commentary

The value of conducting a survey helps provide solid baseline data for the Alumni Association. In this case, the new director had inherited an organization that had been sustained for many years, mostly on the basis of the personal relationships that the previous director had with the membership. The membership was smaller than the new director thought it should be, so the survey was done, in part, to find out how the membership group of graduates compared with the group of graduates who were not members. The process revealed specific data, and the new director learned that the members had different characteristics, in the aggregate, than those who were not members of the association. With some degree of accuracy the new director, Sean, could now predict what the future would hold for association membership unless something changed.

What the quantitative study could not answer was why graduates with certain characteristics were more likely to join than others. The only way to learn more about the motivation and reasons for why the people in the respondent pool behaved the way they did was to ask them. Thus, the quantitative study, at least in part, set the stage for a follow-up study using qualitative methods.

## Learning Still More About EMC Alumns: A Qualitative Study

The third phase of the process led by EMC Alumni Association Director Sean Cunningham, was a qualitative study designed to learn more about why people either joined and stayed engaged with the alumni association or were not members. Sean needed this information so that strategies could be developed to grow the association and meet the needs of the people who were not members while simultaneously staying connected with the members. The primary method that was chosen to collect this information was to conduct a series of focus groups with members and nonmembers.

The number of members of the association was smaller than the number of nonmembers, so in developing this study, the leaders determined that they would need to conduct more focus groups with nonmembers than members. But the nonmembers were not engaged with the association, so organizing the focus groups with these people would be much more challenging than organizing groups with members.

The nonmembers tended to be people who lived farther from the campus than those who were engaged. That was not surprising. They also tended to be more recent graduates and they were people who tended to be graduates of liberal arts programs rather than graduates of the professional programs offered by EMC. In developing a strategy to conduct focus groups with the nonmembers, the decision was made to work with some faculty members who were experts in conducting focus groups. These faculty members would help develop the interview protocol for the two sets of groups, the members and nonmembers. The faculty members would field test the protocols and make modifications as necessary. IRB approval was secured before any of the focus groups were conducted.

Since the nonmembers were located farther from campus than the members, the logistics of organizing groups was daunting. Still, the approach that was taken made sense in that people were invited to participate from the pool of respondents in the ten communities that had the largest number of EMC graduates who responded to the survey instrument. Through electronic mail and telephone calls people were recruited to participate in the focus groups. Those who participated were promised a small honorarium for their time. In the end, two focus groups were planned in each of ten cities, ranging from 750 miles from EMC to the neighboring town. Some of the groups were more successful in terms of participation than others. What the leaders learned was that even when people agreed to participate, the attrition rate was about 70 percent, meaning that about three people in ten who promised to attend actually participated. After having a couple of disappointing experiences, more people were invited to each group than there was space, but with the heavy level of attrition, the last thirty groups were more successful than the first ten.

The heart of the questions asked of the groups of nonmembers was this topic: Why have you not joined the alumni association and participated in its events? A variety of reasons emerged, including distance from campus, people being too busy, and the cost, but the one theme emphasized most frequently was that people did not feel connected to the previous leadership and their feeling was that the association really was for older graduates of EMC; the younger graduates did not see the relevance of joining. That provided useful information for Sean in developing a strategy to recruit these graduates as new members of the association.

Fewer groups of association members were organized. They tended to live closer to campus and they were better known in the alumni association. Ten groups were planned and modest honoraria were provided. Learning from the experience with the focus groups with nonmembers, the same strategies for inviting people to attend were employed. The groups worked out very well. These groups centered on this question: Why did you join the alumni association? After this question was discussed, the groups discussed why the members had stayed engaged with the Association over the years. Not surprisingly, the people had joined because they knew the previous director and they stayed engaged because they liked the director personally and they felt their needs were well addressed by the association.

## Commentary

The focus groups provided a foundation on which Sean could build in developing a strategy for recruiting new members. Because the logistics of conducting the groups were quite complex, a decision was made in advance that twenty groups would be conducted with nonmembers and ten would be conducted with members. This approach is at variance with the preferred approach to determining the number of groups. The preferred approach to determining the number of groups to conduct is to conduct groups until the point of redundancy is reached (Schuh & Upcraft, 2000). Redundancy means that no new information is learned from the last group. Then, to be sure, one more group should be conducted. In this case, given the multiple sites and travel, that was not practical. But the sense of the organizers was that the number of groups organized would provide very useful information, and that the point of redundancy for the sets of groups (members and nonmembers) would be reached.

What has learned was quite predictable. Essentially, people either joined or did not join for the same reason: either they felt as though they mattered and stayed engaged, or they thought the association didn't think they mattered and they did not bother to join. The use of focus groups can be very time consuming and expensive. Thirty focus groups were conducted, twenty with the nonmembers and ten with the members, away from the campus. The costs of travel, conducting the groups, providing honoraria and food, recording the session, and transcribing notes required substantial resources. But in this case, the alumni association had no choice. Either it would gather these data and develop strategies to grow, or it could continue to practice administration by guesswork and anecdote, and perhaps develop a strategy that would not result in attracting new members.

## Mixed Methodologies: Some Final Thoughts

Case studies, even when based on actual situations, are artificial and cannot capture the nuanced experiences of people in real life. Nevertheless, cases can be useful in illustrating general learning principles. In the case of the EMC Alumni Association, the operating climate had deteriorated slowly over time, and a change a strategy was long overdue. But to just do something differently would not necessarily lead to an improved situation in terms of increasing membership or satisfaction with the association. Specific strategies based on data needed to be developed or nothing might improve.

In this case we attempted to illustrate how three forms of assessment could be used to provide foundational data and also provide a basis for securing additional information that could be used to inform that leadership of the alumni association with respect to strategies to grow and strengthen the organization. The institutional database, even with its limitations, was helpful in providing profiles of members and nonmembers. Sean was able to learn some basic facts about how the members and the nonmembers differed. That was useful in developing some preliminary notions about alumni association members. In addition, the information could be discussed with staff, EMC leaders, and alumni association stakeholders in discussing who the members and the nonmembers were with accuracy and authority. Without this information any discussions about the characteristics of the members and nonmembers would be not much more than educated guessing.

The study conducted using the institutional database was useful in providing a basis for the quantitative survey. The quantitative survey was conducted with a standardized instrument because one existed with excellent psychometric properties and, just as important, it included questions that would generate information the leaders needed. A wonderful instrument that asks the wrong questions is not useful. It is similar to handing a violin to a world-class pianist with instructions to entertain a group. The pianist has marvelous skills, but they do fit the situation and the result is disappointment. The same result will occur from using an instrument that does not generate the data that the circumstance warrants: disappointment.

The qualitative study built on the quantitative study. Questions were developed to get at why individuals either participated or did not participate with the association. The quantitative study allowed for comparisons with the members and nonmembers, but the qualitative study got into the questions why and how. These questions could not have been answered as fully and completely with techniques other than focus groups. Although expensive and time consuming, the focus groups generated the information needed to develop strategies to develop the alumni association.

Use of this mixed-methods approach is not without problems. Because this set of studies was so comprehensive, the studies took a long time to conduct. It would be very likely that a series of studies such as the ones described could take an academic year to complete. In addition, they can be quite expensive. Each approach requires a different set of methodological skills, so finding people to lead the studies may not be easy. And things might not work out as well as they did in the case study. Nevertheless, with a situation as complex as what the new director inherited, anything less than a comprehensive look at the association and its membership would have been incomplete and might have resulted in less than adequate information upon which to develop strategies to revitalize the association. Accordingly, one should go into a complex assessment process such as this one with eyes wide open. The challenges expressed earlier in this paragraph are real and need to be considered in developing a strategy that will use all three methodological approaches effectively.

What can be learned from this case study is that the methodologies can complement each other very nicely. By itself, each approach generated useful data but left as many questions unanswered as answered. Taken together, they provided powerful tools for assessment. In situations that demand a comprehensive assessment strategy, use of multiple methodologies has excellent potential to result in generating data upon which to base organizational change and improvement.

## References

Caudle, S. L. (1994). Using qualitative approaches. In J. S. Wholey, H. P. Hatry, & K. E. Newcomer (Eds.), *Handbook of practical program evaluation* (pp. 69–95). San Francisco: Jossey-Bass.

Dey, E. L. (1997). Working with low survey response rates: The efficacy of weighting adjustments. *Research in Higher Education, 30* (2), 215–227.

Mark, M. M., Henry, G. T., & Julnes, G. (2000). *Evaluation: An integrated framework for understanding, guiding, and improving public and nonprofit policies and programs.* San Francisco: Jossey-Bass.

Porter, S. R. (2004). Raising response rates: What works? In S. R. Porter (Ed.), *Overcoming survey research problems* (pp. 5–21). New Directions for Institutional Research no. 121. San Francisco: Jossey-Bass.

Rossi, P. H., Freeman, H. E., & Lipsey, M. W. (1999). *Evaluation: A systematic approach* (6th ed.). Thousand Oaks, CA: Sage.

Schuh, J. H., & Upcraft, M. L. (2000). *Assessment practice in student affairs.* San Francisco: Jossey-Bass.

Taylor, G. R. (2000). Conclusion. In G. R. Taylor (Ed.), *Integrating quantitative and qualitative methods in research* (pp. 195–197). Lanham, MD: University Press of America.

Taylor, G. R., & Trumbull, M. (2000). Major similarities and differences between two paradigms. In G. R. Taylor (Ed.), *Integrating quantitative and qualitative methods in research* (pp. 171–176). Lanham, MD: University Press of America.

## Web Sites

American College Testing Program. (2006). *Alumni outcomes survey.* Retrieved July 28, 2006 from http://www.act.org/ess/fouryear.html

The Education Trust, 2006. *College results online.* Available online at http://www.collegeresults.org/

The Integrated Post Secondary Data System (IPEDS). Available online at http://nces.ed.gov/ipeds/

# 10

# LOOKING TO THE FUTURE OF ASSESSMENT

## Some Ideas and Musings

We have dusted off our crystal ball and peered inside it. A number of trends currently in place are likely to continue in the future, perhaps at an accelerated place, so we conclude this book with some hunches, prognostications, musings, and guesses as to what the future might hold for assessment in student affairs.

### Increased Accountability

Newcomer, Hatry, and Wholey (2004, p. xxxvii) made this observation, which we think applies to assessment in student affairs: "The demand for program evaluation information is growing. The U. S. Congress, state legislatures, local legislative bodies, foundations, and other funding agencies are increasingly demanding information on how program funds were used and what those programs produced."

We see no reason to believe that institutions will be less accountable for their activities and outcomes in the future than has been the case in the past. At the time of this writing, the National Commission on the Future of Higher Education delivered a report that emphasizes how institutions will need to develop more accountability measures in the future (2006). Concomitantly, regional accrediting organizations also are emphasizing accountability on the part of their member institutions seeking reaccreditation (see, for example Middle States Commission on Higher Education, 2002). Without question, national leadership (for example, Miller & Milandra, n.d.) is emphasizing accountability, and institutions of higher education will have to respond accordingly.

## Increased Accountability for Degree-Granting Units

Degree-granting units will be under increasing scrutiny to demonstrate that they are achieving their objectives and contributing to student learning. One of the positions that degree granting units have taken historically is that they measure student learning through the administration of tests or other, traditional demonstrations of student learning such as completing laboratory exercises successfully, they award course credit, and they certify that students have completed the requirements for their degrees. Our sense is that in the future, degree granting units will have to provide additional data. An example of this is the criteria for accreditation of engineering programs as published by the Accreditation Board for Engineering and Technology (ABET) (2005). Among the learning outcomes identified by ABET include an ability to function in multidisciplinary teams and an ability to communicate effectively (p. 2).

## Increased Accountability for Non Degree-Granting Units

Student affairs will not be immune from these calls for greater accountability. In fact, because some of the measures that students affairs have used to measure accountability in the past are considered "soft," such as measures of student satisfaction, these organizations will have to employ assessment strategies that provide more hard data, linked more closely to institutional goals, that support claims of success. Primary among these will be the development of outcome measures related to student learning.

The development of assessment strategies that measure the extent to which various student programs, activities, and services actually contribute to student learning will be central to an assessment program in student affairs. For example, if students participate in leadership development experiences, an outcomes-based measure will need to be employed to demonstrate what students have learned from the experience. Short of this kind of measure, hard questions will be asked about program efficacy, and in periods of very tight financial resources, institutional leaders just might decide to eliminate those programs and experiences that cannot be demonstrated to contributed to student learning.

## Increased Use of Institutional Databases

Institutional databases are underutilized in contemporary higher education. These databases are developed in various offices and departments at virtually every institution of higher education, and are located in such places as the registrar's office, the financial aid office, the student housing office, the office of institutional research, and so on. In fact, our hunch is that many institutions may have many databases, the consequence of which is that no one may actually know how many databases there might be on campus and what information is included in them.

If our hunch is correct, the first thing that needs to occur is that some office ought to develop a master list of extant databases and the information contained in them. Our subtext for this hunch is that many of these databases are overlapping. That is, they contain the same information, and time may have been spent needlessly in creating the databases when they just as easily could have been developed in a more streamlined fashion with less redundancy.

More important, student affairs staff can take advantage of these databases to generate answers to important questions on campus. Some deal with issues of use. For example, which students use which services and how often? What students who might be eligible to use certain services do not choose to do so? For example, presumably every full-time student is eligible to use the student health service but if a substantial proportion of these students do not use the service, why is that the case? Are there some distinguishing characteristics that might account for this? That is, by class standing, race, gender, ethnicity, or some other characteristic are some students more or less likely to use a particular service or participate in a certain activity? By using campus databases, a profile can be developed to determine who uses what services.

But beyond these questions of use, larger questions also can be explored. Among these some have to do with identifying those students who are more likely to drop courses or repeat them, those who are more likely to transfer to other colleges or universities, those who are likely to take more than five years to complete their degree, those who are likely to have financial problems, and so on. These data can be very helpful in developing comprehensive strategies to deal with persistence problems, students' transferring to other institutions, or students having to leave because of financial problems.

Existing databases also can be helpful in dealing with problems as they arise. If the question arises as to why a disproportionate percentage of students at risk have judicial problems, existing databases might be helpful. From studying these students one might learn that they are the last to apply for admission, more likely to miss the summer orientation program, more likely to have to live off campus due to lack of space in campus residence halls, less likely to have selected a major, and more likely to have to work off campus because of unmet financial need. All of these issues can be addressed by specific interventions, but the interventions cannot be crafted until the scope of the problem is understood.

## Increased Use of Other Databases such as the Integrated Post Secondary Education Data System and the Revamped Carnegie System

We think it is highly likely that as national databases are developed and refined, they will provide very useful information to student affairs practitioners literally with the click of a few keystrokes. But this information will be very useful for those who wish to use a comparative lens in their administrative practice. This can be illustrated with an example.

The governing board asks the president, who, in turn, asks the senior student affairs officer what percentage of students of students on campus have received institutional grants and how much, on average, each student received compared with the institution's peers. Twenty years ago that would have meant calling or writing colleagues at the peer institutions for the data. The data very well may not have been available, so these people would have had to contact their offices of institutional research and after quite a bit of analysis the data could have been provided. How useful the data might have been would have depended on the accuracy of those collecting and analyzing the data, and how common the definitions were in shaping the data.

More recently, the Integrated Post Secondary Education Data System (IPEDS) database has developed an executive peer tool that allows simple questions related to institutional comparisons to be answered quickly. In the case of this inquiry, a couple of clicks from the IPEDS home page (http://nces.ed.gov/ipeds/) and the answer can be found. To be sure, inaccuracies persist, but the time and effort spent in securing the information is miniscule compared to the scenario described above.

Other databases and data sets exist as well. Some of these are available through the National Center for Education Statistics (http://nces.ed.gov/datatools/); others are available through private sources. The Carnegie Foundation's data base (www.carnegiefoundation.org/classification/index.htm) provides a service so that institutions can identify peers by using a variety of criteria so that one can complete a fairly detailed search for similar institutions. Databases were discussed in detail in Chapter Two.

## Increased Use of Comparative Data and Data Exchanges

We anticipate that institutions increasingly will be asked to compare their characteristics and outcomes with other institutions. If the call for increased transparency and accountability (see the National Commission's Report, 2006) comes to pass, and we think it will, one of the tools that institutions have at their disposal is to compare how well they do with peers. The problem, of course, is that if the data for one institution are compared with a dissimilar institution, the comparison will not be useful. That is, if the graduation rate from an open admissions institution is compared with that of a highly selective institution, the consequence would result in a comparison that is not useful and could even be misleading. Accuracy in identifying peers takes great care (see Bender & Schuh, 2002), so institutions will have to be cautious in using benchmarking as an assessment technique.

Nevertheless, our sense is that an increasing number of indicators for comparison will be identified for institutions, and they will be asked to provide comparative data along these indicators. That is not to say that these have not been available in the past (see, for example, Taylor & Massy, 1996), but many of the comparisons of the past have been of interest to higher education researchers, not individuals external to their institutions. The transparency feature that is being advocated is for prospective students, their parents, members of the general public, and other external stakeholders. Data will have to be presented in a meaningful, understandable form so that they are useful to these stakeholders.

In addition, we think institutions increasingly will form consortia or other groups for which data sharing will be routine.

To a certain extent this has existed for years, such as the Committee on Institutional Cooperation that was founded in the 1950s (Wells, 1967), but our sense is that this approach will spread to other groups of like institutions. The data will be used for self-studies and other forms of careful, thoughtful introspection and improvement. With databases becoming more readily available, and with the increased external press for data, we think consortia are likely to evolve to answer this call for information.

## Increased Levels of Accountability Will Require More Time for Collecting and Managing Databases

The commitment that institutions will be making in the future, if our hunches are correct, will require substantial time and effort. Even with improved databases and other technological improvements in collecting data, such as the Web-based survey, more time will be required for data collection.

This need for additional time very well may take several forms. One form is that the process of developing instruments and collecting data will require a significant time commitment. Although many excellent instruments have been developed in recent years (for example, the National Survey of Student Engagement [NSSE, http://nsse.iub.edu/]), not all instruments collect the data necessary to answer the wide variety of research questions that student affairs administrators will need to answer. And even if an instrument is on point, many of them provide an opportunity for the development of local questions (see, for example, the *Survey of Academic Advising* from ACT, 2006). Developing local questions can be time consuming even if one is adding just ten additional questions.

The responsibility for developing these additional questions may be assigned to staff members in a unit, or perhaps may require the addition of individuals who will coordinate and support assessment efforts. If the former is the situation, the individual's work assignments may be stretched beyond the person's already heavy workload. If a new person is hired, the costs of the person's salary and other support for the position have to be provided. In a period of budget challenges (Sandeen & Barr, 2006) neither option is particularly attractive. But student affairs staff will have to use creative thinking about how to collect the data and manage databases so that they can respond to the questions that will be raised by various stakeholders, including students, their parents, presidents and board members, faculty, and others associated with their institution.

## Greater Use of Data in Decision Making

One of the institutional characteristics that were identified in Project DEEP (Documenting Effective Educational Practices) was that the institutions were data driven (Kuh, Kinzie, Schuh, & Whitt, 2005). By that the researchers meant that the twenty institutions that were included in the study were led by people who made decisions on the basis of what was learned through empirical study of institutional issues and problems. For example, Miami University embarked on an ambitious plan to benchmark academic programs with peers. The University of Kansas conducted systematic interviews with graduating students. These are just two examples of the kind of inquiry that was found at DEEP institutions.

The consequence of this approach is that decisions were grounded in data rather than being based on opinion. Decisions to continue programs, for example, were on a foundation of examining data. As programs are modified or eliminated, a data-driven rationale for making such a decision is provided, rather than a senior leader's hunch, guess, or most recent electronic message.

This approach to decision making will become increasingly pervasive in the future. As programs or initiatives are begun, the caveat will be that the activity will have to have an evaluation component, we suspect beyond simply determining participant satisfaction. As decision makers consider initiatives in the future, if such initiatives do not have an evaluation component, they will be rejected or returned for revision and inclusion of an evaluation dimension to the proposal.

## Greater Demand for Transparency

There is no question that contemporary students and their parents have much more of a consumer view of higher education than their predecessors (Moneta & Kuh, 2005). Since consumers need data to make decisions, institutions will need to provide much more data than currently is the case and make the data very easy to find.

The federal government has required institutions to provide such data as graduation rates and crime statistics (see College Opportunities Online http://nces.ed.gov/ipeds/cool/). Nevertheless, it is unclear whether prospective students and their parents are aware of this resource, for example, and it is entirely possible that they may seek other information. Among the data not available on this Web site are the extent to which students are able to enroll in the classes they desire, the kinds of support services available to them, and the quality of campus life. Other sources can be accessed for other issues that arise, such as the *Princeton Review* for reports on the quality of campus life or the best food (http://www.princetonreview.com/college/research/rankings/rankings.asp).

It is difficult to determine whether such sources are particularly useful or even whether they have used rigorous assessment technique. The point is that consumers want this kind of information, and it will become increasingly important for colleges and universities to provide easy assessment information about the institution's programs, experiences, and services that is easy to access. An example of how this might be done is found at Penn State University, which for years has published *Penn State Pulse* (http://www.sa.psu.edu/sara/pulse.shtml), a periodic student poll about a wide range of topics. Some of the topics are relatively benign, such as the effectiveness of the Student Newspaper Readership Program at Penn State (Issue 131), but others cut to the heart of the student experience (*Cocurricular Learning*, Issue 138) or examine controversial topics (*Student Drinking*, Issue 141). More institutions will need to follow the lead of Penn State in conducting studies of value to the institution.

## More Sophisticated Studies Will Be Conducted

We anticipate in the future that assessment studies will become increasingly sophisticated. The days of acceptable assessment measures consisting of asking student participants at a residence hall program whether they enjoyed a presentation from a speaker by a show of hands or counting the number of people who showed up at film are in the past.

Two trends are likely to frame assessment in the future. First, the use of descriptive techniques, such as frequency distributions or measures of central tendency, will be replaced by more predictive or analytical techniques. More studies will employ regression analysis so as to make predictions from data (Berger, 2004). This is not to suggest, however, that those planning student affairs assessments in the future necessarily will have to be statistical experts. That, in our view, is unlikely. More important, they will have to have a rudimentary understanding of statistical techniques and what is possible to accomplish, given the dynamics of an assessment study. They will need to be able to ask appropriate questions so that as assessment projects are conceptualized they will be able to assist in developing a design that will yield data that can be analyzed to provide answers to the questions of interest. For example, if we are interested in learning whether participation in a certain kind of experience contributes to student learning, we will have to plan a study that is designed to generate data that can be used to explore that outcome.

Second, assessment will take on increasingly sophisticated approaches. That means that sampling is likely to be something other than convenience (see Chapter Three), and increasing care will be taken to make sure that locally developed instruments are both valid and reliable. Along the same lines, more care will be taken in developing qualitative studies. Instead of simply having not much more than a conversation with a group of program participants, qualitative studies involving focus groups will follow more stringent methodological approaches, following the recommendations of Morgan and Krueger (1998). More focus groups will be conducted, sampling will occur with increasing care, interview protocols will be developed with increased sophistication, and data analysis will be thorough. This is not to suggest that current qualitative assessments lack value, but as expectations for more rigorous quantitative studies are increased, so, too, will expectations for qualitative studies increase.

## More Mixed Methods Studies

In this volume we have observed that mixed methods studies (qualitative and quantitative) have great value (see Chapter Nine). We think in the future more mixed methods assessments will be conducted. Ercikan and Roth (2006) asserted, "The quantitative-qualitative dichotomy not only distorts that conception of education research but also is fallacious" (p. 14). They went on to advocate: "Instead of dichotomizing research into qualitative and quantitative, we need integrative approaches that provide the appropriate forms of knowledge needed by decision makers located differently in society and dealing with different units of analysis (individuals, group, community, etc.)" (p. 23).

These assertions are correct, and in the future studies using both quantitative and qualitative methods will become increasingly common and will be seen as especially valuable. The methodologies can be used to complement each other. For example, in implementing a leadership development program, the planners will need to understand who participated in the experience, their backgrounds, and how their thinking about leadership was influenced, compared with a group of similar students who did not participate. Such an assessment needs to be thoughtfully conceptualized, thoroughly conducted, and crafted so as to answer the questions of program supporters, senior leaders, and other stakeholders. As a consequence assessment will require both quantitative and qualitative inquiry. One or the other approach is likely to be incomplete, that is, the inquiry will not generate the needed information. So in this illustration, a quantitative study and a qualitative study would need to be conducted. In the future we think the use of mixed methods will become increasingly common. The following conclusion of Ercikan and Roth (2006) is instructive: "We suggest focusing on the needs of different people in society, who require different forms of knowledge to make decisions" (p. 23).

## Upgrading Skills Will Be a Growth Industry

Our sense is that few people get into student affairs practice because they want to conduct assessment studies. Rather, the graduate students we work with tell us that they are planning to enter the field because they really enjoy working with students and believe in the educational value of the kinds of experiences, programs, and services that they work to provide. Therefore, although they are required to take courses in research methodology, their primary interest (and we suspect professional passion) has to do with college students and how student affairs practitioners can add value to the student experience. However, if our assertions are correct, then they will need to know how to plan assessments and conduct inquiries that explore the value of student experiences. This leads us to conclude that steps will need to be taken to make sure that student affairs practitioners are able to conduct assessments at an acceptable level.

Even though courses in research methods assessment and evaluation are part of the curriculum recommended by Dean (2006), our sense is that such courses are not the highest priority for students. If our guess is correct, it is imperative that senior students affairs leaders make sure that in-service experiences are available for staff so that they can keep their skills in this area sharp and contemporary. This can be done by having members of the staff with excellent skills serve as mentors and coaches for those who need assistance, bringing in faculty members or staff (such as those from institutional research) to conduct workshops or skill development sessions for staff contemplating conducting assessments, or using consultants external to the institution for these endeavors. It might even be possible for institutions that are geographically proximate to form partnerships for conducting workshops for staff in student affairs interested in sharpening their assessment skills.

We are not suggesting that the goal of this skill enhancement is to turn each staff member into an institutional researcher. Rather, staff members need to understand the questions that can be answered by assessment projects and, as important, the research questions that cannot be answered by such inquiries. Staff members need to understand how to design a study, how to collect data that can be used to answer the questions guiding the assessment, and how to present the results in a user-friendly manner. They need not be transformed into statisticians or methodologists. But they do need to have a working knowledge of good practice in conducting assessments so that they know the appropriate questions to ask and understand what is possible given a specific circumstance.

In an era of tight budgets, it is somewhat rare for a division of student affairs to hire an assessment person to conduct such workshops, coordinate and lead assessments, consult with staff, and so on. But if the funding can be found for such a position, our sense is that such a person can be instrumental in making sure that a division's assessment program stays on track. But we also recognize that hiring a new staff person might not be possible and the other suggestions provided above can be a satisfactory substitute for hiring a full-time assessment coordinator.

## More Use of Technology in Collecting Data

Our sense is that the use of technology will be increasingly common in the development of assessment projects in the future. Whereas in the past conducting assessments meant selecting a sample by hand, developing a instrument locally, printing copies, collecting optical scan sheets for data processing, and using cumbersome statistical analysis programs, the future will consist primarily, although not exclusively, of Web-based survey instruments that have been developed commercially and that locally developed instruments will be prepared with the assistance of technologically sophisticated tools such as Survey Monkey (http://www.surveymonkey.com/), Survey Pro (http://www.apian.com/), or similar software products. These tools can cut down on the time it takes to develop an instrument and collect and analyze data.

We also think that relational databases increasingly will be available to administrators in their offices so that they will be able to answer questions that are posed to them by more senior administrators or other stakeholders with a few keystrokes. Instead of having to ask the unit's assessment coordinator, or having to contact the office of institutional research for information, individuals will be able to access data and develop answers to questions much more easily and more quickly than in the past.

## Human Subjects Scrutiny Will Continue to Increase

At one time researchers did not have to pay attention to the protection of human subjects that we take for granted in the contemporary assessment environment. Subjects were not asked to acknowledge that they were participating voluntarily, and institutional review boards did not review research projects in advance, even if they did exist. This laissez faire approach is in the past and it is highly unlikely that investigators in the future will return to a more casual approach to participants in conducting assessment projects.

In the future investigators will continue to have to submit their projects to institutional review boards, and any deviation from published standards will result in the cancellation of investigations as well as potential sanctions for investigators. The days of resident assistants passing out surveys in a floor meeting without IRB permission are over.

Rather, we anticipate that the pendulum will continue to swing in the direction of protecting human subjects in the future. This trend means that projects are likely to receive increased scrutiny and that they will be reviewed even more carefully in the future than now. Our conclusion is based on the potential that exists for litigation when human subjects are not fully informed or their rights are trampled. Institutions cannot risk such exposure, and one tool that currently is available to limit problems with assessment studies is the careful review of proposals in advance of the inquiry.

Investigators may find the level of scrutiny that they encounter in the development of their projects to be onerous, but the alternative—that is, to allow assessment projects to be implemented without institutional oversight—is a risk that most institutions are not willing to take. Consequently, the cautious, and prudent, approach is to provide careful oversight for all projects, no matter how benign they appear to be. We think this will be the case in the future.

## Students Will Suffer from Survey Overload and Fatigue

Our final thought about the future has to do with students' suffering from survey fatigue (see Chapter Four). Survey fatigue refers to potential survey participants refusing to complete survey instruments for various reasons, among them that they are simply tired of doing so. "Multiple surveys do appear to suppress response rates (Porter, Whitcomb, & Weitzer, 2004, p. 72).

Survey fatigue can be managed to a certain extent, such as by not conducting surveys on consecutive days and by making sure that the instrument has salience for the potential respondents (Porter, Whitcomb, & Weitzer, 2004). Even when those responsible for conducting the assessment are cognizant of factors that may reduce a response rate, such as the time of the year, the number of surveys that have been conducted recently, the length of the surveys, and so on, the potential is great that as more data are sought from students, response rates will decline.

Yet data are needed to satisfy the various reasons for conducting assessments, including ensuring organizational transparency, measuring contributions to student learning, and so on. So our best advice for investigators is to try to manage the number of surveys that are conducted particularly with respect to timing, length, and saliency. Data that can secured from other sources such as institutional databases should not be sought from surveys. Rewards might be contemplated to encourage participation. And investigators should be prepared to conduct multiple follow-ups to the initial data collection process to enhance the rate of participation.

## Conclusion

This chapter has included our perspectives on selected issues that will influence assessment and evaluation in the future. Our perspectives are based on our combined experience conducting assessment projects, discussions with colleagues over the years, and trends that appear in the literature. Whether or not our guesses will prove accurate is unknown, certainly to us. But we think that most, if not all, of these trends are likely to come to pass.

# References

Accreditation Board for Engineering and Technology. (2005). *Criteria for accrediting engineering programs*. Baltimore, MD: Author.

Bender, B. B., & Schuh, J. H. (Eds.). (2002). *Using benchmarking to inform practice in higher education*. New Directions for Higher Education, no. 118. San Francisco: Jossey-Bass.

Berger, D. E. (2004). Using regression analysis. In J. S. Wholey, H. P. Hatry, & K. E. Newcomer (Eds.), *Handbook of practical program evaluation* (2nd ed.) (pp. 479–505). San Francisco: Jossey-Bass.

Dean, L. A. (2006). *CAS professional standards for higher education* (6th ed.). Washington, DC: Council for the Advancement of Standards.

Ercikan, K., & Roth, W.-R. (2006). What good is polarizing research into qualitative and quantitative? *Educational Researcher, 35* (5), 14–23.

Kuh, G. D., Kinzie, J., Schuh, J. H., & Whitt, E. J. (2005). *Student success in college: Creating conditions that matter*. San Francisco: Jossey-Bass.

Middle States Commission on Higher Education. (2002). *Characteristics of excellence in higher education: Eligibility requirements and standards for accreditation*. Philadelphia, PA: Author.

Miller, C., & Malandra, G. (n.d.). *Issue paper: Accountability/assessment*. Washington, DC: The Secretary of Education's Commission on the Future of Higher Education. Retrieved October 10, 2006 from http://www.ed.gov/about/bdscomm/list/hiedfuture/reports.html

Moneta, L., & Kuh, G. D. (2005). When expectations and realities collide. In T. E. Miller, B. E. Bender, & J. H. Schuh (Eds.), *Promoting reasonable expectations: Aligning student and institutional views of the college experience* (pp. 65–83). San Francisco: Jossey-Bass.

Morgan, D. L., & Krueger, R. A. (1998). *The focus group kit*. Thousand Oaks, CA: Sage.

National Commission on the Future of Higher Education. (2006, August 9). *Report draft*. Washington, DC: US Department of Education. Retrieved October 10, 2006 from http://www.ed.gov/about/bdscomm/list/hiedfuture/reports.html

Newcomer, K. E., Hatry, H. P., & J. S. Wholey (2004). Meeting the need for practical evaluation approaches: An introduction. In J. S. Wholey, H. P. Hatry, & K. E. Newcomer (Eds.), *Handbook of practical program evaluation* (2nd ed.) (pp. xxxii–xliv). San Francisco: Jossey-Bass.

Porter, S. R., Whitcomb, M. E., & Weitzer, W. H. (2004). Multiple surveys of stuns and survey fatigue. In. S. R. Porter (Ed.), *Overcoming survey research problems* (pp. 63–73). New Directions for Institutional Research, no. 121. San Francisco: Jossey-Bass.

Sandeen, A., & Barr, M. J. (2006). *Critical issues for student affairs: Challenges and opportunities*. San Francisco: Jossey-Bass.

Taylor, B. E., & Massy, W. F. (1996). *Strategic indicators for higher education*. Princeton, NJ: Peterson's.

Wells, H. B. (1967). *CIC history*. Retrieved October 10, 2007 from http://www.cic.uiuc.edu/AboutCIC.shtml

## Web Site Resources

ACT. (2006). *Survey of academic advising*. Downloaded October 10, 2006 from http://www.act.org/ess/fouryear.html

Integrated Post Secondary Data System. *The Integrated Postsecondary Education Data System (IPEDS)*. Retrieved October 10, 2006 from http://nces.ed.gov/ipeds/

National Center for Education Statistics. (n.d.). *College opportunities online locator*. Retrieved October 10, 2006 from http://nces.ed.gov/ipeds/cool/

National Center for Education Statistics. (n.d.). *Data tools*. Retrieved October 10, 2006 from http://nces.ed.gov/datatools/

National Survey of Student Engagement. (2006). *NSSE 2006 standard version*. Retrieved October 10, 2006 from http://nsse.iub.edu/

Penn State University. *Penn State pulse*. Retrieved October 10, 2006 from http://www.sa.psu.edu/sara/pulse.shtml

Princeton Review. (2006). *New 2007 best 361 colleges rankings*. Retrieved October 10, 2006 from http://www.princetonreview.com/college/research/rankings/rankings.asp

Survey Monkey. Downloaded October 10, 2006 from http://www.survey-monkey.com/

Survey Pro. Downloaded October 10, 2006 from (http://www.apian.com/)

The Carnegie Foundation for the Advancement of Teaching. (n.d). *The Carnegie classification of institutions of higher education*. Retrieved October 10, 2006 from http://www.carnegiefoundation.org/classifications/

# Appendix 1

## EXAMPLE OF A FOCUS GROUP PROTOCOL

*Step 1.* Welcome and thank everyone for coming. Introduce yourself (as the focus group facilitator), the note taker, and the recorder. Ask participants to introduce themselves.
*Script...*

"Hi, I'm [name] and I'll be facilitating our focus group today. I have a couple of individuals who will be helping me with this process, [Name] will be taking notes, and [Name] will be running our tape recorder. I'd like to find out who you are, so could we go around the circle and have each person introduce yourself to the rest of us."

**Introductions**
*Step 2.* Why we are asking for their input. Purpose of the research. Review and collect informed consent forms.
*Script...*

"Before we start there are a couple of things that we need to do, and I'd like to tell you a little bit about why we are here and how we will conduct the focus group. We've got some forms that we are going to pass out to you now. These forms tell you a little bit about our study and this process. We will need your signature on the form, which states that you are consenting to participate in this research project, but before you sign them, I'd like to review them with you."

## Pass out informed consent

*Script...*

"Okay, now I'm going to read through the informed consent form with you. If you have any questions please stop me at anytime."

## Read through form, sign, and collect

*Step 3.* Review the procedures and process for the focus group. Some of this may be repetitious from the informed consent.
*Script...*

"In a minute, I'm going to ask you some open ended questions and I'd like you to share your responses to them. Please share only information with this group that you are comfortable sharing. Everything you say is strictly confidential—your real names will not be used at any time during this research project. Please remember that you can leave at anytime."

*Script...*

"At this time, I'd like you to think of a name that you would like to use instead of your real name. Once everyone has their pseudonym, we'll go around the circle so that the note taker can record your pseudonym."

Now have group members pick a pseudonym to use. Have note taker record pseudonym next to their number.
*Script...*

"I'd like to ask that before you make a comment, if you would please tell us your pseudonym and then make your comment. This helps us when we are transcribing the conversation from the tape to identify who is making a specific comment; sometimes it can get difficult to differentiate voices. For example, if I wanted to make a comment on one of the questions or what one of my peers had said, I would say, I'm [facilitator insert your name], and I agree with what Jim had to say about that, but I'd like to add...."

Note: If they forget to state their pseudonym, don't remind them because it will disrupt the flow of the group. Just make sure the note taker is making notations for who is talking.

*Script.* . .

"OK, are there any questions or concerns before we begin?"

Address any questions or concerns.

## Turn tape recorder on

*Step 4.* "We will now begin and [name] will turn on the recorder."

*Step 5.* Start asking the questions. One at a time. Use your judgment in deciding when to move on to the next question. Watch your time.

Once the recorder is on you might start by saying.. . .

"Again I would like to extend our appreciation for your participation here this evening. Our first question is. . .

Q1. Outside of attending classes, what types of activities, events, or organizations do you participate in? (*Note:* Make sure everyone is heard on this first question. You might want to go around the circle. This is an opening question with little opinion and one that we hope everyone can feel comfortable in answering. Like an ice-breaker.)

Q2. How important is involvement in extracurricular activities to you here at Midwestern University?

Q3. What would you change, if you could, in regard to your current level of involvement?

Q4. What supports do you feel exist (physical, social, personal) that assist your involvement in activities?

Q5. What barriers do you feel exist (physical, social personal) that limit your involvement in activities?

Q6. What role does your diagnosis/disability play in your current involvement?

Q7. To what degree do you feel you limit your own involvement? To what degree do you feel you push yourself to become more involved?

Q8. What could Midwestern University do to assist students with disabilities who wish to participate in activities, events, and organizations?

*Script...*

"That was our final question. Is there anything else that anyone would like to add or any additional comments concerning what we have talked about here today?"

## Allow time for comments
*Script...*

"This concludes our focus group. Thank you for coming and participating. Once we have conducted all of the focus groups and analyzed the transcripts, you will receive an e-mail asking you to comment on the conclusions the researchers have drawn based on their analysis of the comments made during the group discussion. If you have any questions at any time please contact Dr. X (her contact information is on your copy of the informed consent) or X."

*Step* 6. Once everyone has left, briefly review the notes with the note taker.

## Things to Remember When Conducting a Focus Group

- Only facilitate, do not get into any debates or offer your opinions on any of the questions discussed.
- Minimize your involvement; your talking should be very limited (10 percent).

- Keep the group on task; don't let side conversations take center stage.

- Avoid judgment statements, negative or positive.

- Do not rephrase a comment someone has made—allow their words to remain their words. You can ask for clarification if it looks like other group members are confused.

- Don't be afraid of silence. Ask your question and wait for a little while.

- Try to encourage involvement from all members, but don't make a group member feel like he or she is on the spot or pressured to answer a question.

# Appendix 2

## USING MICROSOFT EXCEL TO DEVELOP A RANDOM SAMPLE AND A STRATIFIED RANDOM SAMPLE

The following steps were taken to select the random sample:

1. Using MS Excel's random number function (" = rand()"), a random number was generated for each student in the population. This column of data, titled "random," was then copied, and using the "paste special"—"values" feature, the random number formula was replaced by a particular random number.

2. Select the entire dataset, including the newly created random number. Then sort the data by the "random number."

3. Finally, a new column (labeled "sample") was created. The value of "sample" is 1 for the first 2000 students (from row 2 to 2001, assuming the variable names are in the first row). For the remaining students, the value is set to "0."

The following steps describe how stratified random sampling can be conducted using Microsoft Excel.

1. Using the smoking policy example, two specific countries (country numbers 123 and 145) are identified and all other students. There are many ways to create this group variable. One would be to sort the data by country and then add the field by hand. The second (and more efficient method) would be to create a formula.

Suppose that home country is in column D. Type the following formula in a new column labeled "group":
= if (or(d2 = "123", d2 = "145"), "two_cntry", "rest of pop")
Use the copy and paste feature in MS Excel to copy this formula for ALL students.

2. Create a random number using the same formula described earlier. Copy and "paste special"—"values" features; the random number formula will be replaced by a specific random number for ALL students.

3. Select the entire data set (click in the cell above row 1 and to the left of column 1) and sort by "group" as the first sort variable and "random" as the second sort variable.

4. Create a column called "sample". Since 30 students from these countries are needed and using the average 25 percent response rate, 120 students would need to be sampled. Since 157 are enrolled, we place a 1 by the first 120 students and a 0 by the remaining 37. At this row (158), the group variable switches from "two_cntry" to "rest of pop." Starting from row 158, place a 1 by the next 1880 students (2000–120) and a 0 by the remaining.

5. The final step is to extract the sample population of 2000 students from this MS Excel file. To do this, select the entire dataset, then sort by "sample" using a descending sort. Select the first 2000 students along with the header row to use as the list of students.

# Appendix 3

## LISTING OF COMMONLY USED INSTRUMENTS, PURPOSE, AND INFORMATION COLLECTED

| Instrument | Purpose | Information Collected |
|---|---|---|
| **Entering Undergraduates** | | |
| Cooperative Institutional Research Program (CIRP), Entering Student Survey (ESS) | Collect information on incoming students. | Demographics, expectations of the college experience, degree goals and career plans, college finances, attitudes and values, reasons for attending college |
| Freshman Class Profile Service | Provide characteristics of ACT-tested students by institution | Demographics, high school characteristics, career interests, college plans |
| Student Descriptive Questionnaire (SDQ) | Provide profile of SAT-tested students | Demographics, academic record and course-taking patterns in high school |
| Admitted Student Questionnaire (ASQ) and ASQ Plus | Student perceptions of selected institution and admission process | Student perceptions of programs, admissions process, literature, financial aid, etc. ASQ Plus provides institutional comparisons |
| College Student Expectations Questionnaire (CSXQ) | Assess expectations of new students. Can be compared with actual experiences measured in College Student Experiences Questionnaire | Demographics, expectations for involvement, predicted satisfaction, expected nature of learning environment |

| Instrument | Purpose | Information Collected |
|---|---|---|
| **Enrolled Undergraduates** | | |
| College Student Survey (CSS) | Evaluate experiences and satisfaction. Can be used longitudinally with the CIRP. | Demographics, satisfaction with college experience, degree goals and career plans, attitudes and values |
| Faces of the Future | Assess community college population and role of community colleges | Demographics, current college experiences—access, learning, satisfaction, expected outcomes, transitions |
| College Student Experiences Questionnaire (CSEQ) | Quality of students' experiences, perceptions of environment, satisfaction, progress toward learning and development outcomes | Demographics, engagement level, rating of learning environment, estimate of gains toward learning goals, satisfaction with institution |
| Community College Student Experiences Questionnaire (CCSEQ) | Measure student progress and experiences | Demographics, effort expended in experiences (in-class and out-of-class), progress toward outcomes, satisfaction with institution |
| National Survey of Student Engagement (NSSE) | Outcome assessment, undergraduate quality, engagement in effective educational practices | Demographics, quality of effort, engagement in educational activities, quality of interactions, educational and personal gains, satisfaction |
| Your First College Year (YFCY) | Follow-up survey to CIRP. Assess development in first year. | CIRP post-test items, student experiences, life goals, peer and faculty interaction, adjustment and persistence, degree aspirations, and satisfaction |
| Student Satisfaction Inventory (SSI) | Student satisfaction | Rate importance of and satisfaction with aspects of student experience |

| Instrument | Purpose | Information Collected |
| --- | --- | --- |
| Adult Student Priorities Survey (ASPS) | Student satisfaction of students age ≥ 25 | Rate importance of and satisfaction with aspects of student experience |

### Student Proficiencies and Learning Outcomes

| Instrument | Purpose | Information Collected |
| --- | --- | --- |
| College Assessment of Academic Proficiency (CAAP) | Assess achievement in general education skills | Proficiency in core skills: writing, reading, math, science reasoning, and critical thinking |
| Collegiate Learning Assessment (CLA) | Assess student reasoning and communication skills | Proficiency in critical thinking, analytic reasoning, written communication, and problem solving |
| Measure of Academic Proficiency and Progress (MAPP) | Assess student achievement and student learning | Proficiency in critical thinking, reading, writing, and mathematics; context-based subscores in humanities, social sciences, and natural sciences |
| Major Field Tests | Assess student abilities in major field of study. | Ability to analyze and solve problems, understand relationships, and interpret information. Available for 15 disciplines. |

### Alumni

| Instrument | Purpose | Information Collected |
| --- | --- | --- |
| Comprehensive Alumni Assessment Survey (CAAS) | Assess institutional effectiveness, alumni perceptions of preparation | Demographics (employment, continuing education), personal development, community participation, undergraduate experience |
| College Results Survey (CRS) | Provide institution profile based on alumni responses to values, abilities, occupations, work skills, and continuing education | Demographics, continuing education, values, occupation, work skills |

| Instrument | Purpose | Information Collected |
| --- | --- | --- |
| **Series of Instruments** | | |
| Student Outcomes Information Survey (SOIS) | Collect information about student needs and reactions to experiences | Demographics, personal goals and career aspirations, factors influencing college choice, satisfaction with experiences, activities, educational plans, career information |
| Evaluation/Survey Services (ACT) | Assess needs and opinions of students and alumni | Fifteen standardized instruments including (among others) entering student, satisfaction, nonreturning student, and alumni surveys |

# Appendix 4

## COMPUTER SYNTAX CODE FOR TABLE 6.1

The following SPSS computer syntax code was used to conduct a crosstabulation analysis to ascertain the relationship between whether an undergraduate student participates in a learning community (lc) and whether the student is retained from his or her first fall semester to the second fall semester (fall2r):

```
CROSSTABS
/TABLES = fall2r BY lc
/FORMAT = AVALUE TABLES
/STATISTIC = CHISQ
/CELLS = COUNT ROW COLUMN.
```

This syntax is what gets executed by the computer when you use this sequence of SPSS pull-down menu steps:

Analyze→Descriptive Statistics→Crosstabs

Select the fall2r variable and put that under the heading "Row(s):"

Select the lc variable and put that under the heading "Column(s):"

Click on the Statistics button, and select "Chi-square"

Click on the Cells button, and select "Row" and "Column" under Percentages

Click Continue

Click OK

# Appendix 5

# FURTHER EXPLANATION OF TABLE 6.2

For a crosstabulation table with rows labeled by the values $X_i$, i = 1, 2, . . . r and with columns labeled by the values $Y_j$, j = 1, 2, . . ., c, the crosstabulation table has the number of degrees of freedom equal to $(r - 1) \times (c - 1)$. The Pearson chi-square $(\chi^2_p)$ is defined by

$$\chi^2_p = \Sigma_i \Sigma_j (n_{ij} - m_{ij})2/m_{ij},$$

where $n_{ij}$ is the observed frequency for each cell and $m_{ij}$ is the frequency within each cell that is expected if the two variables are independent.

The *Continuity Correction* (Yates' correction for continuity) result adjusts the chi-square statistic to account for the fact that the cell frequency values that are used in calculating the Pearson chi-square statistic do not properly reflect the fact that the underlying theoretical chi-square distribution is continuous. The continuity correction provides a more conservative (smaller) value, and a bigger difference between the continuity-adjusted chi-square value and the Pearson chi-square result is evident in small samples.

The *Likelihood Ratio* chi-square statistic, also known as the $G^2$ statistic, is computed by ratios between the observed and expected frequencies, with the alternative hypothesis being that there is general association between the two variables. With $(r - 1) \times (c - 1)$ degrees of freedom:

$$G^2 = 2\Sigma_i \Sigma_j n_{ij} ln(n_{ij}/m_{ij})$$

*Fisher's Exact Test* assumes that the row and column totals are fixed, and then uses the hypergeometric distribution to compute probabilities of possible tables with these observed row and column totals. Fisher's exact test is appropriate even for small sample sizes and for sparse tables in which some cells have very few observations.

# Appendix 6

## SAMPLE METHODS PARAGRAPH

This report was designed to ascertain the perceptions of first- and second-year students at MSU about advising services during the past two years. The *Survey of Academic Advising*, produced by the American College Testing program, was the instrument we used in this assessment. The data were collected this past January after the beginning of classes and also were collected the previous January. In each case the instrument was sent to all first- and second-year students electronically and they responded online. The response rate for the study was 64 percent. The university's human subjects review board approved this study.

# Appendix 7

## INFORMED CONSENT CHECKLIST: BASIC AND ADDITIONAL ELEMENTS

**§46.116—Informed Consent Checklist—Basic and Additional Elements**

A statement that the study involves research

An explanation of the purposes of the research

The expected duration of the subject's participation

A description of the procedures to be followed

Identification of any procedures which are experimental

A description of any reasonably foreseeable risks or discomforts to the subject

A description of any benefits to the subject or to others which may reasonably be expected from the research

A disclosure of appropriate alternative procedures or courses of treatment, if any, that might be advantageous to the subject

A statement describing the extent, if any, to which confidentiality of records identifying the subject will be maintained

For research involving more than minimal risk, an explanation as to whether any compensation, and an explanation as to whether any medical treatments are available, if injury occurs and, if so, what they consist of, or where further information may be obtained

An explanation of whom to contact for answers to pertinent questions about the research and research subjects' rights, and whom to contact in the event of a research-related injury to the subject

A statement that participation is voluntary, refusal to participate will involve no penalty or loss of benefits to which the subject is otherwise entitled, and the subject may discontinue participation at any time without penalty or loss of benefits, to which the subject is otherwise entitled

## Additional Elements, as Appropriate

A statement that the particular treatment or procedure may involve risks to the subject (or to the embryo or fetus, if the subject is or may become pregnant), which are currently unforeseeable

Anticipated circumstances under which the subject's participation may be terminated by the investigator without regard to the subject's consent

Any additional costs to the subject that may result from participation in the research

The consequences of a subject's decision to withdraw from the research and procedures for orderly termination of participation by the subject

A statement that significant new findings developed during the course of the research, which may relate to the subject's willingness to continue participation, will be provided to the subject

The approximate number of subjects involved in the study

Further information is available from the Department of Health and Human Services. Procedures may change without notice.

*Source:* Department of Health and Human Services. http://www.hhs.gov/ohrp/humansubjects/assurance/consentckls.htm

# Appendix 8

## CODES OF ETHICS OF RELEVANT PROFESSIONAL ORGANIZATIONS TO CONDUCTING ASSESSMENT STUDIES IN STUDENT AFFAIRS

- American Evaluation Association: http://www.eval.org/Publications/GuidingPrinciplesPrintable.asp
- Joint Committee on Standards for Educational Evaluation. Program evaluation standards: http://www.wmich.edu/evalctr/jc/
- The American College Personnel Association: http://www.myacpa.org/au/au_thical.cfm
- The Association of Institutional Research: http://www.airweb.org/?page = 140
- The Association for the Study of Higher Education: http://www.ashe.ws/ethics.htm
- The American Educational Research Association: http://www.aera.net/aboutaera/?id = 222

# Index

### A

Accountability, 2–7; accreditation and, 5–6; benchmarking and, 7; cost of attendance and, 6–7; expectations for learning and, 3–4; future trends in, 231–232; political environment and, 4–5; retention and, 4

Accreditation, 5–6, 232

Accreditation Board for Engineering and Technology (ABET), 232

ACT. *See* American College Testing (ACT) Program

Action steps, 179–181

Admissions information, 28

Admitted Student Questionnaire (ASQ), 257

Adult Student Priorities Survey (ASPS), 259

African American students, 25, 28–31, 40

Agreement estimate, 125

Alumni association case study, 213–226; background information, 213–215; database research, 216–219; qualitative study, 223–226; quantitative study, 219–223

Alumni Outcomes Questionnaire, 220

American College Personnel Association (ACPA), 269

American College Testing (ACT) Program: Academic Advising Questionnaire, 202; Alumni Outcomes Questionnaire, 220, 229; Evaluation/Survey Services, 260; searching databases of, 28–29; Survey of Academic Advising, 172, 237, 265; Web site information, 229, 248

American Council on Education (ACE), 114

American Educational Research Association (AERA), 269

American Evaluation Association (AEA), 207, 269

*American Imperative: Higher Expectations for Higher Education* report, 3

Analysis of covariance (ANCOVA), 148; factorial, 148; multivariate, 148–149

Analysis of variance (ANOVA), 148; factorial, 148; multivariate, 148–149

Assessment: accountability and, 2–7; codes of ethics for, 269; coordination of, 95–96; cost effectiveness, 14–15; ethical issues in, 191–209; examples related to student affairs, 17–18; existing databases used in, 23–47; future trends in, 231–246; getting started in, 9–11; measuring participation in, 11–12; mixed methodological approach to, 211–229, 241–242; needs, 12; organizational functions and, 8–9; outcomes, 13–14; planning for, 108–110; questions to consider for, 15–17; satisfaction, 13

Association for Institutional Research (AIR), 50, 114, 269

Association for the Study of Higher Education (ASHE), 269

Audit trail, 169

Autonomy, 192–193

Axial coding, 159

### B

Backing up data, 142

*Basics of Item Response Theory, The* (Baker), 124

Benchmarking, 7
Benefiting others, 194–196
Bias, sample, 87
Bivariate correlation, 145–146
Briefings, 183–188; delivering, 187–188; materials for, 184–185; preparing for, 186–187
Buros Institute, 113–114, 115

## C

Canonical correlation, 147
Carnegie Foundation for the Advancement of Teaching, 30, 50, 235–236, 248
Case studies: database research, 25–26; mixed methodological approach, 213–228; usefulness of, 226
Casey, M. A., 68–69, 130–131, 132
Central tendency, 144
Checklists: for developing a sample, 102–103; for enhancing instrument quality, 126; for informed consent, 200, 267–268
Chi-square test statistic, 155–156
Classification tools, 30
Cleaning data, 142
Closed-ended questions, 56
Cluster sampling, 86
Codes of ethics, 207, 269
Coding: qualitative data, 162–164; quantitative data, 142–143
Coefficient of variation, 145
Collecting data. See Data collection
College Assessment of Academic Proficiency (CAAP), 259
College Board database, 28–29
College Learning Assessment (CLA), 259
College Opportunities On-Line (COOL) Data System, 30, 34, 50, 239
College Results Online (The Education Trust), 212
College Results Survey (CRS), 259
College Student Expectations Questionnaire (CSXQ), 257
College Student Experiences Questionnaire (CSEQ), 258
College Student Survey (CSS), 258
Colton, D., 55, 60–61, 117, 124
Commission of the Secretary of Education, 2

Committee on Institutional Cooperation, 237
Common Data Set (CDS) initiative, 44
Community College Student Experiences Questionnaire (CCSEQ), 258
Comparative data, 236–237
Compensation, participant, 64, 98–100
Compliance issues, 198
Comprehensive Alumni Assessment Survey (CAAS), 259
Consumer Price Index, 6
Continuity correction, 263
Continuous variables, 144
Convenience sampling, 58, 85–86, 91
Convergent evidence, 124
COOL Data System, 30, 34, 50, 239
Cooper, R. M., 51, 107, 141
Cooperative Institutional Research Program (CIRP), 37, 38–39, 257
Correlation: bivariate, 145–146; canonical, 147; multiple, 146
Costs: assessing cost effectiveness, 14–15; increasing for higher education, 6–7
Council for the Advancement of Standards in Higher Education, 7
Course management systems, 45
Covariance, analysis of, 148–149
Covert, R. W., 55, 60–61, 117, 124
Crediting contributors, 204–205
Crime statistics, 33–34
Cross-tabulation analysis, 152–156; descriptive statistics, 263–264; SPSS computer syntax code, 261

## D

Dashboard indicators, 44–45
Data: accessing, 39–41, 202–203; analyzing, 141–169; backing up, 142; coding, 142–143; collecting, 51–74; comparative, 236–237; organizing, 160–162; ownership, 203–204
Data analysis, 141–169; ANOVA and ANCOVA in, 148; bivariate correlation and regression in, 145–146; canonical correlation and multivariate regression in, 147; chi-square statistic in, 155–156; coding process in, 142–143, 162–164; cross-tabulation example of, 152–156; descriptive statistics for, 144–145; discriminant analysis in, 149–150;

ensuring goodness in, 168–169; factor analysis in, 150–151; frequency tables in, 147; hierarchical linear modeling in, 151–152; interpreting data in, 167–168; levels of measurement in, 143–144; logistic regression in, 150; logit models in, 147; multiple correlation and regression in, 146; multivariate ANOVA/ANCOVA in, 148–149; organizing data for, 160–162; preparing data for, 142, 160; qualitative studies and, 158–169; quantitative studies and, 141–158; repeated measures in, 149; representing data in, 165–167; software packages for, 142, 156–158, 159; structural equation modeling in, 151; time series analysis in, 152

Data collection, 51–74; database management and, 237–238; document review for, 73–74; field observations for, 70–73; focus groups for, 68–70; future trends in, 244; instruments for, 60; interviews for, 64–70; overview of, 51–52; surveys for, 52–64; time line for, 61–62; Web-based, 57, 62, 63

Data exchanges, 236–237

Data warehouses, 41

Databases, 23–47; accessing, 39–41; building, 46; case study on using, 216–219; CDS initiative, 44; considerations for using, 24; external, 26–35, 36; future trends in using, 233–236; institutional, 233–234; internal, 35, 37–46; IPEDS system, 30–31, 33, 34, 35, 36; issues related to, 41–44; mixed methodological approach and, 213; relational, 41, 244; time required for managing, 237–238; training required to use, 42–43; typical data in, 44–46; Web resources on, 50

Decision making, 238–239

Degree-granting units, 232

Department of Health and Human Services (DHHS), 198–200

Describing qualitative data, 165

Descriptive statistics, 144–145

*Designing and Constructing Instruments for Social Research and Evaluation* (Colton & Covert), 117

Dichotomous responses, 133

Discrete variables, 144

Discriminant analysis, 124, 149–150

Dispersion, 144

Do no harm principle, 193–194

Document review, 73–74; advantages and disadvantages of, 74; protocol for conducting, 135–136

Documenting Effective Educational Practice (DEEP) project, 38

Double-barreled questions, 118

Dropouts, 4

E

Education Trust, The, 50, 212, 229

Effectiveness, organizational, 9

E-mail: for data backups, 142; for Web-based surveys, 62, 94

Ending questions, 131

Enrollment Information Service (EIS), 29

Enrollment Planning Service (EPS), 29

Enterprise systems, 41

Ercikan, K., 241, 242

Errors: checking reports for, 183; sampling, 86–87

Esterberg, K. G., 66, 72, 132, 133, 160–161, 164, 167

Ethical issues, 191–209; being faithful, 197–198; being just, 196; benefiting others, 194–196; codes of ethics, 207, 269; conceptual framework for, 192–198; crediting contributors, 204–205; data access, 202–203; data ownership, 203–204; doing no harm, 193–194; future trends in, 244–245; informed consent, 198–201, 267–268; obligations beyond, 205; respecting autonomy, 192–193; sources of assistance with, 206; Web resources related to, 208–209

Evaluation/Survey Services (ACT), 260

Evaluators: codes of ethics for, 269; guiding principles for, 207; skills upgrade for, 242–243

Excel program, 142, 156, 255–256

Executive summaries, 175–176

Expedited review procedure, 200–201

External data sources, 26–35, 36

Extreme or deviant case sampling, 89–90

## F

Face validity, 123
Faces of the Future survey, 258
Factor analysis, 123, 150–151
Factorial ANOVA/ANCOVA, 148
Faithfulness, 197–198
Family Educational Rights and Privacy
    Act (FERPA), 43
Field observations, 70–73; considerations
    pertaining to, 71–72; dimensions of
    data collection in, 73; observer role
    in, 70–71; protocols for conducting,
    134–135; writing notes about,
    72–73
Filtering questions, 56
First-year assessment instruments, 114
Fisher's exact test, 264
Focus groups, 68–70, 87–93; case study
    using, 223–226; characteristics of, 68,
    92–93; definition of, 88; number and
    size of, 68–69, 91–92; protocols for
    conducting, 129–132, 249–253;
    recruiting participants for, 70;
    sampling strategies for, 87–93; when
    to use, 69
Focus Groups: A Practical Guide for
    Applied Research (Krueger & Casey),
    132
Focused coding, 164
Fontana, A. F., 65
Frequency tables, 147
Freshman Class Profile Service, 257
Freshman Survey, 38
Future trends, 231–246

## G

Gansemer-Topf, Ann M., 77
General questions, 133
Grinnell College, 97–98
Grob, G. F., 184–185
Grounded theory design, 159
Group interviews. See Focus groups
Guiding Principles for Evaluators (AEA),
    207

## H

Handouts, 185
Health Insurance Portability
    Accountability Act (HIPAA), 43
Hendricks, M., 184, 185, 187, 188

Hierarchical linear models (HLMs),
    151–152
HLM software, 158
Honesty, 196
Human resources office, 206
Human subject scrutiny, 244–245

## I

Incentives, participant, 64, 98–100
Individual interviews, 66–68
Informed consent, 198–201, 267–268
Institutional databases, 233–234
Institutional Review Board (IRB), 52,
    192, 199–200
Instruments, 60, 107–138; challenges to
    using, 126–127, 136–138;
    development of, 109–110, 116–121,
    126–127; list of commonly used,
    257–260; locally designed, 112–113,
    116–121; pilot testing, 60–61, 125;
    published, 111–112, 113–116, 127,
    257–260; qualitative, 110–111,
    127–138; quality determination for,
    122–126; quantitative, 110–127;
    reliability of, 124–125; selection of,
    109–110, 113–116; validity of,
    122–124
Integrated Postsecondary Education Data
    System (IPEDS), 30–31; crime
    statistics research, 34; finding existing
    data using, 212, 213; future trends in
    using, 235; information categories, 36;
    strengths and weaknesses, 35; student
    affairs expenditure research, 33; Web
    site information, 50, 229, 248
Intensity measures, 56
Intensity sampling, 89–90
Internal consistency estimate, 124
Internal data sources, 35, 37–46
Internet resources. See Web resources
Interpreting qualitative data,
    167–168
Interval data, 143
Interviews, 64–70; focus group, 68–70,
    87–93; guides for conducting,
    132–134; individual, 66–68;
    semistructured, 66, 132; structured,
    65; unstructured, 66
Introductory questions, 131
Involvement in Learning report, 3
IPEDS. See Integrated Postsecondary
    Education Data System

## J

JMP software, 158
Judicial affairs office, 206

## K

Key questions, 131
Kitchener, K. S., 192
Kleinglass, N., 42
*Knocking at the College Door* (WICHE), 26
Krueger, R. A., 68–69, 130–131, 132

## L

LCD projectors, 186
Learning: expectations for, 3–4; instruments for assessing, 259
*Learning Reconsidered* report, 3
Legal counsel, 206
Likelihood ratio chi-square, 156, 263
LIMDEP software, 158
Locally designed instruments: challenges to using, 126–127; development of, 116–121, 126–127; phrasing questions in, 117–119; published instruments vs., 111–113; response scales for, 119–121. *See also* Published instruments
Logistic regression, 150
Logit models, 147
Log-linear models, 147
Longitudinal studies, 97–98

## M

Major Field Tests, 259
Margin of error, 86–87
Maximum variation sampling, 90
Mean, 144
Measure of Academic Proficiency and Progress (MAPP), 259
Measurement: levels of, 143–144; of participation, 11–12
*Measuring Quality: Choosing Among Surveys and Other Assessments of College Quality* (Borden & Zak Owens), 114, 115
Median, 144
Member checks, 169
*Mental Measurements Yearbook, The* (Buros Institute), 113–114, 115
Merriam, S. B., 191

Methods paragraph, 265
Miami University, 238
Microsoft Excel, 142, 156, 255–256
Microsoft Word, 163–164
Middle States Commission, 5–6
Mixed methodological approach, 211–229; case study, 213–228; database research, 216–219; explanatory overview, 211–213; future trends related to, 241–242; qualitative research, 223–226; quantitative research, 219–223
Mode, 144
Multiple linear correlation, 146
Multivariate ANOVA/ANCOVA, 148–149
Multivariate regression, 147

## N

National Center for Education Statistics (NCES), 27, 30, 235, 248
National Commission on the Future of Higher Education, 231
National Household Education Surveys (NHES), 99
National Survey of Student Engagement (NSSE), 37–38, 96, 116, 237, 248, 258
Needs assessment, 12
Nominal data, 143
Nonprobability sampling, 58, 85–86
Norman, W., 40
North Dakota State University (NDSU), 18
Notes, field observation, 72–73
NSSE. *See* National Survey of Student Engagement

## O

Observations. *See* Field observations
Off-campus services, 14
Office of Institutional Research, 40, 77
Online course management systems, 45
Online surveys. *See* Web-based surveys
Open coding, 159
Open-ended questionnaires, 129
Open-ended questions, 56
Opening questions, 130–131
Operations reports, 176

Oral reports, 183–188; briefing preparation, 186–187; materials preparation, 184–185; presentation delivery, 187–188. *See also* Written reports
*Orange Slice* reports, 182–183
Ordinal data, 143
Oregon State University, 18
Organizational functions, 8–9; organizational effectiveness and, 9; strategic planning and, 8–9
Outcome-oriented information, 54–55
Outcomes assessment, 13–14

**P**

Paper-and-pencil surveys, 62, 63, 93–95
Participation, measuring, 11–12
Pascarella, E. T., 10
Pearson, Karl, 155
Pearson chi-square, 155–156
Peer Analysis System, 30–31
"Peer Ten" comparisons, 32–34
Peer-debriefing, 169
Pell Grants, 6
*Penn State Pulse*, 182, 239–240, 248
Penn State University, 17, 18, 182, 239–240, 248
Pilot tests, 60–61, 125
Planning: instrument selection and, 108–110; strategic, 8–9
Point of redundancy, 91
Policy Center on the First Year of College, 114, 115
Political pressure, 4–5
Population: definition of, 79; target, 81–83
Positionality, 137, 169
PowerPoint presentations, 184–185
Presentations, 183–188; delivering, 187–188; materials for, 184–185; preparing for, 186–187
*Princeton Review*, 239, 248
Privacy issues, 41, 42
Probability sampling, 58, 83–84
Process-oriented information, 54–55
Project DEEP, 238
Prokos, A. H., 65
*Proving and Improving: Strategies for Assessing the First College Year* (Swing), 114

PsychData software, 63
Psychological incentives, 99–100
Public records, 73–74
Published instruments: challenges to using, 127; identification of useful, 113–116; list of commonly used, 257–260; locally designed instruments vs., 111–113; resources for selecting, 115. *See also* Locally designed instruments
Purdue University, 45
Pure random sampling, 83–84
Purposive sampling, 58, 88

**Q**

Qualitative data analysis, 158–169; coding process in, 162–164; describing data in, 165; ensuring goodness in, 168–169; interpreting data in, 167–168; listing assessment objectives in, 168; organizing and preparing data for, 160–162; overview of steps in, 159–160; reading through data in, 162; representing data in, 165–167. *See also* Quantitative data analysis
Qualitative instruments, 127–138; challenges to using, 136–138; document review protocols, 135–136; field observation protocols, 134–135; focus group protocols, 129–132; interview guides, 132–134; open-ended questionnaires, 129; reasons for using, 127–128; selection/development of, 110–111; time issues with, 137–138. *See also* Quantitative instruments
Qualitative studies: case example of, 223–226; data analysis for, 158–169; instruments for, 110–111, 127–138; quantitative studies combined with, 211–213, 241–242; sampling techniques for, 87–91
Qualitative variables, 144
Quality of instruments, 122–126; reliability and, 124–125; strategies for enhancing, 125–126; validity and, 122–124

Quantitative data analysis, 141–158; coding process for, 142–143; cross-tabulation example of, 152–156; forms appropriate for student affairs, 145–152; levels of measurement in, 143–144; simple descriptive statistics in, 144–145; software packages for, 142, 156–158. *See also* Qualitative data analysis

Quantitative instruments, 110–127; challenges to using, 126–127; development of, 110–111, 116–121, 126–127; locally designed, 112–113, 116–121; published, 111–112, 113–116; quality of, 122–126; selection of, 110–111, 113–116. *See also* Qualitative instruments

Quantitative studies: case example of, 219–223; data analysis for, 141–158; instruments for, 110–127; qualitative studies combined with, 211–213, 241–242; sampling techniques for, 83–86

Quantitative variables, 144

Questionnaires: data collection using, 52–64; open-ended, 129. *See also* Surveys; *and specific questionnaires*

Questions: categories of, 130–131; double-barreled, 118; general vs. specific, 133; open- vs. closed-ended, 56; phrasing of, 117–119; scalar, 120–121; sequencing of, 130; specific vs. general, 59–60; tips for generating, 133

R

Random sampling: Excel used for, 255–256; pure, 83–84; simple, 88–89; stratified, 85, 255–256

Range, 144, 145

Ratio data, 143

Recommendations for change, 171, 179, 180–181

Referral sampling, 90

Regression: logistic, 150; multiple linear correlation and, 146; multivariate, 147; simple linear correlation and, 145–146

Relational databases, 41, 244

Reliability, 124–125

Repeated measures, 149

Reports, 171–188; oral, 183–188; written, 173–183

Representing qualitative data, 165–167

Resident assistants (RAs), 193

Respecting autonomy, 192–193

Response rates: incentives/rewards and, 98–100; paper vs. Web surveys and, 93–95; survey fatigue and, 93–101; techniques for increasing, 100–101

Response scales, 119–121

Retention, 4, 107–108, 172

Rewards, participant, 64, 98–100

Rhatigan, J. J., 11

Room and board costs: "Peer Ten" comparison of, 32; tuition and fees compared to, 6

Roth, W.-R., 241, 242

S

Sample bias, 87

Sample size: for focus groups, 68–69; for individual interviews, 68; for surveys, 57

Sampling, 57–58, 79–93; checklist for, 102–103; cluster, 86; convenience, 58, 85–86, 91; definition of, 79; errors in, 86–87; extreme or deviant case, 89–90; factors to consider in, 79–81; for focus groups, 87–93; intensity, 89–90; maximum variation, 90; nonprobability, 58, 85–86; probability, 58, 83–84; purposive, 58, 88; referral, 90; simple random, 88–89; snowball, 58, 90; steps in process of, 81–83; stratified purposeful, 90; stratified random, 85, 255–256; typical case, 89

Sampling variance, 86–87

SAS (Statistical Analysis System), 142, 157

Satisfaction assessment, 13

Saturation point, 91

Saunders, Kevin, 23, 107

Scalar questions, 120–121

Seidman, I., 67–68

Selective coding, 159

Semistructured interviews, 66, 132

Shelley, Mack C., II, 141

Simple linear correlation, 145–146

Simple random sampling, 88–89

Skills development, 242–243

Slide presentations, 184–185

"Small wins" concept, 10
Snowball sampling, 58, 90
Software: data analysis, 142, 156–158, 159; survey, 63, 244
Sonnichsen, R. C., 171, 179, 180
Southern Association of Colleges and Schools, 6
Specific questions, 133
Spell check feature, 183
Spradley, J. P., 73
SPSS (Statistical Package for the Social Sciences), 156–157; computer syntax code, 161; data analysis using, 142
St. Olaf College, 97
Stability estimate, 124
Standard deviation, 144, 145
Stata software, 157
Statistical Analysis System (SAS), 142, 157
Statistical Package for the Social Sciences. See SPSS
Strategic planning, 8–9
Stratified purposeful sampling, 90
Stratified random sampling, 85, 255–256
Structural equation models (SEMs), 151
Structured interviews, 65
Student affairs: accountability of, 232–233; assessment examples, 17–18; data analysis, 145–152; expenditures comparison, 32–33
Student Descriptive Questionnaire (SDQ), 257
Student Learning Imperative report, 3
Student Outcomes Information Survey (SOIS), 260
Student proficiency assessments, 259
Student Right to Know and Campus Security Act (1990), 34
Student Satisfaction Inventory (SSI), 258
Student Success in College (Kuh, Kinzie, Schuh, & Whitt), 38
Survey fatigue, 93–101; future trends and, 245–246; incentives/rewards and, 98–100; longitudinal studies and, 97–98; paper vs. Web surveys and, 93–95; suggestions for combating, 95–97
Survey Monkey software, 63, 244, 248

Survey of Academic Advising, 172, 237, 265
Survey Pro software, 244, 248
Surveys, 52–64; attitude and opinion, 56; case study using, 219–223; considerations for using, 54; identifying participants in, 56–57; implementation of, 62–63; instruments for, 60; multiple use, 59–60; paper-and-pencil, 62, 63, 93–95; participant incentives/rewards, 64, 98–100; pilot testing, 60–61; process- vs. outcome-oriented, 54–55; reasons for using, 53–54; response rates to, 93–101; sample size for, 57–58; sponsorship of, 100; time line for, 61–62; Web-based, 57, 62, 63, 93–95. See also specific surveys
Syracuse University, 18, 182

**T**

Target populations, 81–83; gathering lists of, 82–83; identifying, 81–82; selecting samples from, 83–86
Targeted reports, 176
Taylor, G. R., 211, 212
Technological tools, 244
Terenzini, P. T., 10
Test-retest reliability, 124
Tests in Print (Buros Institute), 114
Three-way frequency tables, 147
Time issues: data collection and, 61–62; qualitative instruments and, 137–138
Time series analysis, 152
Transcribing process, 160
Transition questions, 131
Transparency, 239–240
Triangulation, 168
Trumbull, M., 211, 212
T-test, 148
Two-way frequency tables, 147, 152
Typical case method, 89

**U**

University of Kansas, 238
University of Massachusetts at Amherst, 18
Unstructured interviews, 66
Upcraft, Lee, 1
U.S. News and World Report, 44

## V

Validity, 122–124
Variance, 144, 145; analysis of, 148–149; sampling, 86–87
Volkwein, J. F., 44–45

## W

Web resources: benchmarking standards, 22; database resources, 50; ethical issues in assessment, 208–209; informed consent checklist, 200; published instruments, 114, 115; student assessment examples, 22; written reports, 182–183, 189
Web-based surveys, 57, 62, 63, 93–95
Weick, Karl, 10

Western Interstate Commission for Higher Education (WICHE), 26
"Why?" type questions, 133
Wohlgemuth, Darin R., 23, 77
Written reports, 173–183; acknowledging limitations of, 181; emphasizing findings in, 178; ensuring accuracy of, 183; graphics and tables used in, 181–182; methods paragraph, 265; preparing multiple forms of, 175–177; recommending action steps in, 179–181; samples of, 182–183, 189; steps for preparing, 174; watching for land mines in, 177–178. *See also* Oral reports

## Y

Your First College Year (YFCY) survey, 258